D-DAY 1944
OMAHA AND UTAH BEACHES

American History Archives™

D-Day 1944
Omaha and Utah Beaches

7 8 9 10 11 12 / 16 15 14 13 12 11
ISBN 978 1 58159 246 7

The History Channel Club
c/o North American Membership Group
12301 Whitewater Drive
Minnetonka, MN 55343
www.thehistorychannelclub.com

Published by North American Membership Group under license from
Osprey Publishing Ltd.

Previously published as Campaign 100: *D-Day 1944 (1) Omaha Beach,* and
Campaign 104: *D-Day 1944 (2) Utah Beach & the US Airborne Landings,* by
Osprey Publishing, Midland House, West Way, Botley, Oxford OX2 0PH,
United Kingdom

© 2005 Osprey Publishing Ltd.   OSPREY
                                PUBLISHING

Editor: Lee Johnson
Design: The Black Spot
Index by Glyn Sutcliffe
Maps by The Map Studio
3D bird's-eye views by The Black Spot
Battlescene research Mark Henry
Battlescene artwork by Howard Gerrard
Originated by The Electronic Page Company, Cwmbran, and PPS Grasmere,
Leeds, UK
Printed in China through World Print Ltd.

FRONT COVER
**A view from inside an LCVP of the 16th RCT, 1st Infantry
Division during its run in to Omaha Beach on D-Day. The
protective plastic covers on the men's rifles are very
evident in this view. (NARA)**

Author **STEVEN J ZALOGA** is a senior analyst for an
aerospace research firm and an adjunct staff member of the
Strategy, Forces, and Resources division of the Institute for
Defense Analyses. He has written over 50 books on military
subjects. His grandfather landed at Omaha Beach on D-Day
in an engineer battalion and his father served in an engineer
battalion which landed on Omaha Beach a few days later.

Author's note

The author is indebted to many people who assisted on this project and would
like to thank David Isby for his help with photos. Thanks also go to Randy
Hackenburg and Jay Graybeal of the Military History Institute at the Army War
College in Carlisle Barracks, PA (MHI); Charles Lemons and Candace Fuller of
the Patton Museum at Ft. Knox, Kentucky; Alan Aimone of the Special
Collections at the US Military Academy at West Point, NY USMA; the staff of
the US National Archives and Records Administration (NARA), College Park,
Maryland, and the staff of the US Army Ordnance Museum, Aberdeen Proving
Ground (USAOM), for their help.

For brevity, the normal abbreviations for US and German tactical units have
been used here. So 1/8th Infantry indicates the 1st Battalion, 8th Infantry
Regiment while C/8th Infantry indicates Company C, 8th Infantry Regiment. In
the German case, II./GR.919 indicates 2nd Battalion, 919th Grenadier
Regiment while 2./GR.919 indicates
2nd Company, 919th Grenadier Regiment.

The D-Day chronology used here follows the Allied practice of using British
War Time, so H-Hour on 6 June was 0630. For greater clarity, the location
names used here, such as the names and codes for the beaches and beach
exits, are those of the US Army.

Artist's note

Readers may care to note that the original paintings from which the color
plates in this book were prepared are available for private sale. All reproduction
copyright whatsoever is retained by the Publishers. All enquiries should be
addressed to:

Howard Gerrard
11 Oaks Road,
Tenterden,
Kent
TN30 6RD
UK

The Publishers regret that they can enter into no correspondence upon this
matter.

KEY TO MILITARY SYMBOLS

Illustrator **HOWARD GERRARD** studied at the Wallasey School
of Art and has been a freelance designer and illustrator for
over 20 years. He has won both the Society of British
Aerospace Companies Award and the Wilkinson Sword Trophy.
Howard has illustrated a number of books for Osprey including
Campaign 69: *Nagashino 1575,* and Campaign 72: *Jutland
1916.* He lives and works in Kent.

D-DAY 1944
Omaha and Utah Beaches

CONTENTS

INTRODUCTION   *4*

Part 1
Omaha Beach   **5**
CHRONOLOGY   10
OPPOSING COMMANDERS   11
OPPOSING PLANS   19
OPPOSING ARMIES   34
D-DAY   40
OMAHA BEACH IN RETROSPECT   85
THE BATTLEFIELD TODAY   90

Part 2
Utah Beach   **93**
CHRONOLOGY   95
OPPOSING COMMANDERS   96
OPPOSING ARMIES   100
OPPOSING PLANS   109
D-DAY   114
THE BATTLEFIELD TODAY   177

FURTHER READING   *179*

INDEX   *181*

INTRODUCTION

It was a day of war that would change the course of the world forever, and for the better.

And on June 6, 1944, two battlegrounds in particular became critical to the Allies' success—the beaches called Omaha and Utah.

The Germans were expecting the main Allied assault from across the English Channel to come at Calais. But other potential attack points were vigorously defended, too. In fact, on Omaha Beach, fully one third of the first Allied assault wave became casualties within moments of hitting the beach. The coastline was difficult, and the German soldiers were better and more experienced here than at any of the other four beaches hit that day. A dear price was paid, but the Atlantic wall was breached by nightfall.

Utah was the westernmost beach that the Allies attacked on D-Day. Situated at the base of the Cotentin peninsula, it offered access to Cherbourg, a key port for the Allies' overall strategic plan. From there, the army of freedom could move on to the other ports of Breton.

A fact that many people look past is that the day started not with the landings at dawn, but by airborne landings of paratroopers overnight … daring soldiers dropped behind enemy lines to wreak havoc and start taking key bridges, crossroads and other important points. Under difficult circumstances, they got enough of the job done to make a difference.

In one day, the script was written. The drama then played out through the summer, fall and winter, into the next spring. But it all started on *D-Day 1944*, much of it on *Omaha and Utah Beaches*. Here is the complete story.

HISTORY
THE HISTORY CHANNEL CLUB

D-Day at Omaha Beach as seen by a Coast Guard photographer on an LCVP landing troops of 1/16th Infantry on Easy Red beach. The tank in the foreground is A-9, one of the few M4A1 tanks from the ill-fated 741st Tank Battalion to make it ashore. (NARA)

PART 1
OMAHA BEACH

Of the landings on the five assault beaches in Normandy on D-Day, Omaha Beach was the only one ever in doubt. Within moments of landing, a third of the assault troops in the first wave were casualties. The difficulties encountered on "bloody Omaha" were due to the more difficult terrain on this coastline, the unexpected presence of a first-rate German division at the beach and inadequate fire support. Yet in spite of all these problems, by the end of D-Day, the Atlantic Wall had been breached and the US Army's V Corps was firmly entrenched on the French coast.

THE STRATEGIC SITUATION

The Allied planning to assault Fortress Europe had been under way since 1942 and the Overlord plan began to take shape in 1943. Winston Churchill argued for a traditional maritime strategy of peripheral attack through Italy and the Balkans, but US military commanders and many senior British commanders favored a direct attack on Germany by the most plausible route, through northern France. The most significant disagreement concerned the US intent to stage two amphibious assaults, Operation Neptune in northwestern France, and Operation Anvil through the French Mediterranean coast. Churchill and many senior British commanders were firmly opposed to the southern France assault, realizing it would drain momentum from the Italian theater. With British

There was no more vivid symbol of the Atlantic Wall than the heavy coastal guns of the Kriegsmarine along the Channel coast like this one at Le Havre. These batteries were in their densest concentration on the Pas de Calais where the Wehrmacht expected the Allies to land. (NARA)

5

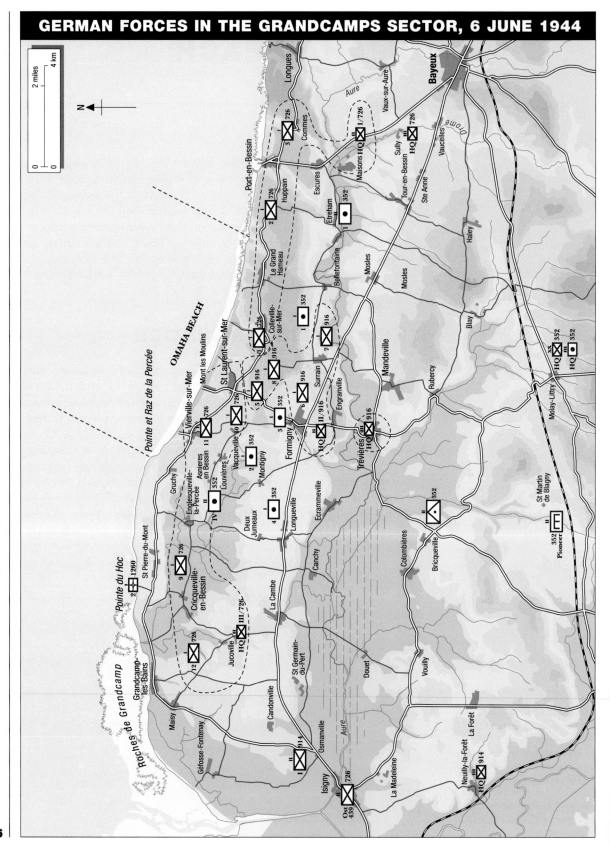

Omaha Beach, known to the Germans as the Grandcamps sector, was 7,000 yards long. This view from east to west shows the E-3 Colleville draw in the foreground and the Pointe-et-Raz-de-la-Percée towards the top. (MHI)

manpower reserves at breaking point and the US Army expected to provide the majority of forces for operations in France, Britain was losing its role as the senior partner in the Allied coalition. The American strategic viewpoint prevailed, although the more experienced British staffs shaped the actual planning for Neptune. In spite of significant controversies, not only between the Americans and the British, but among the combat services of both countries, the Allied coalition remained focused on its shared goal of defeating Germany. The Anglo-American partnership proved to be remarkably resilient in submerging national and service differences when they interfered with the mission.

One of the initial dilemmas was the target for Operation Neptune. The Pas de Calais opposite Dover was the narrowest point of the English Channel and had the added advantage of being closer to the expected route into Germany, through the Low Countries and across the northern Rhine plains. It was also the most obvious target and the area that the Germans were most diligently fortifying in 1943. Normandy was the next most likely area since the Bay of the Seine offered some shelter from weather and there were sufficient beaches with characteristics suitable for amphibious assault. Although more distant from the ultimate objective, Normandy was also less likely to attract the type of heavy defenses the Germans were constructing in the Pas de Calais. The problem in the invasion area was the lack of ports like Le Havre or Calais, but British naval planners had already begun to develop an ingenious artificial harbor that could provide a logistical base until neighboring ports such as Cherbourg were seized. The first draft of the Overlord plan was completed in July 1943, and approved by the Combined Joint Chiefs of Staff in August. Under the plan Operation Neptune would take place in May 1944 and Operation Anvil would follow as soon as it was possible to shift the necessary naval amphibious forces from the English Channel to the Mediterranean.

Overlord consisted of four phases. Operation Pointblank was already under way by the USAAF and RAF aimed at gaining air superiority over the future battlefield by destroying the Luftwaffe and crippling its ability to manufacture, maintain, and fuel its aircraft. The other element of the first phase was an attempt to deceive the Germans about the location of the actual landing site, Operation Fortitude. The second preparatory phase was aimed at isolating the battlefield by air attacks against communication centers, and road and rail networks that linked the Normandy area to reinforcements. Since air attacks limited to Normandy would give away the location of the planned invasion, more missions were actually flown against the Pas de Calais, as part of an effort to reinforce the Operation Fortitude deception. The third phase was Operation Neptune itself, the amphibious landings in Normandy. The fourth phase was the follow-up and build-up phase, aimed at reinforcing the bridgehead in preparation for the campaign in France.

The German view of the invasion beaches in Normandy. In the foreground are two rows of barbed wire, while in the surf are several rows of stakes, usually topped with Teller anti-tank mines. (MHI)

The preparatory work for Overlord took place in the shadow of the failed Dieppe raid of 1942[1]. Dieppe underscored how risky amphibious operations would be against a defended shoreline, but it also provided useful lessons. By 1944 the Allies had further amphibious experience including the landings in North Africa in November 1942 and the Sicily, Salerno, and Anzio landings in Italy in 1943–44. Neptune presented problems beyond the Italian experiences since it would involve landing against a fortified beach, while the previous landings had been conducted against uncontested and largely unprotected beaches. These challenges prompted the development of a host of new innovations such as the artificial harbors, new types of landing craft and assault vessels, specialized armored vehicles, and novel engineer equipment to overcome obstacles.

From the German perspective 1944 was the year of decision. The Wehrmacht had lost the strategic initiative in 1943 following its failed summer offensive at Kursk and the Allied offensive in Italy. Hitler believed that a stout defense in 1944 would lead to cracks in the Allied coalition that might provide the Wehrmacht with opportunities to reverse Germany's declining fortunes on the battlefield. The defeat of an Allied landing attempt in France was a prime opportunity. Hitler's strategic outlook was colored by his experience as a soldier in World War I, where there was no higher objective than the stalwart defense of every last inch of ground. By the beginning of 1944, German forces were scattered all over Europe from Norway and Finland in the north to Greece and the Balkans in the south, and from the Channel Islands in the west to the steppes of Ukraine in the east. "Who defends everything, defends nothing" is a military adage that Hitler ignored at Germany's peril. The Wehrmacht was stretched thin everywhere and Hitler rebuffed attempts to pull troops out of the peripheries to reinforce the most vital sectors. He took ill-advised comfort in the bloated Wehrmacht order of battle, ignoring that it had become a hollow force.

Bled white by the precarious situation on the Eastern Front, the Wehrmacht's innovative traditions in the art of war had stagnated and been overtaken by the Allies' more advanced approach. While some senior

1 See Campaign 127: *Dieppe 1942 – Prelude to D-Day*

German commanders who had fought Britain and the United States had some appreciation of the new style of deep battle, most did not. The Anglo-American style of war emphasized the use of airpower both as a third dimension in the land battle and as a means to deepen the battlefield. At the strategic level, long-range bombers weakened the military might of Germany by attacking its military industries, fuel production, and infrastructure. At the operational level, Allied medium bombers isolated the battlefield by destroying the road and rail networks feeding the forward edge of battle, sapping the Wehrmacht of its mobility and preventing reinforcement. At the tactical level, fighter-bombers outflanked ground formations from the air, extended the firepower of the Allies beyond the range of traditional artillery and disrupted the conduct of Wehrmacht operations with their ability to strike unexpectedly practically anytime, anywhere. The decay of the Luftwaffe undermined attempts to resist the forthcoming invasion of France. Rommel grimly noted that, "even with the most modern weapons, anyone who has to fight against an enemy in complete control of the air, fights like a savage against modern European troops, under the same handicaps and with the same chance of success."

The decline of the Luftwaffe also helped blind German intelligence to the Allied build-up in the ports of southern England facing Normandy. Photo reconnaissance missions over Britain were almost impossible and only two photos of British ports were obtained in the spring of 1944. Other intelligence means proved even more dangerous to German strategy as British counter-intelligence had managed to capture every agent dropped into Britain and had turned many into double agents. Berlin was fed a string of false reports reinforcing their mistaken beliefs about the invasion focus on the Pas de Calais and Picardy coastlines. The British success in breaking the German Enigma codes provided a vital source of information on German activities, but a most dangerous security breach was the US decryption of the code used by the Japanese embassy in Berlin. Ambassador Oshima Hiroshi reported on his frequent meetings with senior Nazi leaders, providing not only insight into Hitler's strategic views, but details of German dispositions such as his November 1943 inspection tour of German defenses on the French coast. The failures of German intelligence and counter-intelligence left the senior German leadership blind while at the same time exposing a remarkably complete picture of German plans to the Allies.

The consensus among German military leaders was that the main attacks would take place against the Pas de Calais or Picardy coast. The landings at Anzio on 22 January 1944 led a growing number of German commanders to believe that the Allies would launch several smaller amphibious attacks to draw off German reserves from the main landing. This greatly confused German defense plans and restricted the actions of German theater commanders because Berlin was increasingly unwilling to commit any reserves until it was evident that an Allied landing was in fact a major operation and not merely another diversion.

CHRONOLOGY

July 1943 First draft of Overlord plan completed

August 1943 Overlord plan approved by Combined Joint Chiefs of Staff

3 November 1943 Führer Directive 51 gives priority to reinforcing Western Front

6 November 1943 Rommel appointed to lead Army Group for Special Employment

4 June 1944 Poor weather forces cancellation of attack on Monday 5 June 1944

5 June 1944 Eisenhower decides that weather will permit execution of Neptune on 6 June 1944

Tuesday 6 June 1944 D-Day

0030hrs Minesweepers clear channel to beachhead

0100hrs German units alerted due to reports of Allied paratroopers

0300hrs Task Force O arrives off Omaha Beach, anchors 25,000 yards from beach

0310hrs General Marcks orders 84th Corps reserves, Kampfgruppe Meyer, to move to junction between Omaha and Utah beach to deal with paratroopers

0415hrs Troops from assault waves begin loading in landing craft

0530hrs DD tanks begin swim to beach

0545hrs Naval bombardment group begins shelling Omaha Beach; firing ends at 0625

0629hrs First wave of tanks begins landing

0631hrs First wave of assault troops and Gap Assault Teams begins landing

0700hrs Tide turns, obstacles gradually submerged by 0800

0700–0730hrs Second wave of troops land

0710hrs Rangers arrive at Pointe-du-Hoc 40 minutes late; reach summit by 0725

0720hrs First advance over the bluffs by group under Lt Spalding, E/16th Infantry

0750hrs Advance over the bluffs begins by 116th Infantry led by Gen Cota and Col Canham

0800hrs Admiral Bryant orders destroyers to close on beach to provide fire support

0810hrs Advance by 5th Rangers over the bluffs begins

0820hrs Regimental HQ of 16th RCT lands, Col Taylor begins rallying troops

0830hrs Beachmaster orders no further vehicles to be landed at Omaha due to congestion

0835hrs General Kraiss directs Kampfgruppe Meyer to stop British advance from Gold Beach except for one battalion aimed at the Colleville penetration

0900hrs WN60 strongpoint falls to L/16th Infantry

0915hrs WN70 strongpoint abandoned due to advance by Cota's force on Vierville

1000hrs 18th Infantry and 115th Infantry move towards beach in LCIs, they are delayed by lack of clear lanes

1100hrs LCI-554 and LCT-30 force their way through to the beach, restoring momentum to the landings

1130hrs E-1 St Laurent draw opened; first exit cleared on D-Day

1300hrs Hour-long naval bombardment of D-1 Vierville draw concludes; survivors surrender

1300hrs Engineers complete makeshift road over bluff near E-1 St Laurent draw; vehicle assembly area completed by 1500hrs

1335hrs Kraiss reports to 84th Corps HQ that invasion force stopped except at Colleville

1630hrs E-3 Colleville draw finally taken

1700hrs Tanks begin moving through E-1 St Laurent draw

1800hrs D-1 Vierville draw finally opened by engineers

1825hrs Kraiss orders 1/GR.914 to retake Pointe-du-Hoc

2000hrs D-3 Les Moulins draw declared open

2000hrs Engineers begin clearing path through E-3 Colleville draw, opens at 0100 on D+1

OPPOSING COMMANDERS

GERMAN COMMANDERS

The Byzantine dynamics of the Nazi political leadership undermined German capabilities to defeat the forthcoming invasion. By 1944 Hitler had lost confidence in the Wehrmacht commanders and had continued to usurp more and more of the decision-making down to the tactical level. Hitler's meddling was erratic and unpredictable and his lazy and disorganized leadership style encouraged the formation of competing factions in the military and the government. This was all too evident in the failed attempts to create a unified command in France where not only was there the usual inter-service rivalries between the navy, army, and air force, but also the Waffen-SS and the Organization Todt paramilitary construction service. The armed forces high command (OKW) headed by Generalfeldmarschall Wilhelm Keitel was a nominal joint staff but in fact the Luftwaffe and navy were represented by junior officers, and Reichsmarschall Hermann Göring and Admiral Raeder circumvented the OKW when it suited them.

The commander in chief in the West (OB West) from March 1942 was **Generalfeldmarschall Gerd von Rundstedt**. The revered victor of the 1940 Battle of France was described by one of his Panzer commanders as "an elderly man ... a soldier of thorough training with adequate experience in practical warfare, but without an understanding of a three-dimensional war involving the combined operations of the Heer [army], Kriegsmarine [navy] and Luftwaffe. He was a gentleman and had the personal confidence and respect of his subordinate commanders and his troops. His authority was limited and quite handicapped. His chief of staff [Blumentritt] was not a suitable complement, either as to capability or character." A post-war US Army study concluded that the lack of unified command in France was a more serious weakness than shortages of troops and equipment.

Workers from Organization Todt scramble for cover as a US P-38 Lightning reconnaissance aircraft piloted by Lt Albert Lanker makes a fast pass over the Normandy beaches on 6 May 1944, a month before the landings. The German construction teams continued to install more anti-invasion obstacles on the beaches until D-Day. (NARA)

While Rundstedt commanded army units, **Generalfeldmarschall Hugo Sperrle** was in charge of Luftflotte 3 including 3rd Flak Korps, and the Luftwaffe paratroop and field divisions. **Admiral Theodor Krancke** commanded Navy Group West along the French coast, including the coastal artillery batteries that would shift to army jurisdiction only after the invasion had begun. German security troops being used for occupation duty were under the control of the two military governors. Tactical control was supposed to shift to OB West once the invasion started, but the disjointed command before the invasion hampered coordinated preparation of defenses and complicated control of the forces during the critical first hours of the invasion.

Rundstedt's limited control was evident in the construction of the Atlantic Wall, a series of coastal fortifications started on Hitler's insistence after the St Nazaire and Dieppe raids of 1942. The fortifications were the responsibility of the Organization Todt paramilitary construction force, which reported to armament minister Albert Speer, not to the army. Furthermore, the navy was responsible for most of the fortified coastal guns, which were positioned as they saw fit. Army artillery officers derided them as "battleships of the dunes," located on the coast vulnerable to Allied bombardment instead of being sheltered further to the rear. Hitler wanted 15,000 concrete strongpoints manned by 300,000 troops by May 1943 – an impossible target. The focus was on the Pas de Calais and in the summer of 1943 further emphasis was placed on this sector due to Hitler's decision to locate the new V-1 and V-2 missile bases in this area. In spite of the rhetoric about an impregnable "Fortress Europe", the poor state of defenses prompted Rundstedt to send a special report to Hitler in October 1943, which led to Führer Directive 51 on 3 November 1943. This reversed former priorities and recognized the need to strengthen defenses in the West in view of the likelihood of a 1944 Allied attack. The most tangible outcome of this debate was the assignment of **Generalfeldmarschall Erwin Rommel** to head the newly created Army Group for Special Employment (later Army Group B), a post directly under OKW for direction of the invasion front.

Rommel's new post partly duplicated Rundstedt's, but both officers attempted to make the best of a confused situation. Rommel's first activities involved an inspection of the Atlantic Wall construction and he invigorated the effort in previously neglected sectors such as Normandy and Brittany. Rommel's appointment brought to a head the debate about the deployment of forces to repel the expected invasion. Rommel argued that the invasion had to be stopped cold on the beaches. It was, therefore, essential that reserves, especially the Panzers, be kept close enough to the beaches for them to intervene promptly. The commander of Panzer Gruppe West, **General Leo Freiherr Geyr von Schweppenburg** argued vociferously that the Panzer divisions and the Luftwaffe should be held back from the coastal zone and kept in reserve to form a counter-attack force that would strike after the Allies had landed. Geyr cited the examples of Sicily, Salerno, and Anzio, where German Panzer forces committed to the coastal battle had been stopped by heavy naval gunfire. Geyr argued that the landings could not be stopped, and that the beach defenses should only be an economy-of-force effort – enough to significantly delay and disrupt but not so much as to drain forces from the decisive battle inland. Rommel retorted that, given Allied air superiority, the Panzers would never be able to mass for a counter-attack and to permit the Allies to win a firm lodgment ensured disaster. The matter came to a head in March 1944 when Rommel asked Hitler for expanded powers to unify the command under his control. Hitler agreed to a compromise, putting three of Geyr's Panzer divisions under Rommel's operational control as the Army Group B reserve, but leaving three other Panzer divisions under Rundstedt's OB West command and the remaining four under direct OKW control as strategic reserves. As a result, the German strategy for Normandy remained a jumble of Rommel's scheme for an immediate defense of the beach and Rundstedt/Geyr's plans for a decisive battle after the landings. On D-Day Rommel was in Germany, hoping to persuade Hitler to give him control of more Panzer divisions.

German forces in Normandy were part of the Seventh Army, which controlled German army units on the neighboring Cotentin peninsula and Brittany as well. The Seventh Army was commanded by **Generaloberst Friedrich Dollman**. He had won the Iron Cross in World War I, commanded a corps in Poland and the Seventh Army in the battle of France in 1940. While he was a highly competent officer, he spent most of the war on occupation duty and many battle-hardened veterans of the Eastern Front were skeptical that his staff was up to the task. Dollman died of a heart attack on 28 June 1944, less than a month after D-Day.

The Normandy sector was the responsibility of the 84th Infantry Corps commanded by **General der Infanterie Erich Marcks**. He was widely regarded as one of the best general staff officers and served early in the war with an army corps in Poland, and with the 18th Army in France in 1940. He was involved in the planning for Operation Barbarossa, and commanded the 101st Jäger Division at the time of the invasion of the Soviet Union in 1941. After he lost a leg in combat in March 1942, he was reassigned to the command of the 337th Infantry Division following his recuperation. His skills as a divisional commander led to his elevation to army corps command, first the 66th Corps in

The commander of the 352nd Infantry Division defending Omaha Beach was Generalleutnant Dietrich Kraiss. (NARA)

September 1942, then the 87th Corps. The Nazis considered him politically suspect as he had been an aide to General von Schleicher, murdered by the SS in 1934, and he was passed over by Hitler for army command. Instead, he was assigned to the 84th Corps in France on 1 August 1943 as part of the process to refresh the command structure in France with Eastern Front veterans. Marcks did not agree with Rommel over tactics to defeat an amphibious landing since he felt that his corps was far too weak and thinly spread to defend the extensive coastline it had been assigned. He favored the construction of a string of field fortifications in modest depth, but relying on a corps reserve of mobile infantry and Panzers within a day's march of the coast to carry out the burden of the defense. Due to the expected bad weather, the Seventh Army had scheduled a series of anti-invasion staff exercises for senior commanders in Rennes for 6 June, with Marcks assigned the role of the senior Allied commander. At 0100hrs on 6 June as the Allied paratroopers were approaching their objectives, Marcks was celebrating his birthday with his staff at St Lô, planning to depart a few hours later for Rennes. He was killed in Normandy during an air attack on 12 June 1944.

The 352nd Infantry Division, commanded by **Generalleutnant Dietrich Kraiss**, defended Omaha Beach. He was a professional soldier, commissioned into the 126th Infantry Regiment in 1909 at the age of 20, and fought in World War I. At the outbreak of World War II he was commander of the 90th Infantry Regiment. His successful leadership in the early campaigns resulted in his appointment to command the 168th Infantry Division in Russia on 8 July 1941, which he led until March 1943. He was transferred to the newly formed 355th Infantry Division, which he commanded until it was disbanded on 6 November 1943 due to the heavy losses it had suffered during the autumn fighting in Russia. Kraiss was then transferred to France to command the newly formed 352nd Infantry Division which was originally earmarked for the Eastern Front. He was wounded during the fighting near St Lô on 2 August 1944, dying of his wounds four days later.

AMERICAN COMMANDERS

General Dwight D. Eisenhower was assigned to command the Supreme Headquarters Allied Expeditionary Force (SHAEF) in December 1943. Eisenhower had served as aide to General Douglas MacArthur in the Philippines in the years leading up to World War II, an invaluable education in the lessons of coalition building and the impact of politics on military planning. Although he was assigned to a regimental command on his return to the US in 1940, his reputation as one of the army's rising stars led the War Department to transfer him to War Plans in Washington. His performance as the chief of staff of the Third Army in the Louisiana maneuvers in the autumn of 1941 caught the attention of the army's chief of staff, George C. Marshall, and ignited his meteoric rise. Eisenhower played a central role in strategic decision making during the early years of the war, and was put in command of US forces for the amphibious landings in North Africa 1942. In contrast to the disjointed German command structure, the Allied command structure was far more centralized. One of

14

Senior commanders of the US forces off Omaha are seen here on the bridge of the cruiser USS *Augusta* on 8 June 1944. In the foreground is Rear Admiral Alan Kirk, commander of the Western Naval Task Force, Major General Omar Bradley, commander of the First US Army, Rear Admiral A.D. Struble, and General Ralph Royce of the Ninth Tactical Air Force. (NARA)

the first challenges to Eisenhower's authority was the resistance of senior US Army Air Force generals to the diversion of their long-range bombers from their strategic missions against Germany to the tactical operations to isolate the battlefield in France prior to D-Day. Although his critics have pointed to Eisenhower's lack of tactical battlefield experience, his visionary views on combined arms warfare as well as his astute political skills made him an ideal commander for a coalition force depending on tri-service cooperation by two Allied armed forces.

The tactical commander of the US Army in Overlord was **Lieutenant General Omar Bradley**, commander of the First US Army. Bradley had been a classmate of Eisenhower's at the US Military Academy at West Point in the class of 1915. Bradley's performance at the infantry school

Commander of the 1st Infantry Division was Major General Clarence Huebner, seen here briefing General Dwight Eisenhower and General Omar Bradley a few weeks after D-Day during the operations near Cherbourg. (NARA)

16th Infantry led the assault on the eastern sector of Omaha Beach, and its officers are seen here shortly before the landings. From left to right are the regimental commander, Colonel George Taylor, Lieutenant Colonel Gibbs (7th Artillery Bn.), Lieutenant Colonel Herbert Hicks (2nd Bn.), Lieutenant Colonel Charles Horner (3rd Bn.), and Major Edmond Driscoll (1st Bn.). (MHI)

in the early 1930s and his work on the General Staff in 1938 attracted Marshall's attention. Bradley raised the new 82nd Division that would later fight as an airborne division in Normandy, and afterwards became deputy commander of George S. Patton's II Corps in the North African campaign. Marshall favored intelligent, conservative planners like Bradley over charismatic leaders like Patton for senior commands and Bradley received the nod to lead First US Army in August 1943.

The force assaulting Omaha Beach came from V Corps, led by **Major General Leonard Gerow**. He was older than either Eisenhower or Bradley, Virginia Military Institute class of 1911, and commanded Eisenhower in 1941 while heading the War Plans division of the general staff. Gerow was regarded by many as the quintessential staff officer, comfortable with planning combat operations but not leading them. Patton despised him, calling him one of the most mediocre corps commanders in Europe and later calling his appointment to head the War College after the war "a joke". But Gerow had Marshall's and Eisenhower's confidence, and was given command of the corps in July 1943 after having led the 29th Division. Bradley had brought in more experienced corps commanders from other theaters, including J. Lawton "Lightning Joe" Collins from the Pacific, to lead at neighboring Utah Beach and probably would not have chosen Gerow had the choice been his. But with his V Corps the first US tactical formation in the UK and with the support of Eisenhower, Gerow would lead the attack. Gerow locked horns with Bradley over many details of the Omaha Beach assault plans and several of his improvements would later prove vital in the success of the operation.

Senior US commanders wanted an experienced unit to land at Omaha Beach and, not surprisingly, the "Big Red One" 1st Infantry Division was selected. Led by the charismatic General Terry Allen and Theodore Roosevelt in North Africa and Sicily, the division had developed a cocksure reputation. Their popular definition of the US Army was "the Big Red One and a million frigging replacements." Bradley relieved the popular Allen on Sicily in August 1943, replacing him with **Major General Clarence Huebner**. Huebner was a veteran of the 1st Division in World War I,

awarded the Distinguished Service Medal for his courageous and skilled leadership of the 28th Infantry. Huebner, a strict disciplinarian, had a hard time asserting control after Allen was sacked. He imposed a strict training regime on the division when transferred to Britain and the rambunctious unit was finally won over. Huebner would later command V Corps under Patton in Germany in 1945.

The second Omaha Beach division, 29th Infantry Division, had been commanded by Gerow until July 1943 when he was replaced by West Pointer and former cavalry officer **Major General Charles Gerhardt**. He had been commissioned in 1917 and served on the staff of the 89th Division in World War I. Gerhardt's excellent performance as a cavalry brigade commander in the 1941 Louisiana maneuvers prompted Marshall to give him command of the new 91st Division. Gerhardt was a very traditional officer demanding a high level of discipline. His stern leadership of the 29th Division helped overcome the friction between the National Guard officers and troops, who formed the core of the unit, and the new influx of regular army officers and conscripts who had filled out the division for war.

In charge of the Engineer Special Brigades was **Brigadier General William Hoge**. His role in the training and planning of the vital engineer operations at Omaha Beach is often overlooked and he would win greater fame for his leadership of Combat Command B of the 9th Armored Division during the battle for St Vith during the Ardennes campaign.

The tactical command of forces landing on D-Day was in the hands of the regimental leaders. The 1st Division's 16th Infantry Regiment was led by **Lieutenant Colonel George Taylor**, an experienced veteran who had headed the regiment since the Tunisian campaign. The 29th Division's 116th Regiment was led by **Lieutenant Colonel Charles Canham**, a strict, by-the-book West Pointer nicknamed "Stoneface" by his troops. Although widely disliked by the enlisted men before D-Day, Canham's heroic performance on Omaha Beach abruptly changed opinions. He had a BAR shot from his hands and fought the rest of the day with one arm in an improvised sling, a .45cal pistol in his good hand. Canham's role has been overshadowed by the presence of the division's assistant commander, **Brigadier General Norman "Dutch" Cota**, who landed on the beach early in the day. Cota was the former chief of staff of the 1st Division and had fought in Tunisia. He was a charismatic combat commander, preferring to be in the field leading his troops rather than behind a desk.

Unlike most of the divisional and regimental commanders, the leader of the Ranger Provisional Group, **Lieutenant Colonel James E. Rudder**, was not a professional soldier. Rudder had graduated from Texas A&M in 1932 and was commissioned a second lieutenant in the Army reserves. He was a high school teacher until 1941, when he was called up to active duty and sent to the infantry school at Ft Benning. After further training at the Army Command and General Staff College in the autumn of 1942, he was posted to the 2nd Ranger Battalion, assuming command in the summer of 1943.

OPPOSING PLANS

THE AMERICAN PLAN

A good portrait shot of two GIs from the 1st Infantry Division onboard a Coast Guard LCI on the approaches to Normandy. The soldier in the foreground is wearing the assault jacket typical of the initial landings, and the Navy M-1926 inflatable life belt can be seen around his waist. (NARA)

Omaha Beach was selected early in the Overlord planning since at the time it was undefended. On the negative side, the bluffs along the beach formed a significant tactical obstacle and were well suited for defense. Even after Rommel began fortifying the beach in the autumn of 1943, it remained an attractive option since it offered a deep-water anchorage only three-quarters of a mile from all parts of the beach with a full 36ft of water at low tide, making it an ideal location for an artificial harbor for follow-on operations. The terrain behind the beach was much more suitable for motor transport than at neighboring Utah Beach. In February 1944, First US Army conducted a study of Omaha Beach which concluded that, if defended by an infantry regiment, the configuration of the beach would multiply the combat power of the German troops and present a formidable defensive position assaulting which would likely result in heavy casualties. If it was defended by a full infantry division, it would be impregnable. The US Army, right up to the time of the landings, thought that the beach was only defended by a single, understrength, poor-quality regiment. As will be discussed further, this would prove to be the most significant mistake in the US plan. The German forces on Omaha Beach were more than three times those anticipated.

The most critical necessity in the Operation Neptune plan was the need for tactical surprise. Allied planners were very concerned that if the Germans suspected a landing in Normandy, they would reinforce the area to the point where an amphibious assault would be impossible. The need for surprise affected the bombardment of the battlefield in the weeks before the landing. Since the Allies did not want to tip their hand, this precluded any concentrated bombardment of the assault beaches by either sea or air. For every bomb dropped in the Normandy area, two or more were dropped in the Pas de Calais and Picardy areas

OMAHA BEACH – CROSS-SECTIONAL VIEW

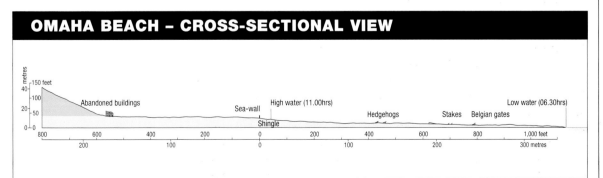

The Omaha Beach Bombardment Group included ten destroyers. This is USS *Thompson* (DD-627) commanded by Lieutenant Commander A.L. Gebelin. She is seen here at the end of May 1944 being replenished at sea from the battleship USS *Arkansas* before setting off for Normandy. On D-Day the *Thompson* began by bombarding the Pointe-et-Raz-de-la-Percée and spent the afternoon providing fire support for the Rangers on Pointe-du-Hoc. (NARA)

to continue the Operation Fortitude ruse. The risk of this strategic choice paid off at all the beaches except Omaha.

Operation Neptune contemplated a dawn landing at low tide due to Rommel's new beach defenses, which placed anti-craft obstacles in the water close to shore. A dawn landing would make it less likely that the Germans would discover the invasion fleet during its movement to the beaches. The landings were scheduled to begin on 5 June 1944 but were postponed due to foul weather in the Channel. Eisenhower rescheduled the assault for Tuesday, 6 June 1944 after Allied meteorological services had discovered a break in the weather that would last for several days. By this time the enormous momentum of the operation also put pressure on Eisenhower to approve the attack, and his decision was reinforced by an intelligence report early in June from the Japanese ambassador in Berlin which indicated that Hitler was still convinced the attack would come on the Pas de Calais.

The amphibious assault was a carefully choreographed plan calling for a series of preliminary though short bombardments of the coast followed by amphibious landings. The initial naval element of Operation Neptune at Omaha Beach was Force O. The naval forces for the American beaches were originally named Forces X and Y, but to make them more comprehensible they were switched first to Omaha and Oklahoma, and then to their final names, Omaha and Utah, monikers that applied to the beaches as well. The bombardment ships consisted of two old battleships and three light cruisers, supported by 15 destroyers and numerous smaller ships and craft. The naval bombardment plan had three phases. At first light (0558hrs) the navy would begin the counter-battery phase, attacking all 14 known German artillery positions. Twenty minutes before the landings (H-20) the bombardment would shift to the attack of beach defenses, especially known fortifications. At H-hour, the fire would shift to targets behind the beachhead, or on the flanks. Admiral Hall was not happy with the "shoe-string naval force" allotted to

One innovation for the Normandy landings was the use of rocket craft. These LCT(R)(3) carry 1,080 5in. rockets. A total of 9,000 rockets were fired in the opening bombardment from nine LCT(R), but most accounts suggest their salvoes missed the beach. (NARA)

Task Force O and he wanted more destroyers. Due to tidal conditions, the landings would begin at Omaha Beach before other beaches and as a result the naval bombardment would be significantly shorter, only 40 minutes. Task Force O had neither the time nor the resources to fulfill its bombardment mission.

Shortly after the naval bombardment began, the US Army Air Force was scheduled to attack the defenses using heavy bombers. The bluff above the beach, the concrete emplacements in the draws, and the areas behind the beach were the primary targets. Contrary to what many Army troops believed, the plan did not call for attacks on the beach obstructions in order to avoid cratering the beach since this would make it difficult later in the day to move motorized transport off the beach. This attack would prove to be one of the most crucial failures at Omaha Beach on D-Day. The US Army Air Force liked to advertise its precision bombing capabilities, but in reality, the bomber commanders knew that there was still a considerable margin of error in their attacks, especially in poor weather. While collateral damage was of little concern when bombing German industrial targets, it was a significant concern when carrying out heavy strikes near US forces. The bombing mission required good weather for even modest precision and when the weather proved poor the Air Force changed the bombing tactics to limit any possible short-falls into the landing force. Due to the use of blind bombing using radar for targeting, the Air Force commanders ordered the bombardiers to delay their bomb release by 30 seconds once the coast was picked up on radar. This guaranteed that the bombs would fall far from the coastline. The lack of a contingency plan, such as the use of bombers under the cloud cover, was a major weakness of the plan, and the Army had unrealistic expectations of the air force's capabilities. There were no plans to use the Ninth Air Force in close-support missions against the beach defenses since the army lacked the communications to call in air strikes and no training had been undertaken.

Since the Allies expected to confront fortifications along the beach, armored support was deemed essential. In theory, each regimental combat team (RCT) would be preceded onto the beach by three companies of tanks to knock out any remaining bunkers not destroyed by the bomber attack. After the Dieppe experience, the British army had developed an assortment of specialized tanks, dubbed "Funnies", to aid in amphibious assaults. The myth has developed over the years that the US Army spurned

Although the US Army Air Force conducted very effective air superiority and interdiction missions on D-Day, the US infantry widely blamed the air force for the lack of preparatory bombardment of Omaha Beach. This B-26C Marauder of the 450th Bombardment Squadron, 322nd Bomb Group is seen over the invasion fleet on D-Day. (NARA)

OMAHA BEACH (WEST)

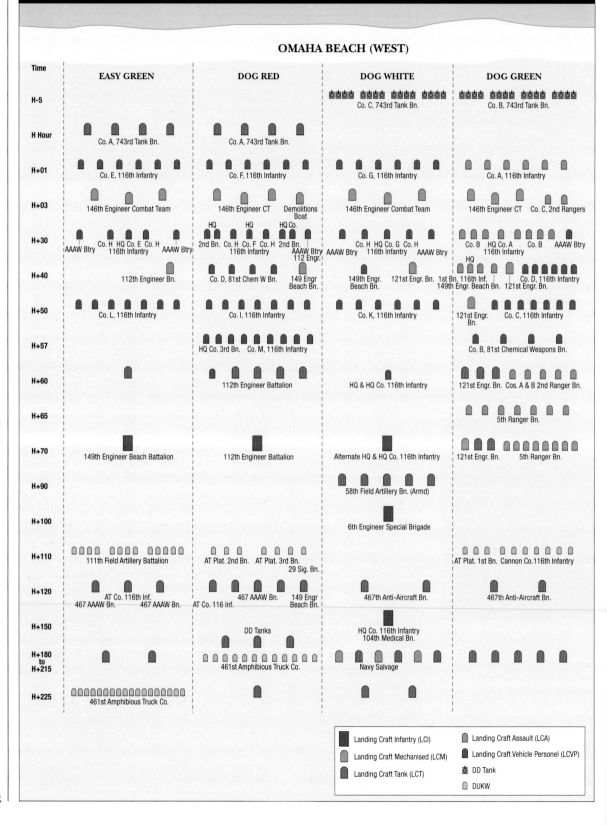

Time	EASY GREEN	DOG RED	DOG WHITE	DOG GREEN
H-5			Co. C, 743rd Tank Bn.	Co. B, 743rd Tank Bn.
H Hour	Co. A, 743rd Tank Bn.	Co. A, 743rd Tank Bn.		
H+01	Co. E, 116th Infantry	Co. F, 116th Infantry	Co. G, 116th Infantry	Co. A, 116th Infantry
H+03	146th Engineer Combat Team	146th Engineer CT Demolitions Boat	146th Engineer Combat Team	146th Engineer CT Co. C, 2nd Rangers
H+30	AAAW Btry Co. H HQ Co. E Co. H AAAW Btry 116th Infantry	HQ HQ HQ Co. 2nd Bn. Co. H Co. F Co. H 2nd Bn. 116th Infantry AAAW Btry 112 Engr.	Co. H HQ Co. G Co. H AAAW Btry 116th Infantry AAAW Btry	HQ Co. B HQ Co. A Co. B AAAW Btry 116th Infantry
H+40	112th Engineer Bn.	Co. D, 81st Chem W Bn. 149 Engr Beach Bn.	149th Engr. Beach Bn. 121st Engr. Bn. 1st Bn. 116th Inf. 149th Engr. Beach Bn.	Co. D, 116th Infantry 121st Engr. Bn.
H+50	Co. L, 116th Infantry	Co. I, 116th Infantry	Co. K, 116th Infantry	121st Engr. Bn. Co. C, 116th Infantry
H+57		HQ Co. 3rd Bn. Co. M, 116th Infantry		Co. B, 81st Chemical Weapons Bn.
H+60		112th Engineer Battalion	HQ & HQ Co. 116th Infantry	121st Engr. Bn. Cos. A & B 2nd Ranger Bn.
H+65				5th Ranger Bn.
H+70	149th Engineer Beach Battalion	112th Engineer Battalion	Alternate HQ & HQ Co. 116th Infantry	121st Engr. Bn. 5th Ranger Bn.
H+90			58th Field Artillery Bn. (Armd)	
H+100			6th Engineer Special Brigade	
H+110	111th Field Artillery Battalion	AT Plat. 2nd Bn. AT Plat. 3rd Bn. 29 Sig. Bn.		AT Plat. 1st Bn. Cannon Co. 116th Infantry
H+120	AT Co. 116th Inf. 467 AAAW Bn. 467 AAAW Bn.	AT Co. 116 Inf. 467 AAAW Bn. 149 Engr Beach Bn.	467th Anti-Aircraft Bn.	467th Anti-Aircraft Bn.
H+150		DD Tanks	HQ Co. 116th Infantry 104th Medical Bn.	
H+180 to H+215		461st Amphibious Truck Co.	Navy Salvage	
H+225	461st Amphibious Truck Co.			

Legend:
- Landing Craft Infantry (LCI)
- Landing Craft Mechanised (LCM)
- Landing Craft Tank (LCT)
- Landing Craft Assault (LCA)
- Landing Craft Vehicle Personel (LCVP)
- DD Tank
- DUKW

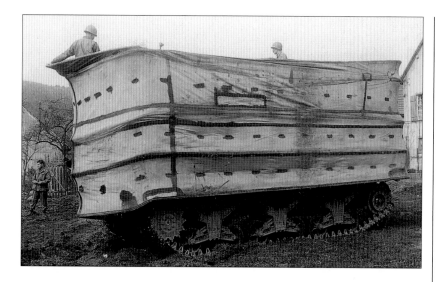

The M4A1 Duplex Drive (DD) amphibious tanks consisted of a normal Sherman medium tank with a folding canvas buoyancy skirt and a modified propulsion system, derisively called "thirty tons of steel in a canvas bucket" by its crews. This DD is seen in Germany in 1945 during later river-crossing operations. (NARA)

the use of these specialized tanks. In fact, by February 1944, the US Army had submitted a request for 25 Sherman Crab anti-mine flail tanks, 100 Sherman Crocodile flamethrower tanks, and other Sherman combat engineer equipment for Overlord. The original US plans expected the use of the Churchill AVRE (Armoured Vehicle Royal Engineers) to support the engineer breaching operations. None of these were provided in time for D-Day as British industry could barely keep pace with the needs of the British Army. Since it would take time for US industry to manufacture these, priority was given to those items deemed most necessary – the controversial DD tanks. In place of the Churchill AVREs, V Corps was allotted 16 M4 dozer-tanks to assist the engineers.

The Duplex Drive (DD) tank was a cover name for an amphibious version of the Sherman medium tank, and was developed in Britain as a means to bring tanks ashore without the need for landing craft. The attraction of this scheme was that the tanks could be sent ashore in the first waves in a less conspicuous and less vulnerable fashion than by using

The alternative to DD tanks was to fit the M4 medium tank with wading trunks as had been the practice on Sicily and in the amphibious landings at Salerno and Anzio during the Italian campaign. One company in each of the two tank battalions landed on Omaha Beach had their tanks fitted with wading trunks, which protected the tanks engine from flooding and allowed the tank to crawl ashore with water up to the top of its turret. The tanks were further waterproofed by sealing gaps and openings to prevent the fighting compartment and engine compartment from leaking. (NARA)

large landing craft. Buoyancy was provided by a large canvas flotation screen around the tank, which folded like an accordion when not in use. The DD tank's canvas screen had only a foot of freeboard when in the water and anything like rough seas threatened to collapse or swamp the fragile screen. A pair of propellers were added at the rear of the hull that were powered off the tank's engine. Since British firms could not produce these in adequate numbers, conversion kits were built by Firestone in the US for M4A1 medium tanks. Of the 350 converted, about 80 tanks were transferred to British units to make up for shortages.

In past amphibious landings, such as Sicily and Salerno, the US Army had preferred to fit tanks with wading trunks, allowing them to be deposited by landing craft in shallow water beyond any beach obstructions and drive ashore. This also allowed the tanks to fire at beach targets during their run into the beach on the landing craft and remain in the surf, with their submerged hull protected by water, while engaging targets on the beach. The new DD tanks were greeted with skepticism by many US officers who doubted their seaworthiness. The V Corps commander, Gerow, opposed their use and would have preferred to land both tank battalions on Omaha with wading trunks. As a result of these misgivings, the US tank battalions slated for Operation Neptune were mixed formations equipped with two companies of DD tanks to land in the initial waves, and one company of tanks with wading trunks to land shortly afterward from LCTs. During pre-invasion exercises at Slapton Sands in Devon, Britain, a number of DD tanks sank, leading doubtful US Navy officials to insist on guidelines for launching them. An arrangement was reached under which the senior officer (army or navy) aboard the landing craft could make the judgment that the sea was too rough for the DD tanks to swim ashore and land them directly on the beach. The loophole in this procedure was that some of the young tank officers outranked the commanders of the landing craft but lacked the experience to evaluate the sea conditions.

One mystery has been why the US Army at Normandy did not use amtracs (amphibious tractors) to land troops as had been done in the Pacific theater since Tarawa in 1943. Bradley had brought back two of the best US divisional commanders from the Pacific to provide some seasoning to the European theater officers and one of these, J. Lawton Collins, was assigned as the corps commander at the neighboring Utah Beach. The other, Major General Charles Corlett, had landed with his 7th Division on Kwajalein in February 1944. Corlett arrived in the UK in April and was surprised to see that the landings would rely on LCVP and LCA landing craft instead of the amtracs now favored in the Pacific. He approached both Eisenhower and Bradley about the issue, but plans were so far along that his opinions were dismissed. The failure to consider the lessons of the Pacific campaign was mainly due to the conviction

A young GI from the 1st Infantry Division on the way to Normandy. He is wearing the distinctive assault jacket worn by the initial waves at Omaha Beach, and his M1 carbine is in plastic wrap to protect it from water. To the left is a pole charge for attacking pillboxes while to the right is an M1A1 bazooka. In front of him are pack charges and behind him bangalore torpedoes, all tied to inflated life belts to provide buoyancy in the water. (NARA)

of the army in Europe that they had much more experience in large-scale amphibious landings than the army in the Pacific or the US Marines. There had been no landings in the Pacific on the scale of North Africa, Sicily, Salerno or Anzio and there would not be until after the Normandy landings. The amtracs had been used at Tarawa specifically to surmount the coral reef surrounding the atoll and this was not a feature of the Normandy beaches. What the US Army commanders in Europe failed to realize and their Pacific counterparts had come to recognize was that the amtracs were a necessity when landing on a contested, fortified beach. The amtracs could put the infantry ashore at the seawall, minimizing their exposure to small arms fire as they struggled from the landing craft, waded through the surf, and raced across hundreds of yards of beach. In fact, the US Army had shipped over 300 amtracs to Europe in 1944, but the lack of demand for their use in the Overlord plan meant that they were reserved for Operation Swordhilt, a contingency operation in which Patton's uncommitted Third Army was intended to reinforce Overlord in the event of a failure at one of the beaches.

American planning for Operation Neptune did not pay enough attention to a key difference between Normandy and previous landings in the Mediterranean, namely the fortified coast. None of the 1943 landings were contested on the shoreline and none involved landings against obstructed beaches. Normandy required tactics and equipment comparable to those for operations against fortifications. While considerable effort went into providing large numbers of engineers to tackle the fortifications at Normandy, neither the M4 tanks nor bulldozers were equipped to survive on a constricted beach targeted by numerous anti-tank guns. In February 1944 the US Army in Europe had requested an assault tank version of the M4A3 medium tank with sufficient armor to confront German bunkers on the Siegfried Line later in the European campaign. This emerged as the M4A3E2 assault tank, which could

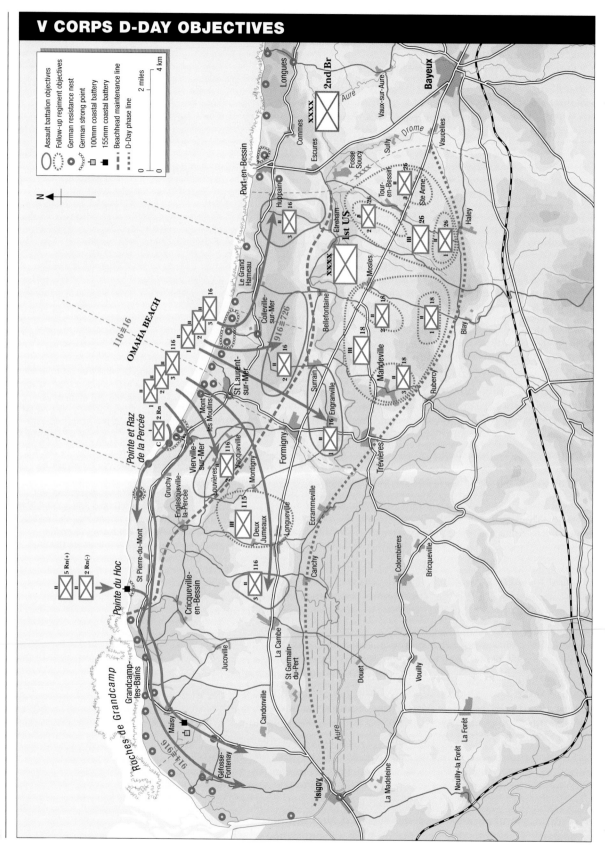

withstand frontal hits from 88mm anti-tank guns, the largest gun encountered in Normandy. These might have made a difference on D-Day had there been more appreciation of the vulnerability of the existing M4 tank to contemporary German anti-tank guns. As it transpired the M4A3E2 did not arrive in Europe until the autumn but did prove very effective in the Siegfried Line campaign. The British already had an effective support tank in their thickly armored Churchill infantry tank and it was used with success on D-Day, including a specialized combat engineer version – the AVRE.

The other specialized forces landing in the first waves were the Gap Assault Teams, of which 16 were assigned to Omaha Beach. They were to blast gaps 50 yards wide through the beach obstructions to allow landing craft to continue to reach the beach once the tide began to rise. The plan gave these teams only about 30 minutes to carry out their tasks due to the rising tide. This was a vital mission since if the gaps were not cleared, the underwater obstacles would prevent follow-up landings by later waves of craft.

The main landings were to be conducted by two regimental combat teams (RCT) each consisting of an infantry regiment with attached engineers and other support troops. The left (eastern) flank would be assaulted by the 16th RCT based around the 16th Infantry Regiment, 1st Division, while the right (western) flank would be assaulted by the 116th RCT, based around the 116th Infantry, 29th Division. The engineers in the first wave were mainly from the divisional engineer battalions, but follow-on waves contained the 5th and 6th Provisional Engineer Brigades to assist in preparing the beach for follow-on forces and supplies. The tasks of the engineers included clearing the beach obstacles, for example using bangalore torpedoes to open gaps in wire obstructions, clearing lanes through minefields to provide the infantry with exits off the beach, and destroying German fortifications. After Dieppe the British army felt that combat engineers required armored support in the form of flail tanks to conduct minefield clearance, and specialized Churchill tanks with petard mortars for demolition work. The US Army ignored the use of armored engineer vehicles, except for armored bulldozers, due to a lack of experience in this type of operation.

The Ranger Provisional Brigade was assigned the most perilous mission of the assault – the capture of the German artillery battery on Pointe-du-Hoc on the western edge of the assault area. This heavily fortified battery could strike both Utah and Omaha Beach and Bradley deemed it essential that it be eliminated. Unfortunately, it was located on a promontory with cliffs all around. One officer remarked that an attacking force could be swept off the cliffs by "three old women with brooms." Pointe-du-Hoc was scheduled to receive special treatment from the naval bombardment force in advance of the Ranger attack but American commanders thought it was the single most difficult aspect of the attack on Omaha Beach.

After the first two regimental combat teams landed at dawn, additional reinforcements would arrive in successive waves bringing the total to four RCTs by midday. Force B would arrive in the afternoon, which would increase the strength on Omaha Beach to two reinforced divisions, with a third division to land on D+1.

Allied intelligence had detected the German 352nd Infantry Division around St Lô and anticipated that it would begin to move against the beachhead sometime on D-Day, and might reach the Aure River or even cross it on the afternoon of D-Day. However, the plan expected that it would delay, but not stop the advance to the D+1 positions.

THE GERMAN PLAN

The defenses along Omaha Beach increased continually after the autumn of 1943 when Rommel was put in charge of reinvigorating the Atlantic Wall. Although Hitler and most senior German commanders expected the main invasion to take place on the Pas de Calais, Rommel believed that a case could be made for landings on the Normandy coast, or in Brittany around Montagne d'Aree. As a result, he ordered the construction of defenses along the most likely areas of coastline and increased the forces ready to defend the coast. Defenses in Normandy were initially based around the 716th Infantry Division, a poor-quality, static division. Omaha Beach was patrolled by a single regiment of this division.

Rommel believed that the sea itself was the best defensive barrier and the terrain around Omaha Beach presented ample defensive opportunities. The initial defensive work began at the water's edge with the construction of obstructions against landing craft. The outer barrier, about 100 yards above the low-tide mark and 275yds from the seawall, consisted of a string of steel obstructions, called Cointet gates by the Germans and Belgian gates or Element C by the Allies. These were designed to block landing craft from approaching the beach. The next line of barriers about 30 yards closer to shore were wooden stakes that were planted in the sand facing seaward and buttressed like an enormous tripod. These stakes were usually surmounted by a Tellermine 42 anti-tank mine. These obstacles were designed to blow holes in the bottom of landing craft. In some sectors these were followed by *Hemmkurven*, called ramp obstacles by the Allies, which were a curved steel structure designed to obstruct the landing craft. Finally there was a row of "hedgehogs" of various types. The most common was the *Tschechenigel*, called "Rommel's Asparagus" by the Allies, which was an anti-craft/anti-tank obstruction made from steel beams. The obstructions on the tidal flats were primarily intended to prevent the approach of landing craft to the seawall during high tide. These were submerged and invisible at high tide, preventing landing craft crews from steering easily through any gaps. There were a total of 3,700 obstacles at Omaha Beach – the highest density of any of the D-Day beaches.

At the high-water mark was a swathe of shingle, round stones the size of golf balls, sometimes backed by a seawall. One or more rows of concertina wire or other barbed wire obstructions were placed immediately inland from this. Until the autumn of 1943 there were many small beach houses and other structures along the shoreline for vacationers and local residents. These were knocked down to deprive Allied infantry of cover. A few of the more substantial buildings along the shore were left intact, but were converted into infantry strongpoints. The beach area was heavily mined, though gaps that contained no mines were also marked with minefield warnings to confuse Allied troops.

In contrast to the other four Normandy beaches, which are relatively flat, Omaha Beach is characterized by bluffs rising up to 150ft from the sea, most noticeably on its western side. The edges of these bluffs provide ideal defensive positions for infantry with clear fields of fire on the exposed troops below. On some of the cliffs on the eastern side of

The most powerful weapons on Omaha Beach were two 88mm PaK 43/41 "Scheunentor" (barn door). These were located in casemates, but one was moved out of the bunker after the landings, as seen here. (NARA)

the beach, 240mm artillery shells were dangled over the cliff with trip-wires to serve as booby-traps for any infantry trying the climb. These were called "roller-grenades" and they were spaced some 330ft apart.

Access from the beach was limited to five gullies, called "draws" by the US Army, and only two of these were readily passable by armored vehicles or motor transport. These became the center point of German defenses at Omaha Beach. Since the tactical objective of the defense was to prevent the Allies from moving off the beach, all five draws were stiffly defended by establishing a fortified belt in and around them. Fourteen strongpoints (*wiederstandnester*), numbered WN60 through WN73, were created along the beach. Most of the draws were covered by a strongpoint on the hilltops on either side of the draw. Two other strongpoints were constructed on the Pointe-et-Raz-de-la-Percée promontory on the eastern side of the beach to provide enfilading fire along the beach, and the three other strongpoints were constructed immediately behind the beach, covering the exits from the draws.

The configuration of each of these strongpoints differed due to terrain, and they were still being built when the Allies landed on 6 June 1944. Generally they consisted of small pillboxes, or concrete reinforced "Tobruk" machine-gun pits, at the base of the bluff obstructing the entrances to the draws. The larger draws were also blocked by barrier walls, anti-tank ditches and anti-tank traps. One of the most effective defenses was the *Bauform 667* anti-tank gun bunkers built into the sides of the bluffs, with their guns pointed parallel to the beach. These

The artillery regiment of the 352nd Infantry Division was deployed in field emplacements about 6 miles behind the beach, like this 105mm leFH 18/40. Pre-sighted on targets along the beach, they proved to be one of the German defenders' most effective weapons on D-Day. (NARA)

bunkers had a defensive wall on the side facing the sea that made it very difficult for warships to engage them with gunfire. By careful positioning they prevented Allied tanks from entering the draw since they could hit the tanks on their vulnerable side armor from point-blank range and, furthermore, the guns were positioned to fire in defilade down the length of the beach. These often contained older anti-tank guns such as obsolete PaK38 50mm. However, such weapons were more than adequate to penetrate the side armor of the Sherman tank and they were also effective against landing craft. In total, there were eight anti-tank gun bunkers along Omaha Beach including two 88mm guns. Besides the fully enclosed anti-tank guns, there were three 50mm anti-tank guns on pedestal mounts in concrete pits, and ten other anti-tank guns and field guns in open pits in the various strongpoints. As an additional defensive installation, the turrets from obsolete French and German tanks were mounted over concrete bunkers. There were five of these on Omaha Beach, the heaviest concentration being in WN66/68 covering the D-3 Les Moulins draw. Generally the strongpoints had a mixture of these types of firing positions. For example, the WN61/62 strongpoint at the E-3 Colleville draw had two 75mm PaK 40 anti-tank guns in casemates to enfilade the beach, two 50mm anti-tank guns on pedestals in open concrete emplacements, a 50mm mortar Tobruk and six machine-gun Tobruks.

Around these fortifications, the German infantry dug out a series of trenches as a first step to creating a series of interlocking shelters and protected passages. However, the shortage of concrete in the spring of 1944 meant that only a small portion of these trench lines were concrete-reinforced. The construction of these defenses was hampered by the haphazard priorities of the army, Luftwaffe, and Organization

Normandy had lower priority than the Pas de Calais for concrete, so many of the German infantry positions were ordinary slit trenches like these from the WN66 strongpoint on the east shoulder of D-3 Les Moulins draw. (NARA)

Table 1: German Beach Strongpoints, Grandcamps Sector

Wiederstandnester	Location[2]	AT Gun Casemates	Panzerstellung	50mm AT gun pit	AT/Field guns	MG bunker/Tobruk	Mortar Tobruk
WN73	Near D-1	1					3
WN72	D-1	2				3	
WN71	D-1					3	1
WN70	D-1/D-3	1			1	4	2
WN68	D-3		2		1	1	
WN66	D-3		1	1	1	1	2
WN65	E-1	1		1	1		2
WN64	E-1				1		2
WN62	E-3	2			3		2
WN61	E-3	1	1	1		4	
WN60	F-1		1		2		3
Total		8	5	3	10	16	17

Todt. The Luftwaffe, for example, built an elaborate concrete shelter for its radar station on the neighboring Pointe-et-Raz-de-la-Percée that was absolutely useless in protecting the radar from any form of attack. At the same time many key infantry trenches on the bluffs, lacking concrete reinforcement, flooded during spring rain and were rendered useless by the time of the attack.

Of all the defenses near Omaha Beach, by far the most fortified was the Pointe-du-Hoc. The site was originally constructed to contain six 155mm guns in open gun emplacements, but the defense was being reconstructed to protect each gun with a fully enclosed *Bauform 671* ferro-concrete casemate. In addition, the site contained a fully enclosed artillery observation point on the seaward side of the promontory and fully protected crew shelters and ammunition bunkers.

Due to Rommel's tactical approach, most of the German tactical defenses were spread as a thin crust along the shoreline with very modest reserve forces behind the main line of resistance. On D-Day itself the tactical plan would simply be to hold the invading force on the beach with the resources at hand.

OPPOSING ARMIES

GERMAN FORCES

The 716th Infantry Division had garrisoned Omaha Beach, called the Grandcamps sector by the Germans, since June 1942. This under-strength, static division was spread from Carentan to the Orne estuary and, therefore, defending all of the Normandy beaches except Utah in the west. 726th Grenadier Regiment (GR.726) was responsible for covering the Omaha Beach area in 1942–43. Of the 58 divisions under OB West on 6 June 1944, 33 were static or reserve divisions. The troops in these static divisions tended to be older conscripts, typically about 35 years old. The fourth battalion of GR.726 was 439th Ost Battalion made up of former Red Army troops. The division was significantly under-strength with only about 7,000 troops compared to a nominal strength of over 12,000. On the other hand, most of its forces were deployed in bunkers or field fortifications with a large number of supplementary weapons including 197 machine-gun pits, 12 anti-tank rifles, 75 medium mortars, and 249 flamethrowers.

On 15 March 1944 the 352nd Infantry Division was ordered to take over defense of the Bayeux sector of the Normandy beaches as part of Rommel's effort to strengthen the defenses in this sector. This division had been formed in December 1943 near St Lô from the remnants of the battered 321st Infantry Division, which had been sent back from Russia to rebuild. The new division was organized as a Type 44 infantry division and most of its personnel were recent conscripts from the classes of 1925/26, meaning young men 18–19 years old. Unlike the old 716th Infantry Division, the 352nd Infantry Division was at full strength. It consisted of three infantry regiments, each with two rifle battalions with their companies numbered 1 through 4 and 5 through 8 respectively. The 13th Company was a cannon company for direct fire support equipped with two 150mm and six 75mm infantry howitzers. The 14th company in each regiment was an anti-tank unit with Panzerschreck anti-tank rocket launchers. The 1944 divisional structure substituted a fusilier regiment for the old reconnaissance battalion, with one company on bicycles and one company motorized. The division's artillery regiment had four battalions, three with 12 105mm howitzers each and the fourth with 12 150mm guns. The division's anti-tank battalion had a company with 14 PzJg 38(t) Ausf. M Marder III tank destroyers, another with ten StuG III assault guns, and a third with improvised 37mm guns on Opel trucks. Divisional training was hamstrung by the lack of fuel and ammunition as well as by the need to divert the troops to work on field fortifications to reinforce the Atlantic Wall. There was little opportunity for training above company level. This unit was reasonably well trained by German 1944 standards, though not by US Army standards. The 1944 German infantry division had less

A young German infantryman enjoys a cup of coffee while on the way to a POW camp in England after having been captured in Normandy. The troops of the 352nd Infantry Division were mostly 18–19-year-old conscripts with their tactical training cut short by the need to do construction work on beach defenses for the three months they were stationed along the Atlantic coast prior to D-Day. (NARA)

manpower than its US counterpart but more firepower, especially in automatic weapons.

The reconfiguration of the defenses along the Bayeux coast in late March 1944 more than tripled their strength. The Omaha Beach area that had been held by two battalions from GR.726 was now reinforced by two regiments of the 352nd Infantry Division along the coastline and a reinforced regiment as corps reserve within a few hours march of the coast. The two battalions of GR.726 in the Omaha Beach sector were subordinated to the headquarters of the 352nd Infantry Division and retained their mission of manning the coastal emplacements and trenches along the beach. 914th Grenadier Regiment (GR.914) was responsible for the Isigny/Pointe-du-Hoc sector west of Omaha Beach, while 916th Grenadier Regiment (GR.916) was responsible for the Omaha Beach sector as well as the eastern section of Gold Beach. The third regiment, 915th Grenadier Regiment (GR.915), and the division's 352nd Fusilier Battalion were formed into Kampfgruppe Meyer and stationed behind the coast near St Lô to serve as the corps reserve.

The reinforced 352nd Infantry Division was responsible for defending 33 miles of coastline, far beyond what was considered prudent in German tactical doctrine. This led to a number of arguments between Rommel and the divisional commander, GenLt Dietrich Kraiss. Rommel wanted all of the infantry companies deployed along the main line of resistance so they could fire on landing Allied troops. Kraiss wanted to adopt a more conventional defense with a relatively thin screen along the beach and most of the companies held in reserve behind the bluffs from where they could counter-attack any penetrations. In the end a compromise was reached. In the Omaha Beach sector one of its infantry battalions moved up to the coastline and deployed two of its companies in the forward defenses alongside GR.726, with the other companies in the villages a few miles from the beach. The other battalion formed a reserve for the regimental sector along with the division's self-propelled anti-tank battalion.

Omaha Beach was covered by 1st Battalion, 352nd Artillery Regiment (I/AR.352) headquartered at Etreham with three batteries of 105mm howitzers. This battalion had forward observation posts located in bunkers along the coast, significantly enhancing their lethality when employed against targets on Omaha Beach. 2nd Battalion, 352nd Artillery Regiment (II/AR.352), headquartered to the east at St Clement, also had Omaha Beach in range. The artillery battalions were provided with only one unit of fire, meaning 225 rounds per 105mm howitzer and 150 rounds for each 150mm gun. No resupply was available for a few days. The final element of the artillery in this sector was added on 9 May 1944 when a battery of heavy artillery rockets (*Nebelwerfer*) of Werfer-Regiment.84 was positioned in this sector. Behind the 352nd Infantry Division was the 1st Flak-Sturm Regiment of the Luftwaffe 11th Flak Division, adding 36 88mm guns to the defense of this sector.

Allied intelligence believed the entire 352nd Infantry Division was in corps reserve around St Lô when in fact only one of its three infantry regiments was in reserve on 6 June 1944. To explain its appearance in the fighting on Omaha Beach on D-Day the myth developed that the division had been deployed near the beach to conduct training a few days before D-Day. This was not the case and the division had been in place near Omaha Beach for more than two months before D-Day.

On the Pointe-du-Hoc promontory between Omaha and Utah beaches was the 2nd Battery of Army Coastal Artillery Regiment 1260 (2/HKAA.1260) equipped with six French 155mm guns and five light machine-guns. By June 1944 four of six casemates for the guns had been completed but heavy Allied bombing raids had reduced the ground around the batteries to a lunar landscape of craters. After the 25 April 1944 bombing, the battery had withdrawn its guns from the casemates to an orchard south of the point. In their place the crews had fabricated dummy guns from timbers that fooled Allied intelligence into thinking the guns were still present. At the time of the invasion the concrete emplacements around the forward observation bunker were reinforced by a company from GR.726.

Luftwaffe support for the beach defenses was nonexistent. On 4 June 1944 Luftflotte 3 had 183 day-fighters in northern France of which 160 were serviceable. There were few ground-attack aircraft due to the policy of hoarding these units on the Eastern Front. Allied air attacks on forward airfields were so intense that on 5 June 124 fighters were withdrawn from the coast to bases further inland and the supplies and support for these aircraft were not available until 6 or 7 June.

ORDER OF BATTLE: GERMAN FORCES, GRANDCAMPS SECTOR

352.Infanterie Division	**Molay-Littry**	**GenLt Dietrich Kraiss**
Grenadier Regiment.914	**Neuilly-la-Foret**	**Oberstleutnant Ernst Heyna**
I/GR.914	Osmanville	
II/GR.914	Catz	
Grenadier Regiment.915		
(detached to corps reserve)	**St Paul-du-Vernay**	**Oberstleutnant Karl Meyer**
I/GR.915	Juaye	
II/GR.915	Lantheuil	
Grenadier Regiment.916	**Trevieres**	**Oberstleutnant Ernst Goth**
I/GR.916	Ryes	
II/GR.916	Formigny	
Infanterie Regiment.726		
(from 716.Infanterie Div.)	**Sully**	**Oberstleutnant Walter Korfes**
I/IR.726	Maisons	
III/IR.726	Jucoville	
Ost-Battalion 439	Isigny	
Artillerie Regiment.352	**Molay-Littry**	**Oberstleutnant Karl Ocker**
I/AR.352	Etreham	
II/AR.352	St Clément	
III/AR.352	La Noë	
IV/AR.352	Asnieres-en-Bessin	
Fusilier Battalion.352		
(detached to corps reserve)	Caumont-l'Éventé	
Panzerjäger Battalion.352	Mestry	
Pioneer Battalion.352	St Martin-de-Blagny	

AMERICAN FORCES

The US plan for Omaha Beach began the attack with a single division that would expand to two divisions by the afternoon. Rather than land the two divisions in column, the left flank of the assault force was the 16th

Regimental Combat Team (RCT) from the 1st Infantry Division, while the right flank was the 116th RCT from the 29th Division, but subordinated for the initial phase of the operation to the 1st Infantry Division.

The 1st Infantry Division, named "Big Red One" after its shoulder patch, was the Army's most experienced division and had been personally selected for the landings by Bradley. The division had already fought in North Africa and on Sicily and was one of the few divisions in the UK with any combat experience. In view of its excellent performance in repulsing a German Panzer attack on the Gela beachhead on Sicily a year before, the 16th Infantry was a natural choice for the initial assault wave.

The 29th Division was nicknamed the "Blue and Gray" for its shoulder patch, symbolizing an amalgamation of the Union and Confederate traditions. This National Guard division was headquartered in Baltimore, Maryland, and as a mid-Atlantic border state between north and south, the division drew its units from Maryland and Virginia. As with nearly all National Guard divisions, the regular army insisted on filling out its senior command posts with professional officers as the National Guard had the reputation for granting ranks as political sinecures. It was also necessary to flesh out the division with conscripts. There was some friction in the unit between the Guardsmen, who were often neighbors with years of peacetime service together, and the new influx of regular army officers and conscripts. Gebhardt's strict training regimen in the UK before D-Day was intended to forge the division into a cohesive fighting force and the 29th Division proved to be one of the better National Guard divisions during the subsequent fighting in France.

Each regimental combat team was allotted a tank battalion for fire support, the 741st Tank Battalion in support of the 16th RCT and the 743rd Tank Battalion supporting the 116th RCT.

The task of eliminating the German artillery battery on Pointe-du-Hoc was assigned to the Provisional Ranger Group, consisting of the elite

2nd and 5th Ranger Battalions. Since the battery was located on a cliff top the battalion developed a number of unique solutions for quickly scaling the cliffs under fire. Ladders were fitted inside the cargo hold of DUKW amphibious trucks. These were difficult to operate unless located firmly against the base of the cliff, so the Rangers also developed a rocket-fired grapnel hook using standard 2in. rockets and portable projectors. The assault teams also carried climbing rope and light-weight ladders. The main assault would be conducted by the 225 men of Force A, with Cos. E and F, 2nd Rangers scaling the eastern side of Pointe-du-Hoc, and Co. D on the western side. Force B, based on Co. D, 2nd Rangers would scale the cliffs on the neighboring Pointe-et-Raz-de-la-Percée promontory to eliminate German positions there. Force C, consisting of the remainder of 2nd Rangers and the 5th Rangers, would remain offshore during the initial assault, reinforcing Force A if the mission proceeded according to plan, but landing with the 116th RCT if the mission failed in order to assault Pointe-du-Hoc from the land side. This mission was widely considered the most dangerous of any assignment on D-Day; the reason the Rangers were given the assignment.

The other key elements in the assault waves were the Gap Assault Teams of the Special Engineer Task Force. Each of these 16 teams was formed by combining a 13-man Naval Combat Demolition Unit (NCDU) with a 28-man army engineer unit. The latter were drawn from the two units supporting the assault wave, the 146th and 299th Engineer Combat Battalions. The task of each team was to blow a gap 50 yards wide in the beach obstructions to permit later waves of landing craft to pass through the obstacles when the tide rose. Each team was allotted a M4 tank-dozer that arrived separately on an LCT.

ORDER OF BATTLE: US FORCES, OMAHA BEACH

V Corps	**MajGen Leonard T. Gerow**
1st Infantry Division	MajGen Clarence R. Huebner
29th Infantry Division	MajGen Charles H. Gebhardt
Provisional Ranger Group	LtCol James Rudder
5th Engineer Special Brigade	Col William Bridges
6th Engineer Special Brigade	Col Paul Thompson

Force O
16th Regimental Combat Team

16th Infantry Regiment	Col George Taylor
741st Tank Battalion	
Special Engineer Task Force (b)	
7th Field Artillery Battalion	
62nd Armored Field Artillery Battalion	
197th AAA Battalion (AWSP)	
1st Engineer Battalion	
5th Engineer Special Brigade (-)	
20th Engineer Combat Battalion	
81st Chemical Weapons Battalion (motorized)	

116th Regimental Combat Team

116th Infantry Regiment	Col Charles Canham
2nd Ranger Battalion	
5th Ranger Battalion	
743rd Tank Battalion	
Special Engineer Task Force	
58th Armored Field Artillery Battalion	
111th Field Artillery Battalion	
6th Engineer Special Brigade (-)	
112th Engineer Combat Battalion	
121st Engineer Battalion	
81st Chemical Weapons Battalion	
467th Automatic Anti-Aircraft Weapons Battalion (SP)	
461st Amphibious Truck Company	

18th Regimental Combat Team

18th Infantry Regiment	Col George Smith Jr.
745th Tank Battalion	
32nd Field Artillery Battalion	
5th Field Artillery Battalion	
5th Engineer Special Brigade (-)	

Force B
115th Regimental Combat Team

115th Infantry Regiment	Col Eugene Slappey
110th Field Artillery Battalion	

175th Regimental Combat Team

175th Infantry Regiment	Col Paul Goode

26th Regimental Combat Team

26th Infantry Regiment	Col John Seitz
33rd Field Artillery Battalion	

D-DAY

The Initial Operations

D-Day was originally scheduled to begin on 5 June, but the appalling weather in the Channel forced a postponement until 6 June. The German meteorology service in the Atlantic had been rolled-up by determined Allied action in the preceding months and, as a result, most senior German commanders were convinced that any landing operations would be impossible for several days until the weather cleared. As a result, Rommel was in Germany and a number of senior commanders were away from their posts to conduct staff exercises. General Dollman had lowered the alert status of all of his troops, believing that the foul weather would preclude any Allied activity.

Around 2215hrs on 5 June the intelligence section of several German headquarters picked up a coded radio message to the French resistance indicating that the invasion would begin in the next 48 hours. Some reconnaissance aircraft were sent to sweep the Channel but many officers thought it was a false alarm. Seventh Army in Normandy was not alerted.

At 0030hrs Allied minesweepers began to clear paths through anticipated minefields, guided by markers placed on the beaches by midget submarines. In fact the Germans had not yet established any significant minefields off Omaha Beach. At 0300hrs Task Force O arrived 25,000yds off Omaha Beach and dropped anchor to prepare the landing craft. At 0330hrs the assault troops were called to their debarkation posts on the assault transports and loaded into the landing craft at 0415. The landing craft gradually set off from the assault transports over the next hour, aiming to arrive at the rendezvous point by 0600hrs. The sea was

LCVPs begin the move to shore on D-Day under the watchful eye of the USS *Augusta*, flagship of the Western Task Force. The landing craft had a 12-mile run to shore in seas with three- to four-foot waves. The navy censor has partly obscured the cruiser's radar masts in this photo. (NARA)

choppy with 3–4ft waves and an occasional interference wave[3] as high as 6ft. The wind was gusting from the northwest at 10–18 knots. As a result, more than half of the assault troops were seriously seasick even before the final approach to the beach.

Wehrmacht units were alerted at 0100hrs when 84th Corps head-quarters first learned of paratroop drops in neighboring sectors of the 716th Infantry Division. Although Omaha Beach was not in the landing zone of the 82nd or 101st Airborne Divisions, the dispersion of the drop resulted in small numbers of paratroopers landing in the GR.914 positions west of Omaha Beach and near the artillery batteries of II/AR.352 behind the beach. Through the early morning hours reports flowed in of paratroop and glider landings in neighboring sectors. At 0310hrs General Marcks ordered the corps reserve, Kampfgruppe Meyer, to begin moving towards Montmartin-Deville in order to keep open the routes between the 709th Division at Utah Beach and the 352nd Division at Omaha. The decision to send the reserves after the paratroopers proved to be premature and a serious mistake. Later in the morning the force would be badly needed in the opposite direction. As a result, Kampfgruppe Meyer spent most of the morning marching westward, only to have their orders changed a few hours later and shifted in the opposite direction, all the while under air attack. The division's artillery positions began to come under air attack around 0320hrs, with especially heavy attacks on Pointe-du-Hoc around 0335. Darkness shrouded the Allied naval force and visibility was only about 10 miles, not enough to see the anchorage. The first reports of Allied naval vessels came from the right flank of the division positions at 0502hrs and by 0520 large numbers of Allied naval vessels had been spotted moving over the horizon.

---

3 An interference wave is an extra-high wave caused by the interaction of two opposing wave patterns.

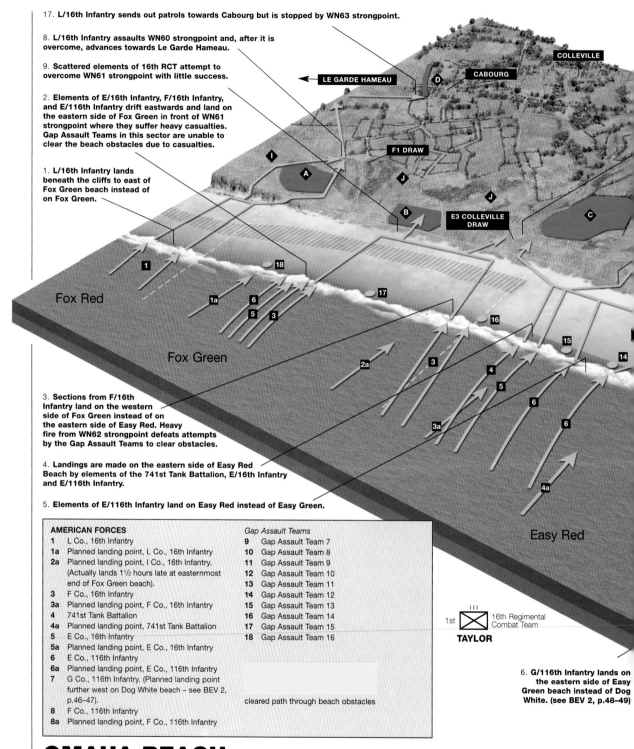

17. L/16th Infantry sends out patrols towards Cabourg but is stopped by WN63 strongpoint.

8. L/16th Infantry assaults WN60 strongpoint and, after it is overcome, advances towards Le Garde Hameau.

9. Scattered elements of 16th RCT attempt to overcome WN61 strongpoint with little success.

2. Elements of E/16th Infantry, F/16th Infantry, and E/116th Infantry drift eastwards and land on the eastern side of Fox Green in front of WN61 strongpoint where they suffer heavy casualties. Gap Assault Teams in this sector are unable to clear the beach obstacles due to casualties.

1. L/16th Infantry lands beneath the cliffs to east of Fox Green beach instead of on Fox Green.

COLLEVILLE

LE GARDE HAMEAU

CABOURG

D

F1 DRAW

I

A

J

J

B

E3 COLLEVILLE DRAW

C

1

18

Fox Red

1a

6

5

3

17

16

Fox Green

2a

3

15

14

4

5

6

3a

6

3. Sections from F/16th Infantry land on the western side of Fox Green instead of on the eastern side of Easy Red. Heavy fire from WN62 strongpoint defeats attempts by the Gap Assault Teams to clear obstacles.

4. Landings are made on the eastern side of Easy Red Beach by elements of the 741st Tank Battalion, E/16th Infantry and E/116th Infantry.

5. Elements of E/116th Infantry land on Easy Red instead of Easy Green.

4a

Easy Red

AMERICAN FORCES		*Gap Assault Teams*	
1	L Co., 16th Infantry	**9**	Gap Assault Team 7
1a	Planned landing point, L Co., 16th Infantry	**10**	Gap Assault Team 8
2a	Planned landing point, I Co., 16th Infantry.	**11**	Gap Assault Team 9
	(Actually lands 1½ hours late at easternmost	**12**	Gap Assault Team 10
	end of Fox Green beach).	**13**	Gap Assault Team 11
3	F Co., 16th Infantry	**14**	Gap Assault Team 12
3a	Planned landing point, F Co., 16th Infantry	**15**	Gap Assault Team 13
4	741st Tank Battalion	**16**	Gap Assault Team 14
4a	Planned landing point, 741st Tank Battalion	**17**	Gap Assault Team 15
5	E Co., 16th Infantry	**18**	Gap Assault Team 16
5a	Planned landing point, E Co., 16th Infantry		
6	E Co., 116th Infantry		
6a	Planned landing point, E Co., 116th Infantry		
7	G Co., 116th Infantry. (Planned landing point		
	further west on Dog White beach – see BEV 2,		
	p.46–47).		cleared path through beach obstacles
8	F Co., 116th Infantry		
8a	Planned landing point, F Co., 116th Infantry		

1st ⊠ 16th Regimental Combat Team

TAYLOR

6. G/116th Infantry lands on the eastern side of Easy Green beach instead of Dog White. (see BEV 2, p.48–49)

OMAHA BEACH
16TH REGIMENTAL COMBAT TEAM SECTOR

6 June 1944, 0630hrs onwards, viewed from the northwest showing 16th RCT's landings on "Fox" and "Easy" beaches, the eastern sector of Omaha Beach. The first wave suffers heavy casualties but with the arrival of the second wave US troops begin to climb the bluffs and overcome the German defenses.

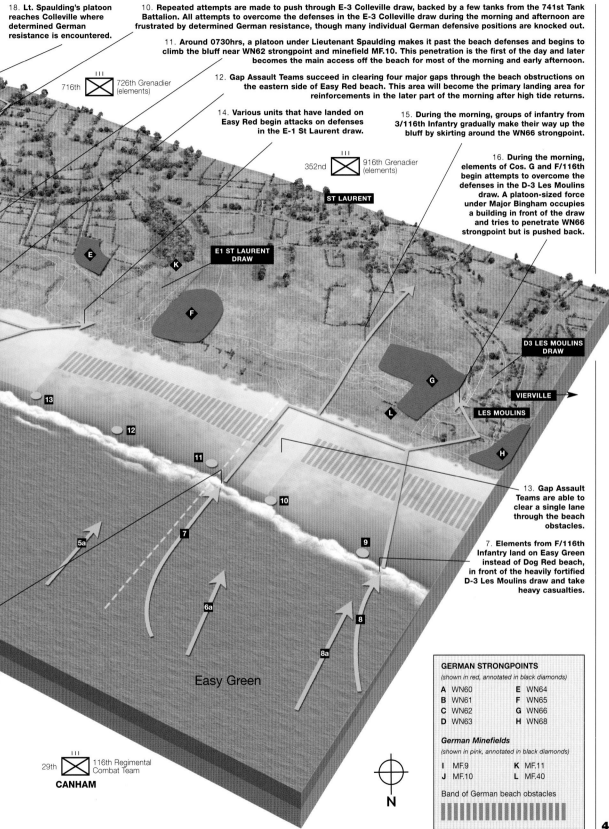

18. **Lt. Spaulding's platoon reaches Colleville where determined German resistance is encountered.**

10. **Repeated attempts are made to push through E-3 Colleville draw, backed by a few tanks from the 741st Tank Battalion. All attempts to overcome the defenses in the E-3 Colleville draw during the morning and afternoon are frustrated by determined German resistance, though many individual German defensive positions are knocked out.**

11. **Around 0730hrs, a platoon under Lieutenant Spaulding makes it past the beach defenses and begins to climb the bluff near WN62 strongpoint and minefield MF.10. This penetration is the first of the day and later becomes the main access off the beach for most of the morning and early afternoon.**

716th ⊠ 726th Grenadier (elements)

12. **Gap Assault Teams succeed in clearing four major gaps through the beach obstructions on the eastern side of Easy Red beach. This area will become the primary landing area for reinforcements in the later part of the morning after high tide returns.**

14. **Various units that have landed on Easy Red begin attacks on defenses in the E-1 St Laurent draw.**

15. **During the morning, groups of infantry from 3/116th Infantry gradually make their way up the bluff by skirting around the WN66 strongpoint.**

352nd ⊠ 916th Grenadier (elements)

16. **During the morning, elements of Cos. G and F/116th begin attempts to overcome the defenses in the D-3 Les Moulins draw. A platoon-sized force under Major Bingham occupies a building in front of the draw and tries to penetrate WN66 strongpoint but is pushed back.**

ST LAURENT

E

K

E1 ST LAURENT DRAW

F

D3 LES MOULINS DRAW

G

VIERVILLE

L

LES MOULINS

13

H

12

11

13. **Gap Assault Teams are able to clear a single lane through the beach obstacles.**

10

7. **Elements from F/116th Infantry land on Easy Green instead of Dog Red beach, in front of the heavily fortified D-3 Les Moulins draw and take heavy casualties.**

5a

7

9

6a

8

8a

Easy Green

29th ⊠ 116th Regimental Combat Team

CANHAM

N

GERMAN STRONGPOINTS

(shown in red, annotated in black diamonds)

A	WN60	E	WN64
B	WN61	F	WN65
C	WN62	G	WN66
D	WN63	H	WN68

German Minefields

(shown in pink, annotated in black diamonds)

I	MF.9	K	MF.11
J	MF.10	L	MF.40

Band of German beach obstacles

Task Force O began to approach Omaha Beach and the battleships and destroyers began the preliminary naval bombardment at 0545hrs, lasting until 0625. Many inland German positions reported these as air attacks. The initial targets were behind the beach and at dawn the warships shifted their sights to specific targets along the beach. Aerial bombardment of positions behind the beach was scheduled to begin at 0600hrs but the decision to delay bomb release for 30 seconds after passing over the coast meant that none of the bombs fell on their intended targets. Most exploded harmlessly in the pastures south of the landing beaches. Of the 446 B-24 bombers taking part, 329 dropped 13,000 bombs. At 0610hrs five LCG(L) monitors approached the beach and added their gunfire to the naval bombardment. A few moments before H-hour nine LCT(R)s approached the beach and fired 9,000 rockets. These were a major disappointment due to their poor accuracy, and none were seen to hit the beach.

THE FIRST ASSAULT WAVE, 0530–0700HRS

The four companies of DD tanks were supposed to be launched from LCT6s around 0530hrs to give them time to swim the 5,000 yards to shore by H-Hour – 0630hrs. The naval officer in charge of the eight craft carrying the DD tanks of the 743rd Tank Battalion was convinced that the water was too rough for the tanks to swim ashore and reached agreement with the tank commander to land the tanks directly onto the beach. The LCTs landed the DD tanks on Dog Green and Dog Red beaches starting at 0629hrs. Company B, coming into the beach at the Vierville draw (Exit D-1), came under heavy anti-tank gunfire. The LCT carrying the company commander was sunk immediately offshore and four other tanks from the company were disabled before reaching the beach. Machine-gun fire from the German pillboxes damaged several other LCTs but all withdrew safely. Company A with the normal M4 tanks with wading trunks landed about the same time, so that 40 out of 48 tanks made it to shore.

An LCVP from the USS *Samuel Chase* with Coxswain D. Nivens at the helm was raked by German machine-gun fire as it approached the beach, which detonated explosives being carried by the infantry and started a fire. The craft safely landed and later returned to the transport. (NARA)

The final approach to the beach by LCVPs carrying the 16th RCT from the USS *Samuel Chase* during the second wave on D-Day around 0730hrs. The troops on the craft ahead have already disembarked and are wading to shore. (NARA)

To the west the situation was much worse. The two captains from the 741st Tank Battalion outranked the senior naval officers and insisted that the DD tanks be launched as ordered 5,000 yards offshore at 0540hrs. The DD tanks immediately encountered problems on entering the water, a few sinking immediately when their fragile canvas screens collapsed. They valiantly tried to swim ashore, but the combination of wind and sea conditions and tidal currents sank all but two tanks from Co. B. Of the tank crews, 33 drowned while the rest were rescued by accompanying vessels. Having watched the first of the four DD tanks on his craft sink immediately after leaving the ramp, the young skipper of LCT-600 decided to drop the remaining three on the beach. As a result, of the 32 DD tanks of the 741st Tank Battalion only five made it to shore on Easy Red beach. Following the two doomed companies of DD tanks was Co. A with M4A1 tanks with wading trunks; each LCT carrying two regular tanks and a dozer-tank. The luckless 741st lost two M4s and an M4 dozer-tank when their LCT struck a mine and sank. As a result, only

The deadliest sector of Omaha Beach for the initial wave was at the western end, Charlie and Dog Green beaches. This aerial view taken in 1945 shows how the German strongpoints on the cliffs of Pointe-et-Raz-de-la-Percée (to the right) could cover the beach with enfilading fire. At the very top of the picture is the D-1 Vierville draw. (MHI)

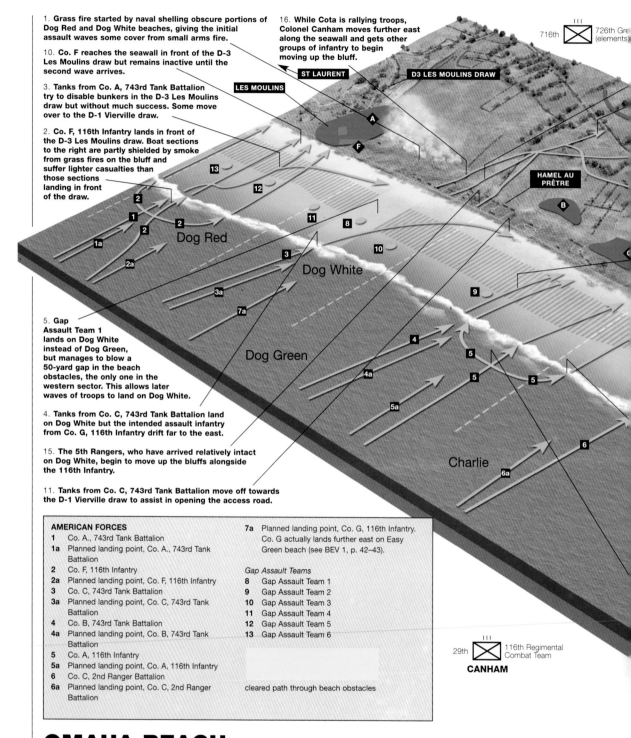

1. Grass fire started by naval shelling obscure portions of Dog Red and Dog White beaches, giving the initial assault waves some cover from small arms fire.

16. While Cota is rallying troops, Colonel Canham moves further east along the seawall and gets other groups of infantry to begin moving up the bluff.

10. Co. F reaches the seawall in front of the D-3 Les Moulins draw but remains inactive until the second wave arrives.

3. Tanks from Co. A, 743rd Tank Battalion try to disable bunkers in the D-3 Les Moulins draw but without much success. Some move over to the D-1 Vierville draw.

2. Co. F, 116th Infantry lands in front of the D-3 Les Moulins draw. Boat sections to the right are partly shielded by smoke from grass fires on the bluff and suffer lighter casualties than those sections landing in front of the draw.

5. Gap Assault Team 1 lands on Dog White instead of Dog Green, but manages to blow a 50-yard gap in the beach obstacles, the only one in the western sector. This allows later waves of troops to land on Dog White.

4. Tanks from Co. C, 743rd Tank Battalion land on Dog White but the intended assault infantry from Co. G, 116th Infantry drift far to the east.

15. The 5th Rangers, who have arrived relatively intact on Dog White, begin to move up the bluffs alongside the 116th Infantry.

11. Tanks from Co. C, 743rd Tank Battalion move off towards the D-1 Vierville draw to assist in opening the access road.

ST LAURENT

LES MOULINS

D3 LES MOULINS DRAW

HAMEL AU PRÊTRE

716th · 726th Gre (elements)

Dog Red

Dog White

Dog Green

Charlie

29th · 116th Regimental Combat Team
CANHAM

AMERICAN FORCES

1	Co. A., 743rd Tank Battalion
1a	Planned landing point, Co. A., 743rd Tank Battalion
2	Co. F, 116th Infantry
2a	Planned landing point, Co. F, 116th Infantry
3	Co. C, 743rd Tank Battalion
3a	Planned landing point, Co. C, 743rd Tank Battalion
4	Co. B, 743rd Tank Battalion
4a	Planned landing point, Co. B, 743rd Tank Battalion
5	Co. A, 116th Infantry
5a	Planned landing point, Co. A, 116th Infantry
6	Co. C, 2nd Ranger Battalion
6a	Planned landing point, Co. C, 2nd Ranger Battalion
7a	Planned landing point, Co. G, 116th Infantry. Co. G actually lands further east on Easy Green beach (see BEV 1, p. 42–43).

Gap Assault Teams

8	Gap Assault Team 1
9	Gap Assault Team 2
10	Gap Assault Team 3
11	Gap Assault Team 4
12	Gap Assault Team 5
13	Gap Assault Team 6

cleared path through beach obstacles

OMAHA BEACH
116TH REGIMENTAL COMBAT TEAM SECTOR

6 June 1944, 0629hrs onwards, viewed from the northwest showing 116th RCT's landings on "Dog" and "Charlie" beaches, the western sector of Omaha Beach. As in the eastern sector, the troops in the first assault wave suffer heavily. However, the efforts of General Norman "Dutch" Cota and Lieutenant Colonel Charles Canham help restore momentum to the US troops and they begin to press inland.

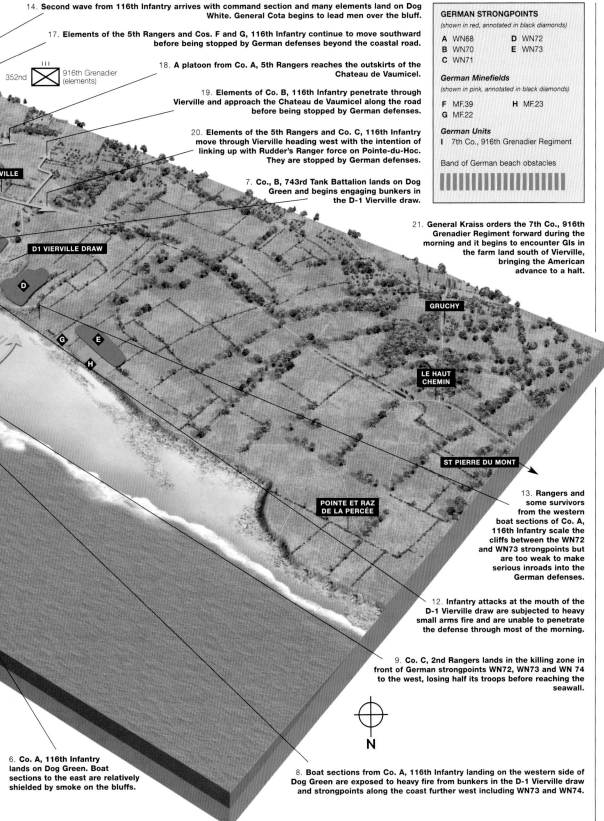

14. **Second wave from 116th Infantry arrives with command section and many elements land on Dog White. General Cota begins to lead men over the bluff.**

17. **Elements of the 5th Rangers and Cos. F and G, 116th Infantry continue to move southward before being stopped by German defenses beyond the coastal road.**

352nd ⊠ 916th Grenadier (elements)

18. **A platoon from Co. A, 5th Rangers reaches the outskirts of the Chateau de Vaumicel.**

19. **Elements of Co. B, 116th Infantry penetrate through Vierville and approach the Chateau de Vaumicel along the road before being stopped by German defenses.**

20. **Elements of the 5th Rangers and Co. C, 116th Infantry move through Vierville heading west with the intention of linking up with Rudder's Ranger force on Pointe-du-Hoc. They are stopped by German defenses.**

7. **Co., B, 743rd Tank Battalion lands on Dog Green and begins engaging bunkers in the D-1 Vierville draw.**

RVILLE

D1 VIERVILLE DRAW

D

G

E

H

21. **General Kraiss orders the 7th Co., 916th Grenadier Regiment forward during the morning and it begins to encounter GIs in the farm land south of Vierville, bringing the American advance to a halt.**

GRUCHY

LE HAUT CHEMIN

ST PIERRE DU MONT

13. **Rangers and some survivors from the western boat sections of Co. A, 116th Infantry scale the cliffs between the WN72 and WN73 strongpoints but are too weak to make serious inroads into the German defenses.**

POINTE ET RAZ DE LA PERCÉE

12. **Infantry attacks at the mouth of the D-1 Vierville draw are subjected to heavy small arms fire and are unable to penetrate the defense through most of the morning.**

9. **Co. C, 2nd Rangers lands in the killing zone in front of German strongpoints WN72, WN73 and WN 74 to the west, losing half its troops before reaching the seawall.**

N

6. **Co. A, 116th Infantry lands on Dog Green. Boat sections to the east are relatively shielded by smoke on the bluffs.**

8. **Boat sections from Co. A, 116th Infantry landing on the western side of Dog Green are exposed to heavy fire from bunkers in the D-1 Vierville draw and strongpoints along the coast further west including WN73 and WN74.**

GERMAN STRONGPOINTS
(shown in red, annotated in black diamonds)

A WN68   D WN72
B WN70   E WN73
C WN71

German Minefields
(shown in pink, annotated in black diamonds)

F MF.39   H MF.23
G MF.22

German Units
I 7th Co., 916th Grenadier Regiment

Band of German beach obstacles

18 of its 48 tanks reached shore and three were knocked out by anti-tank guns almost immediately. In spite of their losses, the tanks attempted to carry out their mission and began engaging the various bunkers and defensive works.

The first assault wave, consisting of 1,450 men in eight infantry companies and the Gap Assault Teams, began landings at 0631hrs. Each LCVP or LCA usually carried 31 men and an officer, with six landing craft to a company. Few of the LCVPs made dry landings, with most grounding on sandbars 50–100 yards out. As the ramps dropped, the landing craft were subjected to a fusillade of machine-guns and gunfire. Some GIs had to wade through neck-deep water under savage fire the entire way. The troops in the assault wave had been issued much more equipment than normal infantry, including explosive charges and additional supplies, which made the passage through the surf especially difficult. Exhausted and sea-sick, when the survivors reached the water's edge there was little refuge. The expected bomb craters were nowhere to be seen and it was a 200-yard dash to the only reliable cover – the shingle and seawall. Many troops simply collapsed, or tried to find cover behind the numerous beach obstructions.

The conditions varied from sector to sector. Company G, 116th RCT landing west of the D-3 Les Moulins draw faced far less gunfire than on other beaches as grass fires started by the naval bombardment helped obscure the landing area. Company F, landing immediately in front of the D-3 Les Moulins draw were partly shielded by the smoke, but the three sections furthest east were exposed and suffered 50 per cent casualties by the time they reached the cover of the shingle. Company A, 116th RCT and Co. C, 2nd Rangers, landing furthest west on Dog Green opposite the D-1 Vierville draw, were slaughtered by the most intense fire encountered in any landing area in the 116th RCT sector. Not only was there a concentration of fortifications in the draw itself but there was enfilading fire from the WN72 and WN73 strongpoints on the

Pointe-et-Raz-de-la-Percée promontory on their right flank. The first Co. A landing craft grounded about 1,000yds from shore in deep water and few men made it to the beach. One LCA was hit by four mortar rounds in rapid succession and disintegrated. Every single soldier in the company commander's LCA was killed. Within moments most of the company's officers and NCOs were dead or wounded and two-thirds of Co. A, 116th Infantry were casualties. The 1/116th Infantry lost three of its four company commanders and 16 junior officers before even reaching the shoreline. Leaderless and under intense fire, the survivors clung to any protection available, mainly the beach obstacles. The company from the 2nd Rangers lost 35 of their 64 men before reaching the base of a cliff at the eastern edge of the beach. (The slaughter depicted in the opening sequence of the film *Saving Private Ryan* depicts this beach.)

On the beaches to the east assaulted by the 16th RCT the situation was bloody chaos. Problems with the control craft and the strong current caused many landing craft to drift eastward and many units landed far from their objectives. The landings on Easy Red between the St Laurent and Colleville draws were the most weakly defended and two sections of Co. E, 16th RCT made it to the shingle with modest losses but with few items of heavy equipment, which were abandoned while swimming ashore. A section from Co. F landing further east came under heavy fire when disembarking from their LCVP in neck-deep water and only 14 men reached the shore. The fire was much more intense on Fox Green beach to the east where Co. F, 16th RCT put ashore, opposite the heavily defended E-3 Colleville draw. Most of the casualties occurred after the ramps were dropped when machine-gun fire from the bunkers cut a swathe through the disembarking troops. On one LCVP only seven of the original 32 GIs reached the beach. Within moments Co. F had lost six officers and half its troops. Company E, 116th RCT had the misfortune of being further from their assigned beach than any other, and landed on Fox Green. They lost a third of their men, including the company commander, before reaching the shingle.

The two other companies of the 16th RCT were also scheduled to land on Fox Green, but Co. L wandered too far east and arrived 30 minutes late at the eastern extreme of Fox Green. Although suffering 35 per cent casualties, it was the only company of the first assault wave to remain a coherent unit. Company I became even more disoriented and drifted much too far east before their navigation was corrected. They landed $1\frac{1}{2}$ hours late in front of the cliffs at the easternmost edge of Fox Green.

The heavy losses amongst the infantry were also suffered by the critical Gap Assault Teams. Team 11 landed in front of the E-1 St Laurent draw and, while dragging ashore their rubber boat loaded with explosives, artillery hit the demolition charges, obliterating the team. Team 15 near the E-3 Colleville draw suffered the same fate and an artillery round struck the explosives of the neighboring Team 14 while still aboard the LCM, killing the entire navy contingent. Team 12 managed to plant their explosives on the obstacles on Easy Red beach but hesitated to detonate them due to the many wounded infantrymen near them. A mortar round hit some primacord, setting off the charges and killing or wounding most of the team and many of the nearby infantry. Team 13 was working on obstacles when German fire set off some of the charges, killing the Navy

Company L, 16th Infantry drifted far east of their intended landing and ended up on the eastern end of Omaha Beach below the cliffs near Fox Green. The company commander was killed, but other officers rallied the unit to attack the WN60 strongpoint on the cliffs above. (NARA)

section of the team. Team 7 was ready to breach a set of obstacles when an LCM crashed into the outer barrier, setting off seven Teller mines. Although these teams were supposed to be supported by M4 dozer-tanks, only six of the 16 made it ashore safely and three of these were quickly knocked out. By the end of the day only one dozer-tank was still operational. In spite of the heavy losses in front of the E-3 Colleville draw, several gap teams landed further east than planned due to the tides and so helped blow four adjacent gaps along the beach between the E-1 and E-3 exits. This accomplishment would prove crucial later in the day, since this was the only gap wide enough to accommodate a large number of landing craft.

The first infiltrations through the German defenses were made here around 0720hrs. Courage is not the absence of fear, but the ability to act in spite of fear. In the face of intense small arms, mortar and artillery fire, a handful of young soldiers began to act. Many young squad and platoon leaders tried to rally their men, but most were cut down by intense small arms fire. After engineers breached some wire obstructions, Sergeant Philip Streczyk from Co. E, 16th RCT ran through a gap at the base of the bluff west of the E-3 Colleville draw. Under covering fire from Co. G, Lieutenant John Spalding rallied a platoon-sized force and followed. Spalding's small force began to attack strongpoint WN62 from behind. In the meantime, the battered Co. F, 16th RCT had begun to attack the WN62 pillboxes from the front, putting one out of action with a bazooka. There were also penetrations into the F-1 draw by scattered groups of GIs who attacked the WN61 strongpoint from both front and rear. At 0720hrs a M4A1 tank of the battered 741st Tank Battalion managed to knock out the 88mm gun casemate at WN61. Around 0745hrs another M4A1 knocked out the top casemate at WN62 on the west side of the E-3 Colleville draw. The commander of GR.726 in this sector radioed back to 352nd Infantry Division headquarters that his telephone lines had been disrupted by the

attack and asked for a counter-attack to throw back the American penetration. The divisional commander, General Kraiss, radioed to the 84th Corps HQ since his GR.915 was in corps reserve as Kampfgruppe Meyer. At 0735hrs the request for a counter-attack was granted and at 0750 Kampfgruppe Meyer began dispatching a battalion towards Colleville that was scheduled to arrive around 0930. It was so far west chasing paratroopers that it didn't arrive until the afternoon. While it was not apparent at the time, the German defenses had already begun to crumble.

The gap teams were far less successful in the 116th RCT sector, in part due to the eastward drift of some landing craft. Team 1 inadvertently missed the killing zone on Dog Green, landing on Dog White instead. They blew a 50-yard gap in textbook fashion in only 20 minutes. The neighboring Teams 2 to 5 had little or no success. Team 2 arrived too late, while Team 3 suffered a direct artillery hit on its LCT and only one of the 40-man team survived. Team 4 suffered heavy casualties in front of the D-3 Les Moulins draw. Team 5 managed to plant its charges, but by the time it was ready to detonate them, so many infantry had huddled around the obstacles for shelter that only a few could be blown. Team 6 landed east of the D-3 Les Moulins draw and managed to create a gap in spite of the infantry using the obstacles for cover. Teams 7 and 8 had an impossible time clearing the obstructions, in part due to casualties and in part due to the recurring problem of the infantry using the obstacles as cover from the deadly German small arms fire. The two narrow gaps in the 116th RCT sector, while not as wide as the gaps to the east, would become the only means for reinforcement during much of the morning. Casualties among the Gap Assault Teams in both sectors were 41 per cent and some of the teams were virtually wiped out.

By 0700hrs the tide had turned and the obstacle belt was slowly inundated, drowning the badly wounded who had taken shelter near the beach obstructions. The surviving members of the eight infantry and one Ranger companies hid behind the shingle and seawalls along 7,000 yards of beach, losing more and more men as German mortar and machine-gun fire took their toll. Many of the GIs had a difficult time engaging the German positions as their rifles had become fouled with seawater or sand. Of the troops who landed in the first wave, more than a third were casualties within the first hour and most units were leaderless, their officers and NCOs dead or wounded.

THE SECOND ASSAULT WAVE, 0700–0800HRS

The second assault wave was supposed to land at 0700 in the midst of an advancing tide. The second wave had as many navigation problems as the first, exacerbated by the remaining, partly submerged obstacles. Company B, 116th RCT landing on Dog Green took heavy casualties like the first wave. Company C landed on Dog White enjoying the cover provided by the grass fires. Company D lost several LCVPs on the way into the beach and landed in a disorganized fashion with heavy casualties. The headquarters company landed at the extreme western area of the beach near the foot of the cliffs and was pinned down by sniper fire for most of the day. Company H and the 2/116th Infantry headquarters company landed on either side of the D-3 Les Moulins draw. Casualties amongst the officers of 2/116th Infantry was particularly heavy with two of the company commanders dead and another wounded. While the second wave landed, the tanks tried to reduce the German strongpoints. Three M4 tanks from the 743rd Tank Battalion began to crawl up the bluff near WN70, while three more began an assault on WN68 on the western side of the D-3 Les Moulins draw, penetrating the first layer of the defense.

The 3/116th RCT was scheduled to follow around 0730hrs. Aside from Cos. A and B, 2nd Rangers which landed in the killing zone near Dog Green, most of the later infantry companies and the 5th Rangers made it to shore with fewer casualties than the preceding waves and

GIs look warily towards the beach during landings on Omaha later on D-Day morning. The beach is already littered with vehicles and tanks knocked out earlier in the day. (NARA)

were soon crowding the beaches on either side of the D-3 Les Moulins draw. Around 0730hrs the regimental command parties began arriving including Col Canham and BrigGen Cota. Two LCIs bringing in the alternate HQ for 116th RCT were hit by artillery fire around 0740hrs and they burned for the rest of the day. To further add to the confusion on the beach, the second wave landings also brought to shore an increasing number of vehicles, which became bunched up along the shoreline and easy targets for German gunners. By 0800hrs the tide had risen by 8ft, covering many obstacles and drowning many of the severely wounded.

Cota and Canham walked along the beach, cajoling the men to move towards the bluffs above. After making a breach in the concertina wire beyond the seawall, around 0750hrs Cota led forward a small group of men from Co. C, 116th Infantry. They waded through tall reeds and marsh grass at the base of the bluffs, finally finding their way up onto the bluffs themselves using the terrain to avoid the German machine-gun positions. Ragged columns of troops followed, some being hit by sniper fire or wandering onto mines. Further east along Dog Red beach, Col Canham led a similar column from Cos. F and G, 116th Infantry

An Air Force reconnaissance aircraft provides a bird's-eye view of Omaha Beach on D-Day. In the center is an LCI(L) while to either side are LCTs. There is a string of DUKW amphibious trucks moving in column ashore. (NARA)

over the bluffs. Around 0810hrs the neighboring 5th Ranger Battalion blew four gaps in the wire. They made their way to the top of the bluffs by 0900hrs, parallel to Cota's and Canham's growing bands. As the groups reached the crest of the bluff, they began to coalesce and send out patrols. A small group of Rangers under Lieutenant Charles Parker set off for Château de Vaumicel to carry out their mission at Pointe-du-Hoc. Sometime after 1000hrs, once enough troops had finally gathered, Cota ordered Co. C, 116th Infantry and a platoon from 5th Rangers into the village of Vierville while other elements of the 5th Rangers moved to the southwest to cut the roads leading out of Vierville.

The first attempt to climb the bluffs east of the D-3 Les Moulins draw failed. Major Sidney Bingham, the 2nd Battalion commander, whose own companies had been decimated by the bunkers in the Les Moulins draw, tried rallying the leaderless men of Co. F who had landed in the first wave. He led them in the capture of a house in the mouth of the D-3 Les Moulins draw and then attempted to attack the WN66 strongpoint on the eastern shoulder of the draw. However, the German defensive positions were too strong and the GIs had to retreat to the protection of the house and neighboring trenches. A number of squads from Co. G had more success on the bluffs east of Les Moulins draw by skirting behind the WN66 strongpoint. When the 3/116th RCT landed relatively unscathed in this area, it provided the momentum to finally push inland and by 0900hrs there were portions of three companies over the bluffs between the D-3 and E-1 draws. By late morning there were about 600 GIs over the bluffs advancing southward. The scattered tanks fought a day-long battle

LANDINGS AT EASY RED BEACH, 0730HRS (pages 54–55)
This boat section of assault troops from 1st Battalion,
16th Infantry huddle inside their LCVP as it approaches
Easy Red beach around 0730hrs during the second wave of
landings. The tide has already started to turn, and some of
the beach obstructions (1) are already awash. A M4A1
medium tank (2) with the number 10 on its wading trunk can
be seen in the water to the left. The intended tactic for
these tanks was to remain in the water with only the turret
exposed, thereby protecting the hull from German anti-tank
gun fire. In the event, most tanks drove onto the beach.
Each LCVP carried one officer and 31 enlisted men. The
standard loading pattern in the craft were three men
abreast in 11 rows. The first two rows were the boat team
leader, in this case a young lieutenant (3), and rifle team
armed with M1 Garand rifles. They were followed by a
four-man wire-cutting team, two BAR automatic weapons
teams, a four-man 60mm mortar team, two two-man

bazooka teams, a two-man flamethrower team, a five-man
demolition team, and the assistant boat team leader (a
sergeant) in the rear. The positioning of the lieutenant in the
front of the craft proved disastrous in the initial assault
waves, as so many of the young lieutenants were the first
men killed when the ramp went down, exposing the craft
hold to German machine-gun fire. The green brassard (4) on
the rifleman in the center is a chemically impregnated panel
that would change color if exposed to chemical weapons.
There was considerable concern that the Germans would
attempt to repel the landings using gas weapons. So the
troops in the assault waves wore battledress impregnated
with a special (and uncomfortable) gas-resistant substance
and carried a gas mask. Rifles were protected by a
plastic wrap (5), though some troops removed this before
disembarking. Many of the landing craft were crewed by
the Coast Guard, one of whom (6) can be seen to the
right. (Howard Gerrard)

This is a view from the WN71 strongpoint on the eastern side of the D-1 Vierville draw looking east towards the neighboring D-3 Les Moulins draw. The initial penetration by General Cota and the 5th Rangers took place over this part of the bluff. (MHI)

with the German beach fortifications. Major Bingham later said that the tanks of the 743rd Tank Battalion had "saved the day. They shot the hell out of the Germans and got the hell shot out of them."

In the 16th RCT sector to the east, Easy Red held out the most promise since there were a few M4A1 tanks from the 741st Tank Battalion providing covering fire, and this area included the only major gap through the obstacles. Company G came in first in the second wave and suffered 30 per cent casualties before reaching the shingle. But in contrast to the first wave, this company was still functional. Company H, 116th RCT landed late a little further west and took heaviest casualties in those boat sections landing nearest the E-1 draw. Three more companies

This view was taken from the junction of Easy Green and Easy Red beaches at the base of the bluffs to the east of the D-3 Les Moulins draw. The draw is the depression in the center of the photo. This was the area where the 3rd Battalion, 116th Infantry staged their advance over the bluff. General Cota advanced over the bluffs on the other side of the draw, seen towards the right side of this photo. (MHI)

DOG RED BEACH, 0740HRS (pages 58–59)

The 29th Division's assistant commander, Brigadier General Norman "Dutch" Cota (1), and the 116th Infantry commander, Colonel Canham, landed on Dog White with the second assault wave. They found the troops from the first wave leaderless due to the heavy losses among officers and NCOs. Canham moved westward, prodding his 116th Infantry troops along Dog White to move forward, while Cota headed eastward along Dog White and Dog Red. Cota cajoled the troops, "Don't die on the beaches, die up on the bluff if you have to die. But get off the beaches or you're sure to die!" On meeting Captain John Raaen of the 5th Rangers nearby, he uttered the phrase that would go down in Ranger legend "We're counting on you Rangers to lead the way!" Here Cota is seen talking to some soldiers from the 116th Infantry (2), distinguished by the blue and gray divisional insignia painted on their helmets and worn as a patch on the left shoulder above the rank insignia. To the right are two soldiers from the 5th Rangers (3), evident from the yellow rhomboid painted on the back of their helmets. The 29th Division rifleman in the right of the scene can be seen still wearing the olive green anti-gas brassard (4) and he still carries the chemical protective mask bag (5) on his chest, as does the lieutenant left of Cota. The weapons of many of the GIs had become fouled with sand or seawater

during the chaotic landings and the rifleman is attempting to clean his using a toothbrush. On the ground to the right of Cota is a set of bangalore torpedoes (6). These were tubes filled with high explosive that would be joined end to end, and then pushed under wire obstructions. Once in place, they would be detonated to clear a path through the wire. A helmet belonging to a member of one of the Engineer Special Brigades, with its distinctive crescent marking (7), lies on the beach behind Cota. Around 0750hrs, small groups of soldiers from Company C, 1st Battalion, 116th Infantry began moving through a gap in the seawall towards the bluff in an area out of sight of the German machine-gun teams. A private placed a bangalore torpedo under a wire obstruction blocking their path but was killed by sniper fire. A platoon leader, Lieutenant Stanley Schwartz, replaced him and detonated the charge, blowing a wide gap. The first man trying to run through the gap was hit by the sniper and his agonized cries demoralized the troops following. Realizing that the advance was faltering, Cota raced through the gap, shouting back: "C'mon! If an old buzzard like me can do that so can you!" The infantry, with Cota at the lead, waded through tall reeds and marsh grass at the base of the bluffs, finally finding their way to the bluffs. It was the first advance off the beach in the 116th RCT sector. (Howard Gerrard)

The entrance to the D-3 Les Moulins draw was dominated by this solid house. It was captured by a group under Major Sidney Bingham, but they were unable to overcome strongpoint WN66 at the top of the draw, seen here in the distance beyond the barbed wire. (NARA)

from 1/116th Infantry landed between 0740 and 0800, followed by two more from 3/116th Infantry. By 0800hrs there were elements of eight infantry companies on Fox Green beach, mainly concentrated in the area where the gaps in the obstacles had been made between the E-1 and E-3 draws. Several defensive positions were created behind the protection of shingle, and some light machine-guns and 60mm mortars were in action. Company G began another wary advance through the minefields at the base of the bluff and eventually managed to join Spalding's group from Co. E on the crest. Company A tried to follow but suffered heavy losses after wandering into a minefield. These scattered units spent most of the morning advancing slowly southward and dealing with German snipers. Strongpoint WN64 was cleared around 1000hrs although a lone pillbox at the head of the draw remained in German control until the evening.

Further to the east, strongpoint WN60 was captured by Co. L around 0900hrs the first of the defensive positions to fall. The companies from 3/116th RCT began to push further into the F-1 draw towards the village of Cabourg but were halted by the WN63 strongpoint.

The command post for the 16th RCT landed around 0820hrs on Easy Red, along with the much-needed regimental medical section. Colonel George Taylor gathered the battalion and company commanders together and prodded them to get their troops off the beach. "Two kinds of people are staying on the beach, the dead and those who are going to die – now let's get the hell out of here!" Taylor continued down the beach urging the infantrymen forward. At 1100hrs Col. Taylor ordered the decimated 741st Tank Battalion to shift all of its tanks to attack the fortifications in the E-3 Colleville draw. Three M4A1 tanks entered the draw and two were knocked out in duels with the anti-tank guns in the bunkers. Besides the tanks, the engineers' D-7 armored bulldozers were very active in trying to clear beach obstacles to assist the infantry in their attacks.

This photograph was taken after the war looking directly into the D-3 Les Moulins draw. Several of the small structures at the opening of the draw were added after the landings. The numerous bunkers that so effectively resisted the US advance down the access road are difficult to identify due to their small size. (MHI)

From the perspective of General Kraiss, the situation on Omaha Beach was far less worrying than that on neighboring Gold Beach, where British tanks had already comprehensively penetrated the defenses by early morning. Since his division was committed to defending the western side of Gold Beach as well as Omaha Beach, he decided to commit his reserves to stemming the more dangerous British advances. At 0835hrs he asked permission from the 84th Corps HQ to shift all of Kampfgruppe Meyer to the eastern sector against the British, with the exception of the single battalion already promised for the repulse of the American penetrations in front of Colleville. Corps headquarters agreed with this plan. Shortly after these decisions had been made the reports from Omaha Beach began to give cause for concern as US troops continued to penetrate over the bluffs. At 0915hrs GR.916 reported that WN65 to WN68 and WN70 had been captured. From east to west these strongpoints stretched from the west shoulder of the E-1 St Laurent draw across to the west side of the D-3 Les Moulins draw. In fact only WN70 had been abandoned due to the presence of Gen Cota's force. The battalion from Kampfgruppe Meyer due to make the counter-attack towards Colleville had not yet returned from its dawn odyssey to the west.

STALEMATE ON THE BEACH

Although the first penetrations of the German defensive line were well under way by 0900hrs, the Operation Neptune plan was already hours behind schedule. The inability of the Gap Assault Teams to clear and mark sufficient paths through the beach obstructions had caused considerable problems when the tide turned after 0800hrs. There were too few safe approaches to the beach for landing craft and those exits that had been cleared were soon jammed with vehicles that could not move off the beach. At 0830hrs the beachmaster ordered that no landing craft with vehicles should land. Even the troop-laden LCT and LCIs could find no marked lanes to enter, so around mid-morning landings ground to a gradual halt. The senior commanders offshore did not appreciate the status of the forces on the beach due to the loss of so many radios during the landings as well as the generally chaotic situation on the beach. However, the evidence of heavy casualties and

As the assault on Omaha Beach seemed to stall in early morning, Navy destroyers came to the rescue, moving perilously close to shore to provide fire support. This photo, taken from the battleship USS *Texas*, shows one of the destroyers firing at shore targets on D-Day morning. (NARA)

burning equipment, evident even from offshore, allowed little doubt that the landing was in jeopardy.

Realizing that the landing was in peril, around 0800hrs the destroyers began moving dangerously close to shore to provide more fire support to the beleaguered troops. Around 0830hrs USS *McCook* arrived off Vierville and began pounding the D-1 Vierville draw as well as the WN73 strongpoint on Pointe-et-Raz-de-la-Percée that had been inflicting so many casualties on Charlie and Dog Green beaches. After about 15 minutes of fire one of the gun emplacements on the cliff fell into the sea and the other exploded. Around 0950hrs Adm Bryant radioed the destroyers "Get on them men! Get on them! They're raising hell with the men on the beach, and we can't have any more of that! We

The critical link between the army units ashore and the navy destroyers were the Naval Shore Fire Control Parties. One is seen in operation using an SCR-284 with hand-operated generator while the soldier to the right is using an SCR-586 handie-talkie. (NARA)

must stop it!" By 1030hrs the *McCook* took up stations a mere 1,300 yards from shore, in only three fathoms of water, and spent most of the day firing at targets of opportunity. Starting around 0800hrs, USS *Carmick* began a pass offshore from Pointe-et-Raz-de-la-Percée towards Fox Red, eventually approaching within 900yds of shore. With only intermittent contact with shore fire-control parties, the destroyer was close enough that the officers watched where tanks and infantry were firing, and then responded with their own 5in. gunfire. Near the D-3 Les Moulins draw, a tank from the 743rd Tank Battalion began engaging targets on the bluff and then the destroyer eliminated the target with 5in. gunfire. When Bingham's small detachment became trapped in the house at the base of the draw, the *Carmick* began smashing up the WN68 and WN66 strongpoints overlooking the draw. USS *Carmick* was soon joined by USS *Doyle*, which spent much of the day shelling the D-3 Les Moulins draw area. In one of the more famous incidents Adm Bryant ordered the USS *Emmons* to eliminate a German artillery spotter in the steeple of the Colleville church, toppling the belfry with the 13th round. Several other

LCI-83 carrying troops of the 20th Engineer Battalion first tried landing at 0830hrs but was unable to do so, transferring some of the troops to shore via LCVPs. Another attempt around 1115hrs, seen here, was more successful but the craft was struck by an artillery round, killing seven and damaging a ramp. Two of the M4A1 tanks of Company A, 741st Tank Battalion can be seen further down the beach. (NARA)

destroyers took part in fire-support missions during the course of the day and they provided what little artillery support was available to the army. One of Gerow's first messages to Bradley after arriving on the beach later in the day was "Thank God for the Navy!"

In spite of the beachmaster's cancellation of any further vehicle landings after 0830hrs, there was a dire need to reinforce the infantry ashore. The next two regiments scheduled to land were the 115th RCT from the 29th Division and the 18th RCT from the 1st Division. These regiments were already onboard the larger LCI(L) "Elsies" and began moving towards the beach around 1000hrs, very behind schedule. The 115th RCT was supposed to land around the D-3 Les Moulins draw, but fire from that area was still so intense the landing site was shifted eastward towards the E-1 St Laurent draw. Not only was this area less subject to German fire but the 115th could follow behind the penetrations already made in this sector. Although there was some sporadic mortar fire during the landings, the regiment suffered relatively light casualties. The WN65 strongpoint on the western side of the draw had been mostly eliminated when G/116th Infantry had advanced over the bluff and tanks and destroyer fire reduced WN64. The 2/115th RCT had to clear a few remaining defenses in WN64, but by 1130hrs the E-1 St Laurent draw had been opened. As a result the 1st and 2nd Battalions, 115th Infantry actually advanced through the draw, while the 3/115th Infantry advanced over the bluff behind the WN64 strongpoint. The Engineer Special Brigade moved into action with bulldozers around 1200 and the E-1 St Laurent draw became the single most important exit route from the beachhead on D-Day.

The situation for the 18th RCT proved somewhat more complicated. Although a gap in the beach obstacles had been made on the eastern side of Easy Red beach, it was poorly marked and by late morning the obstacles were completely submerged. The strongpoints around the E-3 Colleville draw had still not been silenced. For nearly two hours the LCIs carrying the 18th RCT had tried in vain to find clear channels to the

A view from Easy Red beach eastward towards Fox Green and the E-3 Colleville draw shows an LCVP from the *Samuel Chase* in the foreground, and the damaged LCI-553 behind. On the beach are several vehicles including a few tanks from the 741st Tank Battalion. (NARA)

beach. Finally, around 1100hrs the two young skippers on LCT-30 and LCI-554 decided to try to crash through the obstructions and they headed in to Fox Green beach under a hail of gunfire. They began to engage the German gun pits with their own 20mm cannon and .50cal machine-guns and one of the nearby destroyers moved over to provide fire support. Both craft made it to the beach safely and disembarked their troops. LCT-30 was so smashed up by gunfire that it had to be abandoned. LCI-554 managed to pull away from the beach, evacuating a number of wounded at the same time. The example of these two craft convinced other LCI skippers to make an attempt and within moments the shoreline was again swarming with landing craft and the 18th RCT was finally ashore. Casualties were relatively light but a total of 22 LCVPs, two LCIs, and four LCTs were put out of action by beach obstacles while carrying the 18th RCT ashore.

From the German perspective, the defense of Omaha Beach appeared to be holding. Telephone connections to GR.916 were severed at 0855hrs and contact was intermittent through the day. At 1140hrs GR.726 reported that the E-1 St Laurent draw had been breached. However, General Kraiss' attention was focused on neighboring Gold Beach as a result of the rapid advance of British units there. At 1225hrs 84th Corps agreed to transfer the 30th Mobile Brigade to the landing area to be committed opposite Gold Beach. At 1235hrs GR.726 reported that Colleville had fallen into American hands, which was only partly true, and that WN61 on the eastern side of the E-3 Colleville draw was occupied by US troops, which was not true. Through the morning Kraiss had received reports that various strongpoints had fallen to the Americans, to learn moments later that in fact they had not been lost, their communications had simply been cut. He was completely unaware of the penetrations around Vierville by the 116th RCT. By late morning Kraiss concluded that the Allied plan was a two-pronged attack on Bayeux with one arm of the assault emanating out

Later waves of troops approach Easy Red beach on D-Day. The cloudy weather gave way to sunshine after 1100hrs and so this section from the 18th RCT of the 1st Infantry Division is probably heading inshore in the late morning or early afternoon. (NARA)

of the St Laurent/Colleville area and the other out of the British sector. Resources to blunt the attack in the Grandcamps/Omaha Beach sector were limited. He ordered the 14 PzJg 38(t) Ausf. M Marder III tank-destroyers of his anti-tank battalion forward as well as 7/GR.916, which was stationed south of the beach near Trevieres. These forces converged on the area behind the D-3 Les Moulins draw around noon. In the sector south of the St Laurent and Colleville draws he alerted the 5/GR.916 to move forward from its barracks in Surrain and also directed the II/GR.915 from Kampfgruppe Meyer to conduct the counter-attack that had been delayed by the difficulties in moving to the beach. By early afternoon Kraiss believed that the situation on Omaha Beach was under control and at 1335hrs he contacted 84th Corps with the news that the invading forces had been thrown back into the sea except at Colleville, but that his forces were counter-attacking there. This report was forwarded to Army Group B and was one of the few bright spots in view of the dire circumstances on the other Normandy beaches.

Although out of touch with Kraiss and the divisional headquarters, companies of GR.916 were firmly holding defensive positions behind the bluffs, mainly along the road that paralleled the beach. The American infiltrations at this time were not strong enough to overcome these defenses and there were numerous skirmishes through the early afternoon.

The senior US commanders waiting anxiously on ships off the coast were even more confused about the real situation than were the German commanders. Although the situation in the late morning was actually improving on the beach, the news arriving on board the ships reflected the despair of mid-morning. Bradley dispatched an aide by DUKW towards the beach, who sent back alarming reports of the congestion, casualties, and disorder along the beach, concluding at 1130 that "Disaster lies ahead." In fact, by late morning the situation on Omaha Beach was rapidly improving. The reinforcements from the 115th and 18th RCTs, although slow in moving off the beach, solidified

the four penetrations over the dunes. The naval gunfire from the destroyers was wreaking havoc with the German strongpoints and, furthermore, the German gunners were running out of ammunition after the intense firing of earlier in the morning. While the situation was far from secure, the momentum was shifting in favor of the American assault.

THE RANGERS AT POINTE-DU-HOC

The most isolated skirmish of the morning was fought by the three companies of the 2nd Rangers under LtCol James Rudder that had been sent to silence the guns on Pointe-du-Hoc. The rocky promontory had been thoroughly pulverized by naval gunfire and bombers prior to the mission, including 698 tons of bombs in the early morning hours. The assault force of about 200 Rangers were loaded into ten British LCAs escorted by several other craft. The mission began badly when the waterlogged LCA carrying the Co. D commander sank in the assembly area along with a supply craft. The remainder of the flotilla, led by a Royal Navy Fairmile motor-launch and escorted by a pair of British LCS fire-support craft, set off for the objective. The guide boat became disoriented and led the flotilla towards Pointe-et-Raz-de-la-Percée to the east of Pointe-du-Hoc before Rudder realized the mistake and ordered the flotilla westward. The navigation error cost the Rangers about 40 minutes and they had to run a gauntlet of fire from the cliffs. A DUKW and an LCS were sunk by 20mm cannon fire. During the lull between the naval bombardment and the arrival of the landing craft, the German garrison on top of Pointe-du-Hoc exited their concrete bunkers and made their way to the edge of the cliffs.

The nine LCAs landed along the eastern side of Pointe-du-Hoc, with the crews setting off the grappling rockets on touchdown. The early-

A section from the 2nd Rangers is seen loaded in the hold of their LCA in Weymouth, England, before setting out across the Channel for Pointe-du-Hoc. The diamond-shaped Ranger insignia can be seen on the back of several helmets. There is a BAR gunner to the left and a bazooka gunner to the far right. (NARA)

morning naval bombardment by the battleship USS *Texas* had caused a large slab of cliff to fall off, creating a 40ft mound of spoil. This was both a blessing and a curse. It prevented the DUKWs from deploying their scaling ladders, but nearly half the height of the cliff could be climbed without ropes or ladders. German troops began appearing along the edge of the cliffs as the Rangers landed, firing small arms, and causing about 15 casualties. The destroyer *Satterlee* came in close to shore and swept the cliff top with fire, forcing the German garrison back into the shell craters and bunkers. Within five minutes of landing, the first

The preliminary naval bombardment of Pointe-du-Hoc collapsed a large section of the eastern cliff onto the beach. This reduced the height that the Rangers had to climb to reach the top of the promontory in this area. (NARA)

THE 2ND RANGERS AT POINTE-DU-HOC (pages 70–71)
The original plan for the Ranger landing at Pointe-du-Hoc
was to land two companies on the east side of the cliffs, and
one on the west side. Due to the delays caused by a
navigational error all three companies landed on the east
side. LCA-888 carrying a section from Company D landed
along the cliffs where the preparatory naval bombardment
had collapsed a large slab of the rock-face, creating a heap
of spoil (1) about 40ft high. This spoil and the shell craters
along the beach prevented the DUKW amphibious trucks
from placing their ladders up against the cliff. But the spoil
allowed the Rangers from Company D to climb almost half
way up the cliff without the need for ropes or assault ladders
(2). The first ropes were launched over the edge of the cliff
using rocket-propelled grappling hooks. Once the first fire
teams had reached the top, they dropped additional ropes
down the cliff to the troops below. In this scene, the Rangers
are continuing to climb the cliffs after the first teams have
established a toehold above. Many of the Rangers, like the
first wave of assault troops, wore the distinctive assault
jacket (3), best seen on the lieutenant at the left. The
Rangers at the right are wearing the distinctive insignia
of the Rangers including the blue and yellow Ranger
rhomboid patch (4) on their left shoulder and yellow/orange
rhomboid with the battalion number superimposed in
black (5) painted on the rear of the M1 steel helmet. The
horizontal white stripe on the back of the helmet (6) is a
standard US Army marking, indicating an NCO. Officers'
helmets were painted with a vertical white stripe (7). The
British Commando (8) with the bandaged head is serving
as a liaison with the Rangers for the mission. He is armed
with a Sten gun (9) and wears British battledress with
the distinctive Commando insignia (10) on his shoulder.
(Howard Gerrard)

A view up the cliff showing where many of the Rangers climbed on D-Day. This photograph was taken by a navy photographer a few days after the landings. (NARA)

Rangers were on top of the cliffs. The promontory was a lunar landscape of deep bomb and shell craters that provided the Rangers with ample cover. But the terrain was so pockmarked that the Rangers had a difficult time assembling or communicating. By the time the main body of Rangers ascended the cliff, the survivors of the German garrison had withdrawn into the surviving bunkers. Prior to the bombardment the German garrison on Pointe-du-Hoc consisted of about 125 troops of the 716th Division manning the defensive positions, as the 85 artillerymen had withdrawn off the point three days before.

There had been some hints the night before the landing that Allied intelligence had learned that the guns had been withdrawn. When the Rangers reached the casemates they found that this was indeed the case. The only "guns" on Pointe-du-Hoc were a number of dummies made from timber. At least two significant concentrations of German troops remained on the point for much of the morning, the most dangerous being an anti-aircraft position at the southwest corner of the artillery position that resisted repeated Ranger attacks. The observation bunker at the tip of the point was defended by a handful of German troops and there were several small groups of German soldiers in the ruins of the ammunition and troop bunkers. A German strongpoint on a cliff to the east continued to rake the point with harassing fire for much of the morning until a British destroyer spotted it and blasted it into the sea.

Small groups of Rangers gradually set out southward to secure the point and about 50 men reached the highway by 0800hrs after a firefight near two German defensive positions on the southern edge of the base. Small patrols infiltrated south through the farm fields looking for the missing guns. A two-man patrol finally found them, completely unguarded but ready to fire, in an apple orchard in Criqueville-en-Bessin about 600yds south of the battery positions. They were pointed towards Utah beach, with ammunition at the ready. The first patrol placed thermite grenades in two guns and smashed the sights, and further damage was done when a second patrol arrived with more grenades. The Rangers had accomplished their mission.

The other elements of the Provisional Ranger Group still at sea remained unaware of Rudder's success. Although a message at 0725hrs that the Rangers were up the cliffs was acknowledged, a second message at 0745 that the point had been taken was not acknowledged. As a result of Rudder's force landing 40 minutes late, the remainder of the Provisional Ranger Force assumed that the mission had failed and went ashore with the 116th RCT at 0730hrs. This would pose a major problem to Rudder's force as by 0830 it was barely at company strength and attracting an increasing amount of German attention. About 60 Rangers remained in and around the point, establishing a lightly defended skirmish line near the southern edge of the battery positions. At the same time Rudder sent out a number of small patrols, about a half-dozen men each, to scout and clear out isolated pockets of German troops who had withdrawn from the battery positions due to the bombardment.

The headquarters of the German 352nd Infantry Division knew about the attack almost from the outset, but the news was not particularly alarming in view of the disturbing events elsewhere. At 0805hrs GR.916 reported to divisional headquarters that a "weak force" had penetrated into Pointe-du-Hoc and that a platoon from 9/GR.726 was being sent to

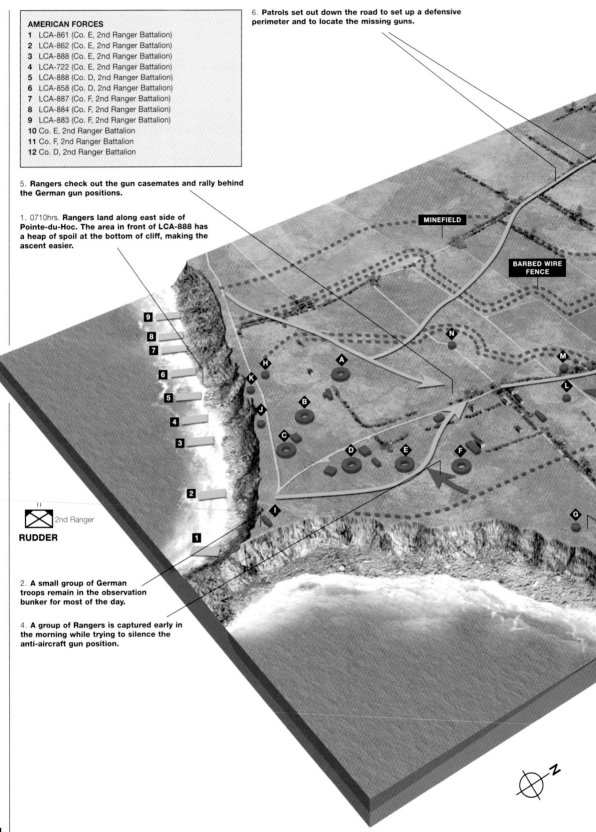

AMERICAN FORCES

1 LCA-861 (Co. E, 2nd Ranger Battalion)
2 LCA-862 (Co. E, 2nd Ranger Battalion)
3 LCA-888 (Co. E, 2nd Ranger Battalion)
4 LCA-722 (Co. E, 2nd Ranger Battalion)
5 LCA-888 (Co. D, 2nd Ranger Battalion)
6 LCA-858 (Co. D, 2nd Ranger Battalion)
7 LCA-887 (Co. F, 2nd Ranger Battalion)
8 LCA-884 (Co. F, 2nd Ranger Battalion)
9 LCA-883 (Co. F, 2nd Ranger Battalion)
10 Co. E, 2nd Ranger Battalion
11 Co. F, 2nd Ranger Battalion
12 Co. D, 2nd Ranger Battalion

6. **Patrols set out down the road to set up a defensive perimeter and to locate the missing guns.**

5. **Rangers check out the gun casemates and rally behind the German gun positions.**

1. 0710hrs. **Rangers land along east side of Pointe-du-Hoc. The area in front of LCA-888 has a heap of spoil at the bottom of cliff, making the ascent easier.**

MINEFIELD

BARBED WIRE FENCE

2nd Ranger

RUDDER

2. **A small group of German troops remain in the observation bunker for most of the day.**

4. **A group of Rangers is captured early in the morning while trying to silence the anti-aircraft gun position.**

N

74

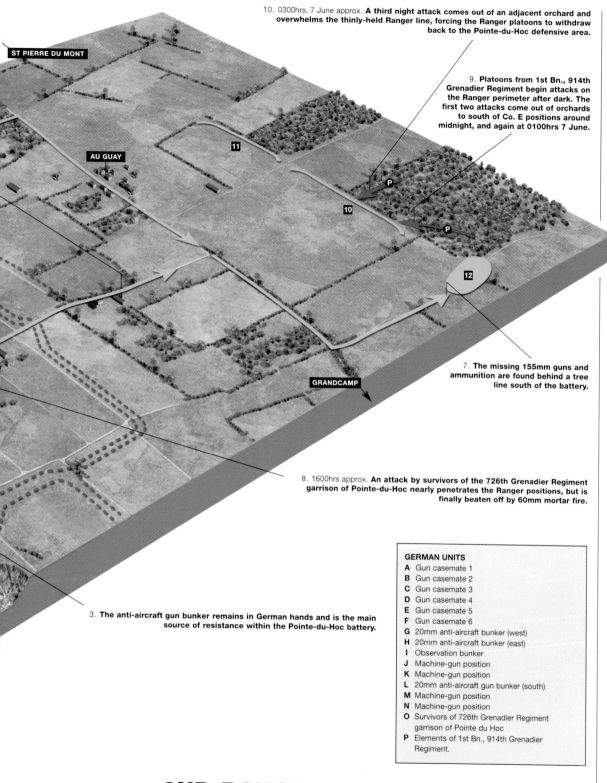

10. 0300hrs, 7 June approx. **A third night attack comes out of an adjacent orchard and overwhelms the thinly-held Ranger line, forcing the Ranger platoons to withdraw back to the Pointe-du-Hoc defensive area.**

9. **Platoons from 1st Bn., 914th Grenadier Regiment begin attacks on the Ranger perimeter after dark. The first two attacks come out of orchards to south of Co. E positions around midnight, and again at 0100hrs 7 June.**

ST PIERRE DU MONT

AU GUAY

11

10

P

P

12

GRANDCAMP

7. **The missing 155mm guns and ammunition are found behind a tree line south of the battery.**

8. 1600hrs approx. **An attack by survivors of the 726th Grenadier Regiment garrison of Pointe-du-Hoc nearly penetrates the Ranger positions, but is finally beaten off by 60mm mortar fire.**

3. **The anti-aircraft gun bunker remains in German hands and is the main source of resistance within the Pointe-du-Hoc battery.**

GERMAN UNITS
A Gun casemate 1
B Gun casemate 2
C Gun casemate 3
D Gun casemate 4
E Gun casemate 5
F Gun casemate 6
G 20mm anti-aircraft bunker (west)
H 20mm anti-aircraft bunker (east)
I Observation bunker
J Machine-gun position
K Machine-gun position
L 20mm anti-aircraft gun bunker (south)
M Machine-gun position
N Machine-gun position
O Survivors of 726th Grenadier Regiment garrison of Pointe du Hoc
P Elements of 1st Bn., 914th Grenadier Regiment.

2ND RANGERS AT POINTE-DU-HOC

0710hrs 6 June–0300hrs 7 June 1944, viewed from the northwest showing the successful assault on the Pointe du Hoc battery by Lieutenant Colonel James E. Rudder's 2nd Ranger Battalion.

counter-attack. The German resistance forced the Rangers to set up a defensive line south and east of the Pointe-du-Hoc fortifications. The first significant counter-attack by 9/GR.726 came out of St Pierre-du-Mont to the eastern side of the Ranger defensive line in the early afternoon. It was repulsed by rifle fire. A more dangerous attack began around 1600hrs on the western edge of the defenses near the anti-aircraft pit. This attack was finally broken up by the Ranger's sole surviving 60mm mortar. The V Corps headquarters knew nothing of the fate of the Rangers until the afternoon when a message was passed via the *Satterlee*, which remained off the point for most of the day providing fire support. The message was simple and to the point: "Located Pointe du Hoe – mission accomplished – need ammunition and reinforcements – many casualties."

The 2nd Rangers landing at Pointe-du-Hoc were led by Lieutenant Colonel James Rudder. He is seen here at his command post at the edge of the cliff a few days after the landing with an EE-84 signal lamp behind him, which was used to communicate with ships at sea due to the loss of most of the unit's radios. (MHI)

The Rangers on Pointe-du-Hoc remained isolated for most of the day, expecting the planned relief force from the 116th RCT and 5th Rangers to arrive at any time. At dusk around 2100hrs, a patrol of 23 soldiers from Co. A, 5th Rangers led by Lieutenant Charles Parker made their way into the defensive line. Parker's group had been with the force that had made the penetration into Vierville earlier in the day and, facing modest resistance, they gradually infiltrated through German defenses to Pointe-du-Hoc.

In view of the lack of success of GR.726 in overcoming the Rangers, at 1825hrs Gen. Kraiss ordered 1/GR.914 to regain control of Pointe-du-Hoc. Nightfall came late, around 2300hrs, and the Ranger defensive line of about 85 soldiers stretched along a series of hedgerows south of

The 2nd Rangers take a break near the unit headquarters on Pointe-du-Hoc after a relief column from the 116th RCT had reached them on D-Day+2. Note the British Commando in the lower right of the photo. (MHI)

the battery complex and the hamlet of Au Guay. German infantry began probing the defenses shortly after dark and skirmishing began in earnest around 0100hrs. A concerted German attack around 0300hrs overwhelmed a portion of the defensive line, capturing 20 Rangers. This forced the Rangers in the outlying positions to withdraw back from the orchards and into the battery positions behind the road. By dawn on D+1 Rudder's force had been reduced to 90 Rangers capable of bearing arms and several dozen wounded. Naval gunfire kept the 1/GR.914 at bay and in the afternoon a landing craft finally arrived with provisions, ammunition and a relief platoon. But throughout D+1 the Rangers on Pointe-du-Hoc could do little more than hold on for the relief force to arrive. During the night of D+1 a patrol from the relief force arrived, by which time the 116th RCT had reached St Pierre-du-Mont only 1,000yds away. The relief of the Rangers at Pointe-du-Hoc finally came on the morning of D+2, spearheaded by tanks of the 743rd Tank Battalion.

CONSOLIDATING THE BEACHHEAD

The senior US commanders did not have an accurate appreciation of the situation on the beach until well into the afternoon of D-Day. The first favorable reports by Col Talley of the Forward Information Detachment did not arrive at Gerow's V Corps HQ on the USS *Ancon* until 1225hrs and spoke vaguely of "men advancing up slopes" and "men believed to be ours on skyline." At 1309hrs Talley sent the first optimistic report back to the ships: "Troops formerly pinned down on beaches Easy Red, Easy Green, Fox Red advancing up heights behind beaches."

As the second group of regiments landed in late morning, the situation along the beach was shifting from total chaos to mere disorder. By noon the Engineer Special Brigades had enough troops ashore to begin the complicated task of preparing the beachhead for subsequent waves of troops and equipment. Some significant portions of the beach, especially in the Easy Red sector, were relatively free of small arms fire although still subject to occasional mortar and artillery fire. The beaches were littered with the dead and wounded, smashed and burning equipment and a significant traffic jam of troops and vehicles unable to move off the beach. None of the draws had been cleared sufficiently to permit traffic off the beach and the troops moving inland were all walking over the bluffs.

One of the engineers' first tasks was to finish removing the beach obstructions. High tide was around 1100hrs and then the sea began to recede, making it easier to tackle the obstacle problem. The areas along the bluffs were still heavily mined and these minefields had to be cleared to permit troops to safely pass southward. The worst beaches of the morning had been Charlie and Dog Green to the west. Like the infantry landing there, the engineers had taken heavy casualties. By late morning C/121st Engineers had landed along with bulldozers and explosives. Between 1200 and 1300hrs navy shore fire-control parties directed four salvoes from the battleship USS *Texas* against surviving bunkers in the D-1 Vierville draw. Stunned by the barrage, about 30 surviving German soldiers exited the bunkers and surrendered. A few moments later Gen. Cota walked down the draw from the other side to try to get more troops moving to Vierville. At 1400, as he watched, the engineers breached the

anti-tank wall there with a half-ton of explosives. The road to Vierville was finally open around 1800hrs although still subject to artillery fire. The D-3 Les Moulins draw remained the most stubborn of the defenses and no progress was made until late evening when it was declared open at 2000hrs. The E-1 St Laurent draw had been one of the first German strongpoints overcome in the morning, but progress was slow in clearing the many minefields, filling in anti-tank ditches, clearing barbed wire obstructions and removing accumulated debris. Under continual sniper fire, bulldozers plowed a new road up the bluff west of the draw by 1300hrs. The availability of a road off the beach led the beachmaster to open Easy Red and Easy Green to vehicles again, the first DUKWs arriving around 1400hrs.

The E-3 Colleville draw was strongly defended and the last pillbox was not silenced by tank fire until 1630hrs. The draw remained dangerous through most of the evening as it was registered for artillery fire, with salvoes arriving every 15–20 minutes. Engineer work to clear the

Beached landing craft and debris clog the shores of Fox Green beach at the end of D-Day while medical teams set about the task of recovering the dead and the wounded. (NARA)

obstructions at the front of the draw began around 2000hrs when artillery fire slackened. Tanks began moving through the draw around 0100hrs on D+1, but wheeled vehicles did not use the exit until dawn. By the evening of D-Day the engineers had fully cleared 13 of the 16 gaps that planners had expected to be open after the first wave landed. About 35 per cent of the beach obstacles had been cleared as well.

Efforts to land artillery on the beach for fire support proved frustrating. The field artillery battalions attached to the infantry regiments had their 105mm howitzers on DUKWs. But these amphibious trucks were heavily loaded and in rough seas they began to ship water. All but one of the DUKWs of the 111th Field Artillery Battalion (116th RCT) sank. The 7th Field Artillery Battalion (16th RCT) lost six on the way in and the remaining six were unable to land in mid-morning due to the beach

Engineers from 5th Engineers Special Brigade come ashore from LCT-538 on Easy Red around 1130hrs. The engineers had the distinctive crescent marking on their helmets as seen here. The photographer who took this photo, Captain Herman Wall of the 165th Photographic Company, was wounded shortly after this picture was taken. (NARA)

congestion. The two armored field artillery battalions with M7 105mm self-propelled howitzers participated in the early bombardment from offshore and had no more luck landing. Five of the LCTs of the 58th Armored Field Artillery Battalion struck mines or were sunk and the 62nd Armored Field Artillery Battalion was unable to land. The 7th Field Artillery Battalion plus a single 105mm howitzer from the 111th Field Artillery Battalion fired their first mission from the beach at 1615hrs against German machine-gun nests near Colleville. Six M7 105mm self-propelled howitzers from the 62nd Armored Field Artillery Battalion finally made it ashore by 1830, but were not ready for action on D-Day. Seven M7 105mm self-propelled howitzers of the 58th Armored Field Artillery Battalion arrived in the afternoon and were sent to support the fighting near St Laurent. In total, five artillery battalions were eventually landed on D-Day, but lost 26 of their 60 howitzers and saw very little use.

THE BATTLES FOR THE VILLAGES

Throughout the afternoon a series of skirmishes raged all along the coastal road, centered on the small villages located behind the bluffs. The first of these to be taken was Vierville on the western side of Omaha Beach. The American control of the Vierville sector remained precarious throughout D-Day due to the extremely heavy losses suffered by the units landing on Charlie and Dog Green beaches and the diversion of the reinforcing wave of the 115th RCT to beaches further east. In addition, the German 352nd Infantry Division had an unbloodied regiment west of Pointe-et-Raz-de-la-Percée. A company from the 5th Rangers and 116th Infantry headed west out of Vierville around noon but were stopped by German defensive positions. The remainder of the Ranger force arrived by late afternoon but the 116th RCT commander, Col Canham, decided against pushing on to Pointe-du-Hoc that day due to the weakness of his force. This was a realistic assessment as the German forces opposite Vierville were the strongest in any sector. To the immediate south of Vierville was the III/GR.726, which was reinforced by elements of the 352nd Infantry Division's engineer battalion and the 7/GR.916 later in the day. To the west were two companies of GR.726 and a battalion of GR.914, reinforced late in the day by a battalion from the 30th Mobile Brigade.

With the D-1 Vierville draw finally cleared by late afternoon, the surviving 17 tanks of the 743rd Tank Battalion moved into Vierville for the night. US tank losses on D-Day were 79 and if it had not been for the four reserve tanks landed later in the day, the 741st Tank Battalion would have been without tanks. Several of the disabled tanks were put back into service over the next few days.

The advance towards St Laurent in the center had progressed more slowly even though there were about five battalions of US infantry in the immediate area. The hedgerows and orchards made the area well suited for defense and the US units were scattered and uncoordinated. To deal with the US attack, Kraiss ordered his dozen 75mm PzJg 38(t) Ausf. M Marder III tank-destroyers forward to support local counter-attacks by the 7/GR.916. The tank-destroyers were spotted by naval observation aircraft and pummeled by naval gunfire well south of the beach. Their attack came to an end before reaching US lines. The two companies of 3/116th Infantry fought a number of skirmishes with the newly arrived 7/GR.916 and their advance slowed as a result. In addition, strongpoint WN67 covered the crossroads where the road from the beach intersected the coastal road. Unknown to the 3/116th Infantry, the 2/115th Infantry was advancing southward along the eastern side of St Laurent and spent most of the afternoon skirmishing with German troops inside the village. The area was hit by a naval barrage around dusk, which halted the US attack. Around 1700hrs four M4A1 tanks from the 741st Tank Battalion were ordered through the E-1 St Laurent draw to reinforce the attack on the village but, not finding the infantry, they formed a defensive line on the eastern side of the village. By this time 1/115th Infantry had bypassed St Laurent and bedded down in the fields south of the village. The 2/115th Infantry joined them there by nightfall. The tanks finally linked up with some scattered infantry units, and conducted a few missions with the infantry to clear out snipers and machine-gun nests shortly before nightfall.

Although few field artillery batteries were able to take part in the fighting on D-Day, the 81st Chemical Weapons Battalion landed on D-Day morning, armed with 4.2in. mortars. It was split between the 16th and 116th RCTs and provided the only shore-based artillery support in the morning and early afternoon. (NARA)

Scattered platoons from the 16th Infantry began the fighting for Colleville in mid-morning. Around noon the US forces had coalesced into a force of about 150 men and began moving into the western side of the village. While this was taking place, elements of the II/GR.915 from Kampfgruppe Meyer appeared on the scene and began to reinforce the German positions around Colleville. Company G, 16th Infantry was forced onto the defensive until the arrival of 2/18th Infantry around 1500hrs. This was the counterattack ordered by Kraiss earlier in the morning but it was not well organized and failed to push back the US penetration as planned. Further American penetration into the village was halted when naval gunfire hit the village in the late afternoon. The 2/18th Infantry made its way south of Colleville, while the three under-strength battalions of the 16th Infantry were deployed in a band along the coastal highway southwest of Colleville. The situation in this area was extremely confused, as not only were the US units facing local attacks by II/GR.915, but numerous small groups of German troops were retreating from the defensive works near the beach and bumping into US patrols.

On the eastern side of the beach, the small village of Le Garde Hameau was taken early in the day and occupied by 3/16th Infantry. When the third regiment of the 1st Infantry Division began arriving later in the day one of its battalions, 1/26th Infantry, was sent through

Company A, 741st Tank Battalion provided the 16th RCT with critical fire support against German strongpoints during the morning of D-Day. This tank, A-13 "Adeline II", was hit on the rear bogie by a 50mm anti-tank gun during fighting against the bunkers in the E-1 St Laurent draw. The tank could still move in spite of the damage, but it could not surmount the seawall to exit the beach. It was later recovered by the battalion's T2 tank recovery vehicle and is seen being towed through Colleville after D-Day for repair. (NARA)

the F-1 draw and bivouacked north of Cabourg, while the other two battalions went over the bluff west of the E-3 Colleville draw to secure the area between the 1st and 29th Divisions between St Laurent and Colleville.

ABOVE **US troops spent the next few days after D-Day clearing up isolated pockets of German troops and snipers in the countryside around the beach. This soldier's choice of a surrender flag was maybe not the best, but seems to have worked! (NARA)**

ABOVE, LEFT **Reinforcements continued to arrive through D-Day and this platoon is seen moving through a mine-cleared lane west of the E-1 St Laurent draw. The engineers marked lanes with white tape as seen here. (NARA)**

OMAHA BEACH IN RETROSPECT

ABOVE **Following the landings, engineers were kept very busy clearing the beaches and the immediate coastal areas of the thousands of mines that the Germans had laid. This engineer is using the standard SCR-625 mine-detector near the beach on 13 June 1944. The painted insignia on his helmet identifies him as belonging to one of the Engineer Special Brigades.**

RIGHT **Dog White beach is littered with shattered vehicles and craft at low tide on the evening of 6 June 1944. The M4 tank, C-13 "Ceaseless" is from Co. C, 743rd Tank Battalion and was disabled on the beach after losing a track. General Cota led the breakthrough in the 116th RCT sector across the bluffs in this area earlier in the morning. (NARA)**

By the end of D-Day, the US Army had a firm toehold on Omaha Beach, clinging to a ragged line about a mile inland from the beach. This fell far short of the plan but was, in view of the serious underestimation of German strength, a significant accomplishment. A total of about 34,200 troops landed at Omaha Beach on D-Day. In spite of the large numbers of troops landed much of this force was still congregated on or near the beach at the end of the day. The assault forces south of the beach were too scattered, disconnected and weak to make a push forward until the next day. The senior US commanders had not expected the landings at Omaha Beach to be difficult. The decisive action would come when the Germans launched a violent counter-attack within a day or two of the landings. In the event, the landings proved to be more costly than expected, but the German counter-attack never materialized.

Precise US casualties for D-Day will never be accurately determined. The V Corps history places the total at 1,190 for the 1st Infantry Division, 743 for the 29th Division and 441 for V Corps troops for a total of 2,374. Of these, 694 were killed, 331 missing and 1,349 wounded. No breakdown is available by rank, but from written reports the casualties amongst the combat leaders – the young majors, captains, lieutenants, and sergeants – had been disproportionately high. The 1st Division later reduced their casualty figures as the missing were gradually located and a total of about 2,000 army casualties is the generally accepted figure for Omaha Beach on D-Day. This exceeded the casualties of all the other beaches combined. There has been a tendency to exaggerate these losses in recent years,

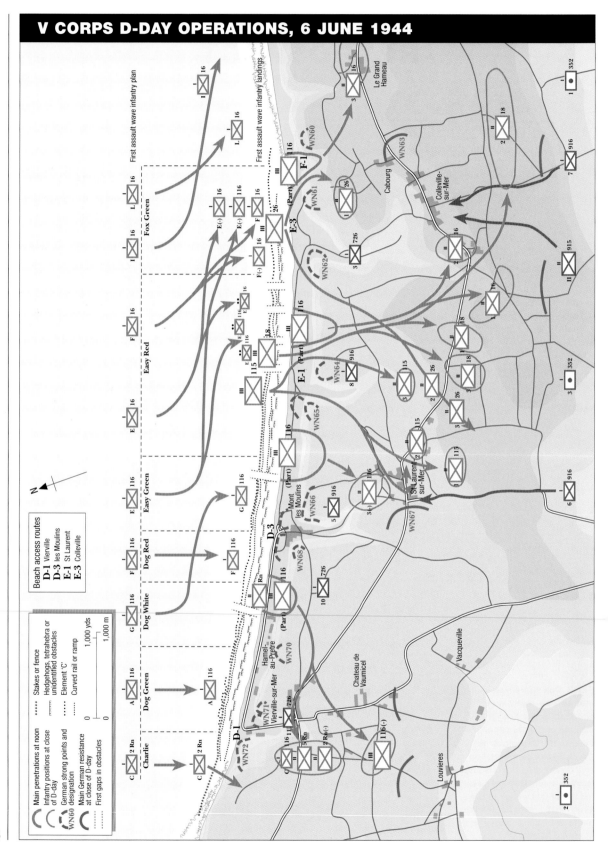

To stiffen the Normandy defenses, Rommel had pressed obsolete WWI field guns into service including German 77mm guns re-bored to 75mm and Czech Skoda 76.2mm guns. Old or not, these weapons were very effective against exposed infantry on the beaches below. This particular one has taken a direct hit, probably from a tank gun, on the right side of its splinter shield, which has also blown off one of the wheels. (NARA)

especially in view of the difficulty of the assignment. As dreadful as they were it should be remembered that the US Army suffered an average of 1,200 casualties a day during the fighting in Normandy in July 1944. What marked out Omaha Beach from later Normandy fighting was the high level of losses among the first assault waves in such a short period of time. Yet the bloodletting should not obscure the fact that Hitler's vaunted Atlantic Wall had withstood the Allied onslaught for less than a day. The sacrifice at Omaha was the foundation for the forthcoming liberation of France.

The reasons for the high casualties are not difficult to identify. Omaha Beach was much more heavily defended than any other beach and its high bluffs posed a much more substantial defensive obstacle than the relatively flat beaches elsewhere. A classified wartime British study noted that the three beaches in the British/Canadian sector were defended by an average of nine anti-tank guns per beach compared to 30 anti-tank and field guns at Omaha, four mortars per beach compared to six at Omaha and 21 machine-guns compared to 85 at Omaha. In addition Omaha was subjected to fire from two artillery battalions, compared to a battalion or less at most of the other beaches. Finally, the preparatory bombardment of Omaha Beach was shorter than those at the neighboring British/Canadian beaches, in some cases by as much as an hour, as the Omaha landing took place earlier due to tidal variations.

Although the initial bomber attack on Omaha Beach had been a failure, the activity of the Allied air forces over Normandy on D-Day had been extremely effective. The most important consequence of Allied air superiority over the beach was that it gave free rein to Allied bombers and fighter-bombers to isolate German reserves from the beachhead. Movement by any type of motorized transport became difficult or impossible. The US Eighth Air Force conducted 1,729 heavy bomber missions on D-Day and IX Bomber Command added a further 823 medium bomber attacks for a combined total of 5,037 tons of bombs delivered. The Eighth Air Force conducted 1,880 fighter sorties on D-Day and the Ninth Air Force a further 2,065 fighter-bomber missions.

The performance of the US Navy at Omaha Beach had been exemplary. The US Navy, Coast Guard and Royal Navy crews of the landing craft had contended with fearsome difficulties through the day and had landed the force in the face of intense fire. When the landings appeared to falter, the young destroyer skippers skillfully maneuvered in shallow water to bring their vital firepower to bear on the German fortifications. These actions helped turn the tide of the D-Day fighting and Omaha Beach was a combined arms battle in the fullest sense of the term.

The German perspective at the end of D-Day was far more pessimistic than in the afternoon when it appeared that the invasion had been thwarted on Omaha. General Kraiss retained little hope of stemming the Allied forces unless substantial reinforcements arrived. Casualties on D-Day had not been particularly high compared with US losses; about 1,000 men. But his artillery was out of ammunition, his units were thinly spread and no units remained in reserve. He was primarily concerned

about the breakthrough by British armor in the neighboring Gold Beach sector next to Omaha. The counter-attack by Kampfgruppe Meyer near Bazenville during the afternoon and evening of D-Day had been decisively smashed by the British. Oberstleutnant Meyer had been killed and his three battalions reduced to less than 100 effectives. This consumed the 84th Corps reserve except for the 30th Mobile Brigade, which was being fed in piecemeal to cover gaps in the line. Kraiss did not have a firm idea of the status of Omaha Beach since communication had been lost with most of the forward strongpoints, and his forces along the coastal highway received contradictory stories from the stragglers retreating back from the beachhead strongpoints. Nevertheless, his defensive line opposite Omaha Beach appeared to be holding, which was far better than could be said for the situation on either side of Omaha Beach. The following day, he sent his operations officer to the surviving WN76 strongpoint on Pointe-et-Raz-de-la-Percée. The trip took five hours instead the usual 30 minutes due to Allied aircraft. Oberstleutnant Fritz Ziegelmann later wrote: "The view from WN76 will remain in my memory forever. The sea was like a picture from the Kiel review of the German fleet. Ships of all sorts nestled close together on the beach, and echeloned at sea in depth. And the entire concentration remained there intact without any real interference from the German side! I clearly understood the mood of the German soldier who was pleading for the Luftwaffe. That the German soldiers fought here hard and stubbornly is, and remains, a wonder."

The Luftwaffe, battered by months of Allied air action, played practically no role in the fighting. The commander of Luftflotte 3, Generalfeldmarschall Hugo Sperrle, did not authorize the "Impending Danger West" signal until mid-morning on 6 June 1944, even though his reconnaissance aircraft had spotted the Allied fleets before dawn. As a result, the many fighter units that had been moved inland to avoid Allied fighter sweeps did not return to the forward fields near the Channel until the evening of D-Day. The only Luftwaffe aircraft over the beaches on D-Day were a pair of Fw-190 from I/Jagdgeschwader 26 led by the squadron commander, Oberstlt Josef "Pips" Priller, which took off from Lille around 0800hrs and made a fast pass over the Normandy beaches before landing, out of fuel, at Creil. The units near the coast were able to launch only about 100 daylight sorties on D-Day of which 70 had been by fighters. The Luftwaffe fighters claimed 24 Allied aircraft, but lost 16 fighters in the process. One attempted raid on the beaches by a dozen Ju-88 bombers led to the entire force being shot down. The Luftwaffe attempted to redeem itself with a concerted night attack by the bombers and torpedo-bombers of Fliegerkorps IX, but few of the 175 sorties managed to reach the Allied fleets due to Allied night-fighters and anti-aircraft fire. The Kriegsmarine had even less effect on the landings and its warships and coastal artillery played no role whatsoever at Omaha Beach.

The reaction by higher German commands on D-Day was tentative and indecisive. There was the belief through most of the day that the Normandy landings were a diversion, and not the main invasion. Hitler was reluctant to commit the Panzer reserves and insisted that the landings be crushed with local resources. This indecision would linger through much of June. Rommel began moving the Panzer divisions under his control against the Allied beaches, but none of this force was directed against Omaha Beach. Nor did the Panzers have a decisive impact once deployed over the next few days. Not only was it difficult to move the Panzer divisions forward due to air attack but the area of coastal farmland behind the beaches, known as the *bocage*, was broken up by thick hedges and constricted by a poor road network that made maneuver impossible. The battles in Normandy, especially in the American sectors, would be an infantry battle.

The US V Corps gradually expanded the Omaha beachhead, finally reaching the Aure River and the D-Day objectives two days late. The 352nd Infantry Division continued to offer stiff resistance but the advantage was clearly shifting to the growing American forces. On 9 June V Corps launched its first offensive out of the beachhead, a three-division attack that pushed 12 miles inland and seized the dominating terrain at the Cerisy forest. On 12 June the attack was resumed and the Utah and Omaha beachheads joined by seizing Carentan. By 13 June V Corps had pushed 20 miles beyond the beachhead, linking with both Utah and Gold beaches on either flank. In the neighboring Utah Beach sector Collins' VII Corps faced far less formidable defenses and reached the seaport of Cherbourg on 20 June. But the Germans had demolished the harbor facilities, rendering it a hollow victory. Over the next seven weeks the Allies would fight a bitter battle for the *bocage* and the city of Caen, before finally breaking out of Normandy during Operation Cobra[4] in the last week of July.

4 See Campaign 88: *Operation Cobra 1944 – Breakout from Normandy*

THE BATTLEFIELD TODAY

Due to their dramatic history the Normandy beaches have become a popular tourist attraction, with many preserved artifacts. The drive through the Norman countryside is very picturesque and Normandy is accessible from the Channel ports or Paris. The area around the Normandy beaches is still rural, so the road network becomes restricted near the coast. There are numerous markers and orientation maps along the beach, although it is a good idea to obtain one of the many guidebooks available to better appreciate the significance of many of the locations. A good map is essential, as some of the more significant sites can be easily overlooked. In addition, some areas are privately owned and wandering tourists are not welcome. The landing areas at Omaha Beach stretch for about 7,000yds (3miles/5km) so the beach can be visited on foot in one day, depending on the amount of time spent at the many sites. The neighboring D-Day beaches are also within easy reach by car so if time is limited, it is useful to determine in advance which sites are of special interest. Some of the museums located near the other beaches are dedicated to the D-Day landings in general and should not be overlooked. For readers interested in uniforms and military equipment, many of these contain an interesting display of preserved artifacts. For example, the private "Musee Sous-Marins" at Commes contains one of the DD tanks recovered from offshore along with other equipment sunk on D-Day.

The toll of war. A temporary grave for one of the Rangers killed on Pointe-du-Hoc was created amongst the litter of war. (NARA)

One of the most impressive sites is Pointe-du-Hoc, which remains little changed from 1944, still pockmarked with bomb craters. The site has become overgrown with grass and weeds over the years, but the sense of the devastation there in 1944 is still obvious. Most of the concrete bunkers remain, cleaned up a bit and the debris removed. The view over the cliff is a vivid reminder of the courage of the Rangers. Pointe-du-Hoc is separated from the main landing beaches by the Pointe-et-Raz-de-la-Percée promontory and so is best reached by car before or after visiting the landing beaches. It is readily accessible from the coastal road (D.514).

Probably the best known of the sites at Omaha Beach is the US military cemetery located on the bluffs near St Laurent, and most ceremonies dedicated to the US forces on D-Day have been held here. More than 9,000

Reinforcement of the 1st Infantry Division sector began on the evening of 7 June with the arrival of the 2nd Infantry Division. Here we see a column moving up the bluff near the E-1 St Laurent draw on the morning of 8 June 1944. (MHI)

GIs are buried in the cemetery, mostly from the fighting after D-Day, and the row upon row of markers stand as a very tangible reminder of the cost of the Normandy campaign. There are numerous memorials located along and above the beach dedicated to units which took part in the D-Day landings or during later fighting in France.

The beach itself has seen many changes from 1944, since Normandy remains a popular seaside attraction in France. Most of the smaller beach obstructions have long since been cleaned away, although there are remains of the Mulberry harbor near the Vierville draw. Since the Vierville draw was the primary route from the Mulberry harbor off the beach, it was heavily reworked by US engineers in 1944, and so bears little resemblance to the defensive position of June 1944. The National Guard memorial was placed on the location of the 75mm gun casemate of the WN72 strongpoint. Some of the other draws are less important for access to the beach and so remain closer to their original condition. Many of the concrete casemates located in the draws are still in place, some of them dedicated as monuments to the fighting. The anti-tank gun casemate of the WN65 strongpoint shown in one of the photos has been preserved. Many of the bunkers and other shore fortifications have been removed or altered over the years. For example, none of the *Panzerstellung* turreted tank bunkers are still preserved, and other bunkers have been sealed up. Casual tourists should not wander into bunkers at Omaha Beach or elsewhere along the Normandy coast, except for those clearly intended for tourist visits. Many have ammunition sub-basements at the bottom of the access stairs that present a serious hazard to the unwary as the doors have often been removed or rotted away.

On the way to Utah Beach. Task
Force U sets sail for Normandy
on 5 June with a flotilla of LCI
(landing craft, infantry) ahead, as
seen from the bridge of an LST
(landing ship, tank). (NARA)

PART 2
UTAH BEACH

he plans for the US Army at Utah Beach were a bold attempt to use airborne units to overcome the difficult terrain behind the beachhead. In the largest combat airdrop of the war so far, two airborne divisions were delivered at night behind enemy lines with the aim of securing the key bridges and access points. Due to the inherent risks of such a night operation, the paratroopers were very scattered and unable to carry out many of their specific missions. Yet in spite of these problems, the gamble paid off. The landings at Utah Beach were never in doubt, and within a day the US Army had a firm foothold in Normandy. The previous section on Omaha Beach provided a detailed account of the planning and preparation for US Army operations on D-Day. The chapters that follow provide a more detailed look at US Army operations subsequent to D-Day. With the capture of Cherbourg and the Cotentin peninsula, the Wehrmacht lost any hope that the Allies could be dislodged from France.

THE STRATEGIC BACKGROUND

Allied planning for Operation Overlord recognized the need for extensive port facilities to supply the armies for later operations in France. The German army presumed that the Allies would conduct their invasion in the Pas de Calais where there were many excellent ports. Consequently, the main German defensive effort was concentrated in this area, making it far less attractive to Allied planners, who turned instead to Brittany and Normandy. Brittany had several excellent ports such as Brest, but the Breton peninsula was more distant from English ports than either the Pas de Calais or Normandy. In addition, had the Allies landed in Brittany, German forces might have contained their advance by sealing off the relatively narrow exit from the Breton peninsula. As a result, Brittany was dropped from consideration. The Normandy coast had few large port facilities except for Cherbourg on the Cotentin peninsula. Nevertheless, Normandy was attractive for many other reasons including its proximity to the English Channel ports, and the relatively weak German defenses in the region, especially in mid-1943 when Allied planning started in earnest. A two-step solution was found to the problem of port facilities. In the short term, the Allies would rely on the creation of a pair of artificial harbors that would be located at the landing beaches. The next objective would be to seize suitable port facilities. This was a task assigned to the US Army: first, the seizure of Cherbourg and then the Breton ports. Utah Beach was selected with this objective in mind. It was the westernmost of the five

This propaganda photo of the Atlantic Wall was released by Germany in December 1943. The Cotentin peninsula, especially around Cherbourg, was one of the few portions of the Normandy coast with a substantial number of heavy coastal defense guns like these. (USAOM)

D-Day landing beaches, at the base of the Cotentin peninsula, offering the best access toward Cherbourg.

German defense of the Cotentin peninsula was based on the mistaken assessment that the main Allied effort would be against the Pas de Calais. As a result, German defensive efforts in 1943 concentrated on creating the "Atlantic Wall" along this stretch of coastline. The Allied landings in Italy in 1943–44, particularly the Anzio landing in January 1944, convinced senior German commanders that the Allies would land in more than one location, using smaller landings to draw off German reserves and weaken the main defenses. As a result, the German strategy was to deploy second-rate units behind mediocre beach defenses on other areas of the French coast such as Normandy and Brittany as an economy-of-force approach. These forces would prevent an uncontested Allied landing and would be reinforced in early 1944 as resources permitted.

CHRONOLOGY

1943

July First draft of Overlord plan completed
3 November Führer Directive 51 directs priority to reinforcing Western Front
6 November Rommel appointed to lead Army Group for Special Employment

1944

1 February Operation Neptune plan adds Utah Beach to the Overlord operation
28 May Landing zone for 82nd Airborne Div. shifted from St Sauveur to Merderet River
3 June OSS teams drop into Normandy to set up beacons for pathfinders
4 June Luftwaffe meteorologist forecasts rough seas and gale-force winds through mid-June
5 June Eisenhower decides that break in weather will permit execution of Neptune on 6 June 1944

D-Day, Tuesday, 6 June, 1944
00.15 Pathfinders begin landing in Normandy to set up beacons for air drops
01.30 Albany mission begins and 101st Airborne paratroopers start landing in Normandy
02.30 Boston mission begins and 82nd Airborne paratroopers start landing in Normandy
02.30 Task Force U arrives off Utah Beach, anchors in transport area
03.10 Gen Marcks begins to move Kampfgruppe Meyer to counter paratroop drops
04.00 Chicago mission begins and 101st Airborne gliders start landing
04.07 Detroit mission begins and 82nd Airborne gliders start landing
04.30 Cavalry detachment lands on St Marcouf island off Utah Beach, finds it deserted
05.05 German coastal batteries begin engaging Allied warships
05.50 Preliminary naval bombardment of Utah Beach begins
06.05 Bomber attacks on Utah Beach begin
06.30 Assault waves begin landing on Utah Beach
09.00 Combat Team 8 (CT8) begins moving off Utah Beach via Exit 2
21.00 Elmira mission delivers glider reinforcements to LZ W; Keokuk to LZ E

POST-D-DAY

7 June Galveston mission delivers gliders to LZ W at 07.00; Hackensack at 09.00
7 June German counterattack on Ste Mère-Église repulsed with tank support
8 June Rommel receives set of captured VII Corps orders, decides to reinforce Cotentin peninsula
9 June La Fière causeway finally captured by 82nd Airborne Division
10 June 101st Airborne seizes causeway leading to Carentan
10 June 90th Division begins attempt to cut off Cotentin peninsula
11 June Fallschirmjäger Regiment 6 (FJR 6) retreats from Carentan
12 June 101st Airborne occupies Carentan in effort to link up with V Corps at Omaha Beach
13 June Counterattack on Carentan by 17th SS-Panzergrenadier Division fails with heavy losses
15 June Failure of 90th Division leads to substitution of 9th Division and 82nd Airborne Div. in westward attack
16 June Hitler meets Rommel and Rundstedt in France, insists on last-ditch defense of Cherbourg
17 June 60th Infantry, 9th Division reaches the sea at Barneville, cutting off Cotentin peninsula
19 June Final drive on Cherbourg begins as a three-division assault
21 June VII Corps reaches outer ring of defenses of Fortress Cherbourg
25 June US infantry begin entering outskirts of Cherbourg
26 June Senior Wehrmacht commanders in Cherbourg forced to surrender
28 June Final outlying German positions in Cherbourg harbor surrender
30 June Last pocket on Cap de la Hague surrender to 9th Division
1 July 9th Division reports that all organized German resistance on Cotentin peninsula has ended

OPPOSING COMMANDERS

GERMAN COMMANDERS

The Wehrmacht had developed a hard-won reputation for tactical excellence during World War II, due in large measure to a style of war epitomized by "*aufsträgtaktik*": senior commanders briefed their subordinate commanders on the goals of the mission, and then permitted them to carry out the assignment as they saw fit, allowing them considerable tactical flexibility. This flexibility was eroded as the conflict dragged on, particularly in the final year of the war. By 1944, the Wehrmacht's capabilities in the field were degraded by an increasingly Byzantine command structure. At the strategic level, Hitler had gradually usurped more and more command authority due to his growing distrust of the professional army officers. He made all major strategic decisions, but interfered at the tactical level as well. Given the sheer complexity of modern industrial war, management of combat operations was beyond the capabilities of a single great commander as might have been possible in centuries before. Hitler's interference was inevitably erratic and episodic. He would allow the usual chains of command to exercise control over most operations, but would become involved in some operations at his whim. Hitler's leadership style was more feudal than modern, encouraging the dispersion of power away from professional organizations like the general staff and into the hands of enthusiastic amateurs like himself, cronies such as the Luftwaffe head Hermann Göring and the SS chief, Heinrich Himmler.

Field command was in the hands of the professionals, but with inefficient constraints on their freedom of action. **Generalfeldmarschal Gerd von Rundstedt** was the nominal supreme commander of western forces (OB West). In reality the Luftwaffe and Navy units in the West were outside his jurisdiction, and some occupation units were under the control of regional governors. Rundstedt's control was further confused by Hitler's decision in the autumn of 1943 to dispatch one of his favorites, **Generalfeldmarschal Erwin Rommel**, to command the amorphous "invasion front". Rommel and Rundstedt attempted to cooperate under difficult circumstances. Rommel took it upon himself to reinvigorate the construction of beach defenses along the Channel coast. This had the greatest impact in Normandy, which had previously been neglected. Rommel was less certain than many senior commanders about the inevitability of landings on the Pas de Calais, and felt that even if the main attack did fall there, there still might be significant secondary operations on other coasts. At his instigation, coastal defenses in Normandy were significantly strengthened during the winter and spring of 1943–44. Rommel's role eventually became the leadership of Army Group B, which clarified his command relationship with Rundstedt. However, this could

Commander of Army Group B was Field Marshal Erwin Rommel. It was Rommel's initiative in the autumn of 1943 that set in motion the fortification of the Normandy beaches. (MHI)

A veteran Panzer commander from the Russian front, GenIt Karl von Schlieben commanded the 709th Infantry Division, which defended the Normandy coast from Utah Beach to Cherbourg. In late June, he was placed in charge of Fortress Cherbourg by Hitler. (NARA)

The hapless 91st Luftlande Division had three commanders within a few days after Gen Wilhelm Falley was killed by paratroopers on D-Day. He was finally succeeded by Generalmajor Eugen König seen here. (NARA)

not solve the divergent tactical approaches sought by the two senior commanders. Rommel and Rundstedt had serious disagreements over the way that reserve Panzer formations should be deployed, an argument that proved even more complicated due to Hitler's personal interest and involvement in the issue. This controversy was not settled prior to the invasion, and indeed continued to rage through most of June 1944 even after the Allied landings.

Defense of the Cotentin peninsula was the responsibility of the 7th Army, responsible for all German army units along the Normandy coast and Brittany and commanded by **Generaloberst Friedrich Dollman**. Dollman was a corps commander in Poland in 1939, assigned command of the 7th Army in the battle of France in 1940, and remained in command during the years of occupation. Some Eastern Front veterans serving in France felt that the years of occupation duty had softened him and his staff. Dollman died of a heart attack on 28 June 1944, less than a month after D-Day.

The Normandy sector, including the Cotentin peninsula, was the responsibility of the 84th Infantry Corps commanded by **General der Infanterie Erich Marcks**. He was a highly regarded commander and served as a staff officer in Poland in 1939 and France in 1940. He was involved in the planning for Operation Barbarossa, and commanded the 101st Jäger Division at the time of the invasion of the Soviet Union in 1941. After he lost a leg in combat in Russia, he was reassigned to the command of the 337th Infantry Division following his recuperation. His skills as a divisional commander led to his elevation to army corps command, first the 66th Corps in September 1942, then the 87th Corps. The Nazis considered him politically suspect as he had been an aide to General von Schleicher, murdered by the SS in 1934, and he was passed over by Hitler for army command. Instead, he was assigned to the 84th Corps in France on 1 August 1943 as part of the process to refresh the command structure in France with Eastern Front veterans. The 84th Corps headquarters was located at St Lô. Marcks was killed in Normandy during an air attack on 12 June 1944.

Utah Beach fell within the defense zone of the 709th Infantry Division, commanded by **Generalleutnant Karl Wilhelm von Schlieben**. He was appointed to command the division in December 1943 as part of the process to refresh occupation forces in France with hardened veterans from the Eastern Front. He was not the most likely officer to be assigned to a static division, having spent most of the war in the Panzer forces. He had commanded a Panzergrenadier regiment, a rifle brigade, and then 18th Panzer Division in two and a half years of fighting in Russia. The western side of the Cotentin peninsula was defended by another static division, the 243rd Infantry Division, commanded by **Generalleutnant Heinz Hellmich**. The division had been raised in July 1943, and Hellmich was its second commander, assigned on 10 January 1944. Hellmich was killed in action on 17 June 1944. A third division, the newly formed 91st Luftlande Division, was sent to the Cotentin peninsula in May 1944 and had been commanded by **Generalleutnant Wilhelm Falley** since 25 April 1944.

Of the three divisional commanders in this sector, two were in Rennes on D-Day participating in a *Kriegsspiel* (wargame) along with many of their staff. Schlieben did not arrive back at his command post in Valognes until

noon, and Falley was killed by US paratroops near Picauville while returning to his headquarters around dawn. Command of the 91st Luftlande Division was temporarily taken over by **Generalmajor Bernhard Klosterkemper** later on D-Day, awaiting the arrival of a new commander, **Generalmajor Eugen König**, who was assigned the post on 7 June. He arrived at the command post on the afternoon of 10 June.

AMERICAN COMMANDERS

The First US Army was responsible for the conduct of the D-Day landings and was commanded by **Lieutenant General Omar Bradley**. The assault force for Operation Neptune consisted of the V Corps at Omaha Beach and the VII Corps at Utah Beach. VII Corps was commanded by **Major General J. Lawton Collins**, better known by his nickname, "Lightning Joe". Collins graduated from West Point in April 1917, but did not arrive in Europe until after the Armistice. He received a divisional command in May 1942, taking over the 25th Division in the Pacific. Formed from cadres of the peacetime Hawaiian Division, this unit had a poor reputation. Collins whipped it into shape for its first assignment, relieving the 1st Marine Division on Guadalcanal in early 1943. The codename for the division headquarters on Guadalcanal was "Lightning", from which Collins picked up his nickname. He had been brought back from the Pacific theater to provide combat experience. Bradley described him as "independent, heady, capable, and full of vinegar" and he would prove to be one of the most aggressive and talented US field commanders in Europe. He later served as the army chief of staff during the Korean War.

With few exceptions, Collins was blessed with excellent commanders. Not surprisingly, the two airborne division commanders stood out. The 82nd Airborne Division had been commanded by **Major General Matthew Ridgway** since June 1942 when it had first converted from a regular infantry division into a paratroop division. Ridgway had led the unit during

One of the most highly regarded infantry commanders in Normandy was MajGen Manton Eddy, commander of the 9th Infantry Division, seen here talking over a field telephone during the fighting in Cherbourg at the end of June 1944. (MHI)

The first major American victory in France was the capture of Cherbourg, and "Lightning Joe" Collins is seen here on a hill overlooking the port talking to Capt Kirkpatrick from the 79th Division. (MHI)

its first major combat jump over Sicily in 1943, and after the Normandy operation would be pushed upstairs to lead the XVIII Airborne Corps in time for Operation Market Garden in September 1944. He would go on to a distinguished career after the war as supreme NATO commander and army chief of staff. The 101st Airborne Division was led by **Major General Maxwell Taylor**, who had served as the artillery commander of the 82nd Airborne Division during the Sicily campaign. Taylor became best known for a cloak-and-dagger affair in 1943 when he was smuggled into Rome to confer with Italian officers about a plan to land the 82nd Airborne Division to capture the city. Taylor quickly appreciated that the hare-brained scheme would lead to the destruction of the division, and he was able to avert it in the nick of time. He also enjoyed a distinguished post-war career, and was the Army chief of staff in the mid-1950s after Collins.

The infantry division leading the assault on Utah Beach was the 4th Infantry Division, commanded by **Major General Raymond "Tubby" Barton** since July 1942. Barton led the division through the autumn campaign, culminating in the ferocious Hürtgen Forest campaign that gutted the division. He was relieved for medical reasons by George Patton in December 1944. His assistant divisional commander was **Brigadier General Theodore Roosevelt Jr.**, son of president Teddy Roosevelt, and a distinguished soldier in his own right. Roosevelt had been assistant commander of the 1st Infantry Division in North Africa and Sicily, and when the divisional commander was relieved in 1943 due to personality conflicts with Bradley, Roosevelt was given the boot as well. He was reassigned to the 4th Division, where he proved to be a popular and effective leader. He died in Normandy from a heart attack, but his inspirational leadership at Utah Beach led to his posthumous decoration with the Medal of Honor.

Following the initial phase of the Utah Beach operation, the 82nd and 101st Airborne Divisions were withdrawn to Britain for refitting. Three other infantry divisions would play a central role in the fighting on the Cotentin peninsula. The 9th Infantry Division, headed by **Major General Manton Eddy**, was a veteran of the North Africa and Sicily fighting and widely regarded as one of the army's best divisions. Eddy was a particularly capable officer and in August was given command of the XII Corps in Patton's Third Army. The 79th Division was commanded by **Major General Ira Wyche**, West Point class of 1911. Wyche had served in the field artillery until assigned to command the 79th Division in May 1942, leading it in its combat debut in 1944. Of all the divisions in Collins' VII Corps, the only one to suffer from serious leadership problems was the 90th Division, led by **Major General Jay MacKelvie**. An artilleryman by training, MacKelvie had little feel for infantry operations and was relieved by Collins on 12 June after five days of combat along with two of his regimental commanders.

OPPOSING ARMIES

GERMAN FORCES

By the summer of 1944, the Wehrmacht had been bled white by three years of brutal conflict in Russia. The enormous personnel demands of the Eastern Front led to the cannibalization of units in France. Hitler "wanted to be stronger than mere facts" and so the Wehrmacht order of battle became increasingly fanciful in the last year of the war, with impressive paper strength but increasingly emaciated forces.

In response to Rundstedt's strong criticism of the state of the forces in France in October 1943, Hitler issued Führer Directive 51 to reinvigorate the Wehrmacht in the West. Rundstedt's command increased from 46 to 58 divisions, partly from the transfer of burned-out divisions from the Eastern Front to France for rebuilding, and partly from newly formed divisions. The units on the Cotentin peninsula were second-rate formations. In 1942 Rundstedt had initiated the formation of static divisions. These were under strength compared to normal infantry divisions, lacked the usual reconnaissance battalion, and had only three battalions of artillery. In addition, their personnel were mostly from older age groups. Through much of the autumn of 1943, the better troops were siphoned off to satisfy the insatiable requirements for more replacements on the Eastern Front. In their place came a steady stream of Ost battalions manned by "volunteers" from Red Army prisoners. Colonel Von der Heydte of the 6th Fallschirmjäger Regiment recalled that: "The troops for a defense against an Allied landing were not comparable to those committed in Russia. Their morale was low; the majority of the enlisted men and noncommissioned officers lacked combat experience; and the

A severe shortage of German conscripts prompted the Wehrmacht to employ former Soviet prisoners-of-war in infantry units. This soldier, from one of the Soviet Union's Central Asian republics, wears the swastika-less eagle insignia peculiar to these troops above his right breast pocket. (NARA)

Many German units on the Cotentin peninsula were over-extended, second-rate units. The lack of motor transport led to expedients such as the use of bicycles in some units such as the 243rd Infantry Division. This is a bicycle-borne *Panzerschreck* anti-tank rocket unit. Note that the lead bicycle carries spare rockets in a seat over the rear wheel. (MHI)

officers were in the main those who, because of lack of qualification or on account of wounds or illness were no longer fit for service on the Eastern Front." The weapons were "from all over the world and seem to have been accumulated from all periods of the twentieth century." For example, during the fighting along a 1⅓ mile (2km) stretch of the Carentan front, von der Heydte's unit was equipped with four calibers of mortars from 78mm to 82mm, of German, French, Italian, and Soviet design. General Marcks summed up his assessment during the Cherbourg maneuvers in 1944: "Emplacements without guns, ammunition depots without ammunition, minefields without mines, and a large number of men in uniform with hardly a soldier among them."

The occupation divisions were bedeviled by the petty mindset of an army assigned to years of peaceful occupation duty. General Schlieben recalled that "For someone who had served only in the east, the flood of orders, directives, and regulations which continually showered the troops was a novelty for me. This paper flood impressed me more than the tide along the Atlantic coast. Higher headquarters concerned themselves with trivial affairs of subordinate commanders. For example, it became a problem whether a machine-gun was to be placed 20 meters more to the right or the left ... A senior commander wanted to have an old ramshackle hut demolished to create a better field of fire so a written application had to be filed with the appropriate area HQ, accompanied by a sketch." This practice began to change in February–March 1944 after Rommel's arrival. Rommel was insistent that beach defenses be strengthened. There were not enough workers from the paramilitary Organization Todt to carry out this work, since they were involved in the construction of a series of massive concrete bases for the secret V-1 and V-2 missiles. Instead, the construction work was carried out by the infantry in these sectors, at the expense of their combat training.

The 709th Infantry Division deployed *Goliath* remote control demolition vehicles from special underground hiding places as seen here. They were popularly called "doodlebugs" or "beetles" by the US troops who found many on the beach or in the countryside beyond. (NARA)

The 709th Infantry Division defending Utah Beach provides a clear example of the problems. The division had been formed in May 1941 as an occupation division and in November 1942 it was converted into a static division. One of its battalions was sent to Russia in October 1943, and in June 1944 three of its 11 infantry battalions were manned by former Red Army prisoners of war. Two of these were attached Ost battalions formed from various Red Army prisoners while another was recruited from Georgian prisoners. The division was further weakened by the incorporation of a high percentage of troops recruited from *Volkliste III*, mostly Poles from border areas incorporated into Germany after 1939. The divisional commander later noted that their reliability in combat was doubtful, and he did not expect that the eastern battalions would "fight hard in cases of emergency." German troops in the division were over age with an average

The workhorse of the German infantry divisions was the StuG III Ausf. G assault gun which combined the excellent 75mm anti-tank gun on the old PzKpfw III chassis. This one was knocked out in the fighting near Ste Mère-Église with the 82nd Airborne Division. (NARA)

German units in France exploited the large inventory of captured French armored vehicles to flesh out their meager armored reserves. The small Renault R-35 infantry tank was fitted with a Czech 47mm anti-tank gun, resulting in a lightly armed and thinly armored tank destroyer. On the Cotentin peninsula, these vehicles served with Panzer Abteilung 101, a training unit attached to the 709th Infantry Division. (NARA)

of 36 years. In spite of the mediocre quality of the troops, the division was relatively large for a static division with 12,320 men, and it had 11 infantry battalions instead of the nine found in the new pattern 1944 infantry divisions. Of these troops, 333 were Georgian volunteers and 1,784 were former Red Army POWs. The divisional artillery had three battalions; one with mixed French/Czech equipment, the second with French guns, and the third with Soviet guns. For anti-tank defense, it had 12 towed 75mm anti-tank guns and 9 self-propelled 75mm tank destroyers. Tank support was provided by Panzer Abteilung 101, a training unit weakly equipped with ten Panzerjäger 35R, an improvised combination of Czech 47mm anti-tank guns on obsolete French Renault R-35 chassis. The division originally was spread along the entire Cotentin coastline, a distance of some 150 miles (240km). With the arrival of the 243rd Infantry Division in May, its

German Panzer forces on the Cotentin penisula were mostly composed of training units equipped with obsolete, captured French tanks. The Hotchkiss H-39 of Pz.Abt. 100 would figure prominently in the fighting against the paratroopers around Utah Beach. (NARA)

frontage was reduced. It still stretched from Utah Beach all the way to the northern coast around Cherbourg, a distance of about 60 miles (100km). As a result, its defenses were simply a thin crust along the shore with very little depth. Rommel hoped to compensate for the paucity of men with concrete defenses, but the construction along the Cotentin coast received less priority than in other sectors.

A large group of GIs from the 4th Infantry Division are seen on the deck of an assault transport on the way to Utah Beach in June 1944. (NARA)

The 243rd Infantry Division was formed in July 1943 as a static division and reorganized in January 1944. Two of its infantry battalions were converted from static units to bicycle infantry, though in the process, the division lost an infantry battalion. The division was originally in reserve, but in late May was shifted to defend the western coast, taking over from the over-extended 709th Infantry Division. On D-Day it included about 11,530 troops, somewhat under strength. Its artillery was mostly captured Soviet types, but it had a self-propelled tank destroyer battalion with 14 75mm Marder III and ten StuG III assault guns. The division was reinforced by Panzer Abteilung 206, equipped with a hodgepodge of old French tanks including 20 Hotchkiss H-39, 10 Somua S-35, 2 Renault R-35 and 6 Char B1 *bis*. This was deployed on the Cap de la Hague on the northwestern tip of the Cotentin peninsula.

The 91st Luftlande Division was formed in January 1944 to take part in Operation *Tanne* (pine tree), an aborted airborne operation in Scandanavia planned for March 1944. When this mission fell through, the partially formed division was transferred to Normandy, arriving in May

Tank support for Combat Team 8 came from the 70th Tank Battalion. Several M4 and M4A1 medium tanks of Company C are seen here fitted with deep wading trunks for the Utah Beach landing while in the foreground, one of the unit's T2 tank recovery vehicles backs on board the landing craft before setting off from Kingswear, Devon, England. (NARA)

Additional armored support for Utah Beach came from the 899th Tank Destroyer Battalion, which later played a role in the efforts to overcome the German coastal fortifications at Crisbecq and Azeville. Here a number of M10 3in. Gun Motor Carriages with deep wading trunks are loaded aboard LSTs in England for the D-Day operation. (NARA)

1944 to reinforce the two static divisions. At the time of the invasion, it was under strength with only two infantry regiments and a single fusilier battalion, and numbered about 7,500 men. However, 6th Fallschirmjäger Regiment (FJR 6) from the 2nd Fallschirmjäger Division was attached to the division during the Normandy fighting. Colonel Von der Heydte of FJR 6 considered that the combat efficiency of the division was poor, especially compared to his elite Luftwaffe troops. The division artillery was based around the 105mm Gebirgs-haubitze 40 mountain gun, which did not share the same type of ammunition as the normal 105mm divisional gun. Once the division had expended its one basic load of ammunition, its guns were useless. During the course of the fighting, its artillery regiment was re-armed with a mixture of captured artillery types including Czech and Soviet types. Panzer Abteilung 100, headquartered at Château de Francquetot, provided armored support. It had a motley collection of captured French tanks including 17 Renault R-35, 8 Hotchkiss H-39, one Somua S-35, 1 Char B1 *bis*, and 1 PzKpfw III.

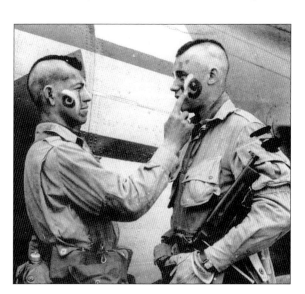

Some paratroopers of the 506th PIR, 101st Airborne Division, decided to get Mohican haircuts and daub their faces with their idea of Indian warpaint. This is demolition specialist Clarence Ware applying the finishing touches to Pvt Charles Plaudo. The censor has obscured the "screaming eagle" divisional patch on his shoulder. (NARA)

There were a number of smaller formations in the area as well. Sturm-Abteilung AOK 7 was an assault infantry battalion attached to the Seventh Army headquarters. On D-Day, it was redeployed from Cherbourg to the 701st Infantry Division during its actions near the Vire River.

Even if the German units on the Cotentin peninsula were not the best in the Wehrmacht, they were still a credible fighting force. Training and tactics were based on hard-won battle experience, and there were Eastern Front veterans in many of the divisions. During the fighting, General Barton visited one of his battalions that had been stalled by the German defenses and assured the officers that the German troops facing them were second-rate. A young lieutenant replied: "General, I think you'd better put the Germans on the distribution list. They don't seem to realize that!"

Besides the infantry formations, there were a significant number of coastal gun batteries located around the Cotentin peninsula. The army controlled two coastal artillery regiments (*Heeres-küsten-artillerie-abteilung*), HKAA 1262 on the west coast of the peninsula and HKAA 1261 on the east coast. Some of these took part in the later land actions, most notably the Azeville and Crisbecq battery of HKAA 1261 near St Marcouf. The navy's MAA 260 (*Marine-artillerie-abteilung*) was responsible for the seven naval batteries located mainly in the area around Cherbourg while MAA 608 protected the port of Granville on the western side of the peninsula.

Order of battle: German Units, Cotentin Peninsula, June 1944

84th Corps	**St Lô**	**General der Artillerie Erich Marcks**
709th Infantry Division	***Chiffremont***	***Generalleutnant Karl von Schlieben***
Grenadier Regiment 729	Le Vast	
Grenadier Regiment 739	Cherbourg	
Grenadier Regiment 919	Quineville	
243rd Infantry Division	***Bricquebec***	***Generalleutnant Heinz Hellmich***
Grenadier Regiment 920	Quett	
Grenadier Regiment 921	Lessay	
Grenadier Regiment 922	Sortosville	
91st Luftlande Division	***Etienville***	***Generalmajor Wilhelm Falley***
Grenadier Regiment 1057	Hauteville	
Grenadier Regiment 1058	Vindefontaine	
Fallschirmjäger Regiment 6	Hotellerie	
Coastal Artillery Units		
Army Coastal Artillery Regiment 1261	Quineville	Oberst Gerhard Triepel
Army Coastal Artillery Regiment 1262	Grosseville	
Naval Artillery Regiment 260	Cherbourg	Korvettenkapitän Karl Weise
Naval Artillery Regiment 608	Granville	Korvettenkapitän Hubbert

US FORCES

The US units taking part in the initial landings contained the two best light infantry divisions in the army, the 82nd and 101st Airborne Divisions. The 82nd Airborne Division had already seen combat in Sicily and Italy, though in June 1944, more than half of its paratroopers were replacements. Normandy was the first combat jump for the 101st Airborne Division, but like the 82nd, it was formed on the basis of volunteer troops and had exceptionally thorough training. In addition, its officer ranks were stiffened by transferring veterans from the 82nd Airborne Division. Both were elite units in the true sense of the word.

The 4th Infantry Division had been reactivated in 1940 and at first was equipped as a motorized infantry division. This concept was eventually dropped, and the division reverted back to a conventional organization in August 1943 prior to being sent to England. While Bradley had insisted on using at least one experienced division in the assault at neighboring Omaha Beach, Utah Beach was viewed as a less demanding mission. Nevertheless, it required the use of a well-trained and ably led division, and

the 4th Division was chosen. The assault would be conducted by Combat Team 8 (CT8) with the division's 8th Infantry Regiment forming its core.

Armored support for CT8 came from the 70th Tank Battalion, the most experienced separate tank battalion in the US Army, which had previously seen combat as a light tank battalion in North Africa and Sicily. For D-Day, two of its companies were equipped with M4A1 Duplex Drive (DD) amphibious tanks. These tanks were modified by the addition of a folding canvas skirt to provide buoyancy, and a pair of propellers for propulsion in the water. In order to deal with beach obstacles, especially the seawall, there were plans to equip the third medium tank company with 7.2in. demolition rockets in a T40 launcher over the turret. The first four rocket launchers were delivered in May and tested against simulated beach obstructions. The rockets were not particularly effective, but the tank crews showed that two or three high explosive rounds from the tank's 75mm gun were adequate to breach seawalls. As a result, Company C was landed without the rocket launchers. The battalion's light tank company was landed later on D-Day and assigned to support the 82nd Airborne Division.

In the build-up immediately after D-Day, three more infantry divisions were gradually injected into the Cotentin fighting. The 90th Division was based around National Guard units raised in the Texas–Oklahoma area, hence its nickname "Tough Ombres". It developed a bad reputation in Normandy due to poor leadership, which in turn led to poor training. It

went through a series of leadership changes and by the fall, the problems had been largely corrected. It fought with distinction with Patton's Third Army in Lorraine in September 1944. In contrast, the 9th Division was widely regarded as one of the army's best infantry divisions, with previous combat experience in North Africa and Sicily. It would play a critical role in the capture of Cherbourg. The 79th Division was activated in 1942 and shipped to Britain in April 1944. It was a fairly typical US infantry division with good training and leadership.

One of the most significant Allied advantages was the availability of continual air support. At this stage of the war, cooperation between ground and air units was still in a formative stage, and did not come to fruition until late July during Operation Cobra. Nevertheless, continual air operations over the Cotentin peninsula by roving fighter-bombers made any concentrated daytime movement by German units impossible. Some measure of air power's impact can be surmised from the significant percentage of senior German commanders killed by air attack while trying to move between their units.

Order of Battle: US Army, Cotentin Peninsula, June 1944

VII Corps	MajGen J. Lawton Collins
4th Division	**MajGen Raymond Barton**
8th Infantry	Col James Van Fleet
12th Infantry	Col Russell Reeder
22nd Infantry	LtCol James Luckett
9th Division	**MajGen Manton Eddy**
39th Infantry	Col Harry Flint
47th Infantry	Col George Smythe
60th Infantry	Col Frederick de Rohan
79th Division	**MajGen Ira Wyche**
313th Infantry	Col Sterling Wood
314th Infantry	Col Warren Robinson
315th Infantry	Col Poter Wiggins
82nd Airborne Division	**MajGen Matthew Ridgway**
505th Parachute Infantry	Col William Ekman
507th Parachute Infantry	Col George Millett Jr.
508th Parachute Infantry	Col Roy Lindquist
325th Glider Infantry	Col Harry Lewis
90th Division	**BrigGen Jay MacKelvie**
357th Infantry	Col Philip Ginder
358th Infantry	Col James Thompson
359th Infantry	Col Clarke Fales
101st Airborne Division	**MajGen Maxwell Taylor**
501st Parachute Infantry	Col Howard Johnson
502nd Parachute Infantry	Col George Moseley Jr.
506th Parachute Infantry	Col Robert Sink
327th Glider Infantry	Col George Wear
4th Cavalry Group	**Col Joseph Tully**
4th Cavalry Squadron	LtCol E.C. Dunn
24th Cavalry Squadron	LtCol F.H. Gaston Jr.
6th Armored Group	**Col Francis Fainter**
70th Tank Battalion	LtCol John Welbron
746th Tank Battalion	LtCol C.G. Hupfer

OPPOSING PLANS

US PLANS

The original Operation Overlord plans did not envision any Allied landings to the west of the Vire River at the base of the Cotentin peninsula. In January 1944 when General Montgomery was first briefed, he insisted that the frontage of the assault be widened. Montgomery was not entirely convinced of the viability of the artificial harbors and wanted a landing west of the Vire to facilitate an early capture of Cherbourg. The preliminary Operation Neptune plan of 1 February 1944 and the First US Army (FUSA) plan of 25 February expanded the US beachheads to two, one in the Grandcamps sectors (Omaha), and one further east near Les Dunes de Varreville (Utah).

Although many beaches on the eastern Cotentin coast were suitable for landing, the areas behind the beach were a problem since many had been flooded by the Germans. Access between the beach and inland areas was over a small number of narrow causeways that could be defended easily by small German detachments. The second problem was the terrain of the peninsula itself. The Douve River runs through the center of the peninsula, and the low-lying areas of the peninsula were naturally marshy. The Germans exploited this to reduce the number of possible airborne landings by using locks to flood many lowland fields. The planners wanted a beach with at least four causeways to permit the transit of a single division off the beach on D-Day, compared to two on neighboring Omaha Beach. The coast immediately west of Omaha Beach was the obvious solution.

The Cotentin coast was dotted with coastal artillery batteries, including the St Marcouf battery of 3/1261 HKAA in Crisbecq. This ferro-concrete Bauform 683 casemate was armed with a Czech Skoda 210mm gun of the type ordered by Sweden and Turkey but taken over by Germany in 1938. The prolonged defense of the position earned its commander, Oberleutnant zur See Ohmsen, the Knight's Cross after he escaped to Cherbourg on 14 June. (NARA)

One of the most effective types of bunker on the Normandy coast was the Bauform 667 casemate, which were positioned parallel to the shore to permit enfilade fire along the beach. This Bauform 667 casemate of the W5 strongpoint at Utah Beach was armed with a 50mm anti-tank gun, and it was knocked out by tank gun fire directed against the embrasure from close range. (NARA)

To make certain that the causeways remained open, an airborne division would be landed behind the beach before H-Hour on D-Day. Many planners were reluctant to place too much faith on paratroop operations, especially in light of the fiasco on Sicily in 1943. On that occasion the aircraft transporting the 82nd Airborne Division were brought under fire by the naval forces, and the paratroopers subsequently landed in widely scattered and ineffective groups. However, Eisenhower believed that the Sicily operation had merely shown that the airborne force had to land in a more concentrated fashion, and he agreed with General Ridgway to expand the existing US airborne divisions. The initial plan in February envisioned using the 101st Airborne Division immediately behind Utah Beach to secure the causeways. Bradley's FUSA planners wanted the 82nd Airborne dropped further west to permit a rapid cutoff of the Cotentin peninsula, preventing the Germans from reinforcing Cherbourg.

These plans were viewed as extremely risky but Eisenhower decided that they were essential to the operation and that the risks would have to be accepted. The plans continued to evolve well into May, only days before D-Day. Allied intelligence learned of the move of the German 91st Luftlande Division into the central Cotentin peninsula in mid-May. This made the planned landing of the 82nd Airborne Division around St Sauveur-le-Vicomte too risky. Instead, its drop zone was shifted to the Merderet River area, and the 101st Airborne drop zone was shifted slightly south so that both divisions would control an easily defensible area between the beaches and the Douve and Merderet rivers.

GERMAN PLANS

German defensive plans were in a state of flux due to serious disagreements between Rundstedt and Rommel over the deployment and control of the Panzer reserve. To some extent this debate was irrelevant to the Cotentin peninsula, since no senior German commander was particularly concerned that this area would be the focus of an Allied invasion. Until May 1944, the defense of the entire 155 miles (250km) of coastline on the Cotentin peninsula was the responsibility of a single

There was considerable controversy among senior Allied commanders about how to use gliders to reinforce the paratroopers. Here a C-47 of the 90th Troop Carrier Squadron (TCS), 438th TCG (Troop Carrier Group) lifts off from Greenham Common with a Horsa glider in tow on 6 June 1944. (NARA)

Like a medieval knight, a fully loaded paratrooper sometimes needed help simply to move due to the enormous weight of gear and equipment he carried. This is T/4 Joseph Gorenc of the 506th PIR climbing aboard a C-47 on the evening of 5 June 1944. (NARA)

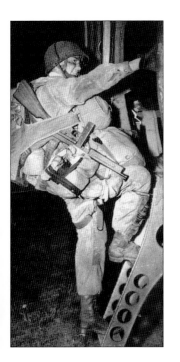

second-rate division. The western coast was lightly guarded since the navy had argued that the heavy seas off the west coast as well as the heavily defended Channel Islands made amphibious landings unlikely. In mid-May, the navy staff had a change of heart, and began to suggest that the Allies might land on both the east and west coasts, with simultaneous attacks on either side of Cherbourg. Shortly afterwards, Rommel visited the area, and later had a conference with Dollman and Marcks about the state of defenses in this sector. Von Schlieben argued that the port facilities in Cherbourg should be sabotaged immediately to make the port an unattractive target, and to permit units to withdraw to the base of the Cotentin peninsula rather than becoming trapped. The navy would not even consider such a plan and the proposal was ignored. Instead, the defense of the Cotentin peninsula was substantially increased. The 243rd Infantry Division was shifted from its location further south in reserve, and placed along the west coast. The partially formed 91st Luftlande Division was placed at the base of the peninsula to back up the two static divisions.

Defense of the Cotentin coast did not have as high a priority as other sectors further east, which were judged to be more likely objectives for an Allied amphibious assault. The forces along the coast were spread very thin, locally concentrated in strongpoints "like a string of pearls." Defenses were not particularly heavy along Utah Beach, since it was presumed that such a beach would be an unattractive objective given the tidal marshes behind it. Two battalions of GR.919 held a total of 25 strongpoints from Le Grand Vey in the south to the Aumeville beach in the north, a distance of about 15 miles (25km). The strongpoints were categorized into two types, *wiederstandnest* (Wn = reinforced position) and *stutzpunkt* (StP = support position). These strongpoints typically consisted of a platoon of 40 troops with several small bunkers, a few machine-gun pits or concrete reinforced "Tobruks", and a few anti-tank guns or obsolete field guns. To make up for the shortage of troops, the formations along the coast had more firepower than a normal infantry unit, even though the weapons were a motley selection of obsolete or captured types.

Paratroopers of the 101st Airborne have their chutes and equipment checked by Lt Bobuck prior to boarding their C-47 for the flight to Normandy. The C-47 in the background has had the black and white D-Day invasion stripes hastily painted on. (NARA)

The strongpoint that figured most directly in the subsequent fighting was WN5. It was manned by a platoon from 3./GR.919 and was commanded by Leutnant Arthur Jahnke, a young veteran of the Eastern Front and holder of the Knight's Cross. It included a 50mm anti-tank gun in a Bauform 667 casemate, two 50mm anti-tank guns in open concrete pits, one French 47mm anti-tank gun in a concrete pit, a Bauform 67 with a French tank turret and 37mm gun, four mortar and machine-gun Tobruks, and a half-dozen other bunkers and shelters. One of the platoon's more exotic weapons was a group of *Goliath* remote control demolition vehicles, a type of wire-guided tracked vehicle designed to be used like a land torpedo to attack high-value targets such as tanks and landing craft. These were deployed from small caves facing the beach. A second strongpoint, WN4, was located immediately to the west of WN5, covering the main access causeway off the beach.

The regimental commander, Oberstleutnant Gunther Keil, did not agree with Rommel's tactic of placing all of his troops in the forward bunkers. Instead, he placed a minimal number of troops on the coast, and the rest of each platoon as an "alert unit" (*alarmeinheiten*) in the buildings behind the beach. Artillery in this sector included a battery from Sturm-Abteilung AOK 7 west of Foucarville, and a battery of multiple rocket launchers from I./Nebelwerfer Regiment 100 south of Brucheville. There were also three batteries from an army coastal artillery regiment (HKAA.1261) in this sector; the 1./HKAA.1261 in St Martin-de-Varreville with four ex-Soviet 122mm guns, the 2./HKAA.1261 in Azeville with four French Schneider 105mm guns, and the 3./HKAA 1261 in Crisbecq with three massive 210mm Skoda guns.

Unlike neighboring Omaha Beach, the Utah Beach sector was relatively flat, not affording the excellent fields of fire to be found further east on the coast. The beach obstacles in front of WN5 were far less extensive than those at neighboring Omaha Beach, and the obstacles largely petered out in the area in front of Grande Dune where the landings actually occurred. Although GR.919 had attempted to reinforce these defenses, the tidal conditions simply washed many of the obstacles ashore. The main reserve in this sector was the Georgian Battalion 795 Ost, which was located further west near Criqueville, and GR.1058 from the 91st Luftlande Division located in the central peninsula in the landing zone of the 82nd Airborne Division.

The Kriegsmarine lacked sufficient forces to seriously entertain the idea of repelling the Allied invasion at sea. Marinegruppe West, under Vizeadmiral Theodor Krancke, was divided into sectors with Konteradmiral Rieve's Channel Coast responsible for the Normandy coast through to the Dutch border. The port nearest to Utah Beach was Cherbourg, which contained two torpedo flotillas, totaling 16 S-boats. Krancke had attempted to inhibit the invasion activities by a program of minelaying off the Normandy coast to coincide with Rommel's fortification efforts. Unbeknownst to him, the Allies were aware of the location of nearly all of these minefields due to the breaking of the Enigma codes. In addition, Enigma allowed the Royal Navy to vigorously disrupt minelaying in the weeks before D-Day. Attempts to mine the Seine bay on 24 May were met by a force of British torpedo boats and Coastal Command aircraft that put an end to any further attempts. The lack of bombproof U-boat shelters along the Channel inhibited Krancke from deploying submarines in the invasion area.

The Luftwaffe played virtually no role in the fighting in the Cotentin sector during June. Allied air superiority was so great, and the Luftwaffe so weak that there was little hope for conducting Luftwaffe operations so far west from the air bases near Paris.

On 4 June 1944, Major Lettau, the chief Luftwaffe meteorologist in Paris released a forecast indicating that the Allies were unlikely to launch an invasion over the next fortnight due to rough seas and gale-force winds that were unlikely to weaken until mid-June. This forecast convinced OB West that it would be an appropriate opportunity to conduct a major command wargame in Rennes to study possible counter-strokes against Allied airborne attacks in Normandy. As a result, about half the divisional commanders and a quarter of the regimental commanders were on their way to a wargame in Rennes. Indeed, the weather forecast was so bad that many units were using the opportunity to give their men rest from the strenuous construction program along the coast. Rommel used the spell of bad weather to visit Germany, hoping to convince the Führer to release more Panzers to his control for a forward defense of the coast.

D-DAY

The first troops to land in France in preparation for Operation Neptune were OSS teams (Office of Strategic Service), usually consisting of two US soldiers trained in the operation of signal devices, teamed with three British commandos for site security. A half-dozen of these teams were flown into France around 01.30hrs on 3 June to mark airborne drop zones for later pathfinder teams who would bring in more extensive marking equipment.

The troops of the two airborne divisions began final preparations for the Normandy airdrops on 5 June at 15 separate airfields in southern England. The air delivery of the two divisions was assigned to the IX Troop Carrier command. Operation Albany, the delivery of the 101st Airborne Division, was assigned to the 50th Troop Carrier Wing and Operation Boston, the delivery of the 82nd Airborne Division, was assigned to the 52nd Wing. The initial wave used 821 troop-laden C-47 and C-54 transports. Each aircraft carried a "stick" of paratroopers, usually 18–20 per aircraft in most aircraft, but 9–10 in parachute artillery units due to the amount of other equipment carried.

To conduct a nighttime drop, the transport pilots were dependent on visual and radar signals to locate the drop zone. Pathfinders were parachuted into the drop zones ahead of the main wave to set up both types of signals – a set of seven color-coded Aldis lamps in the shape of a "T" and an AN/PPN-1 "Eureka" radar beacon. The Eureka set was a useful aid for the approach to the drop zone, but became less effective about two miles out, requiring the use of the Aldis signal lamps for the final approach. Nineteen aircraft carrying the pathfinders departed before midnight and they began landing in France around 00.15hrs on 6 June 1944. The following waves of C-47 transports were fitted with a "Rebecca" system to pick up the signal emitted from the Eureka ground beacon, and some were also fitted with "Gee" navigation aids.

On approaching the drop zones, the pathfinder aircraft encountered an unexpected bank of cloud that created navigational problems. In the 101st Airborne sector, only the teams allotted to Drop Zone C parachuted close to the target. Likewise in the 82nd Airborne Division sector, only one batch of pathfinders was accurately dropped into Drop Zone O. In the case of the other four drop zones, the pathfinders were dropped so far away from their target that they did not have enough time after their landing to reach their designated drop-zone. As a result, some of the pathfinder teams set up their landing beacons in areas away from the planned drop zones, while other teams were able to set up only the Eureka beacons since the presence of German troops nearby made it impossible to set up the Aldis lamps.

The main wave of C-47 transports began taking off from England around midnight. The two skytrains coalesced over the English Channel, and then followed a route around the Cotentin peninsula, passing between the Channel Islands, and entering enemy air-space over the west Cotentin coast, heading northeastward toward the drop zone, and exiting over Utah Beach. In parallel, a force of RAF Stirling bombers flew a diversionary mission, dropping chaff to simulate an airborne formation and dropping dummy paratroopers and noisemakers into areas away from the actual drop zones. The weather conditions were a full moon and clearing skies. The flight proved uneventful until the coast, and the aircraft flew in tight formation in a "V-of-Vs". On reaching the coast, the problems began. The aircraft encountered the same dense cloud that had frustrated the pathfinders. The pathfinder transports had not radioed back a warning about this due to radio silence. The clouds created immediate dangers due to the proximity of the aircraft in formation, and C-47s began to frantically maneuver to avoid mid-air collisions. Some pilots climbed to 2,000 feet to avoid the clouds, others descended below the cloud bank to 500 feet, while some remained at the prescribed altitude of 700 feet. This cloud bank completely disrupted the formation and ended any hopes for a concentrated paratroop drop.

Anti-aircraft fire began during the final approach into the drop zones near the coast. Although they had been instructed to maintain a steady course, some pilots began jinking their aircraft to avoid steady streams of 20mm cannon fire. It was an inauspicious start for an inherently risky mission.

Table 1: D-Day Airlift Operations, IX Troop Carrier Command

Mission	Albany	Boston	Total
Aircraft sorties	433	378	811
Aborted sorties	2	1	3
Aircraft lost or missing	13	8	21
Aircraft damaged	81	115	196
Aircrew killed or missing	48	17	65
Aircrew wounded	4	11	15
Troops carried	6,928	6,420	13,348
Troops dropped	6,750	6,350	13,100
Howitzers carried	12	2	14
Cargo carried (tons)	211	178	389

ALBANY MISSION

The 101st Airborne Division was the first to land around 01.30hrs on 6 June 1944. Its primary objective was to seize control of the area behind Utah Beach between St Martin-de-Varreville and Pouppeville to facilitate the exit of the 4th Infantry Division from the beach later that morning. Its secondary mission was to protect the southern flank of VII Corps by destroying two bridges on the Carentan highway and a railroad bridge west of it, gaining control of the Barquette lock, and establishing a bridgehead over the Douve River northeast of Carentan.

The 502nd Parachute Infantry Regiment (PIR) and 506th PIR (less one battalion) were assigned to the primary objective. The first wave of the 502nd PIR consisted of the 2/502nd PIR and HQ/502nd PIR. The transport aircraft carrying these units were scattered by cloud cover and flak, landing far from Drop Zone A. Most of the 2/502nd PIR was dropped compactly but inaccurately on the far edge of Drop Zone C, three miles south of intended Drop Zone A. The battalion landed in an area divided up by a maze of dense hedgerows, the Normandy *bocage*, and had a great deal of difficulty assembling and orienting themselves. These units spent most of D-Day regrouping and took no part in the initial fighting.

The 3/502nd PIR landed in very scattered fashion to the east of Ste Mère-Église. The battalion commander, Lieutenant Colonel Robert Cole, gathered about 75 men and began moving on the coastal battery at St Martin-de-Varreville. They found that the guns had been removed and the position deserted due to pre-invasion bombardment, so they moved on to their next objective, the western side of Audouville–la-Hubert causeway (Exit 3), arriving there around 07.30hrs. German troops of the I/GR.919 abandoning strongpoint WN8 began retreating across this causeway around 09.30hrs and were ambushed by the concealed paratroopers, losing 50–75 men. This battalion also attempted to clear Exit 4, and while they found it undefended, the location of the nearby German batteries made this causeway unusable for exiting the beach. Contact was made with the 4th Infantry Division around 13.00hrs, and the battalion spent the rest of the day collecting their scattered and missing men.

Lieutenant Colonel Patrick Cassidy's 1/502nd PIR landed near St Germain-de-Varreville, with 20 of the 36 aircraft within a mile of the beacon. One group led by Cassidy moved toward the stone buildings near Mésières, the garrison for the German coastal battery at St Martin-de-Varreville. Cassidy's group occupied the crossroads outside Mésières and determined that the two northern exits assigned to his battalion were clear. On meeting another group of about 45 men from his unit, he ordered them north to create a defensive perimeter near Foucarville. Cassidy kept about a company of troops near the crossroads to prevent any intervention against the beach from the west, and sent a squad to the eastern side of Mésières to clean out any German troops. A team led by Staff Sergeant Harrison Summers killed or captured about 150 German troops in a series of one-sided encounters. As this action was winding down, the regimental commander, Lieutenant Colonel John Michaels arrived with 200 men. This freed up the remainder of Cassidy's men at the crossroads, who then followed the other paratroopers to the Foucarville area. Cassidy's force advanced to

Paratroopers sit on the canvas benches along the fuselage of the C-47 during the trip to Normandy with a captain closest to the camera. These men are probably from the 82nd Airborne, which was not as keen on facial camouflage as the 101st Airborne. (MHI)

C-47s pass over the ships of Task Force U after their runs over Normandy. These are probably from the glider serials that delivered the gliders around dawn on D-Day. (NARA)

the west, since a secondary mission of his unit was to link up with the 82nd Airborne Division that was scheduled to land near Ste Mère-Église. In doing so, a company became engaged in a series of encounters with German infantry around the village of Fournel that lasted through much of D-Day. The 1/502nd PIR held the northern perimeter throughout D-Day without serious challenge from the Germans except at Fournel.

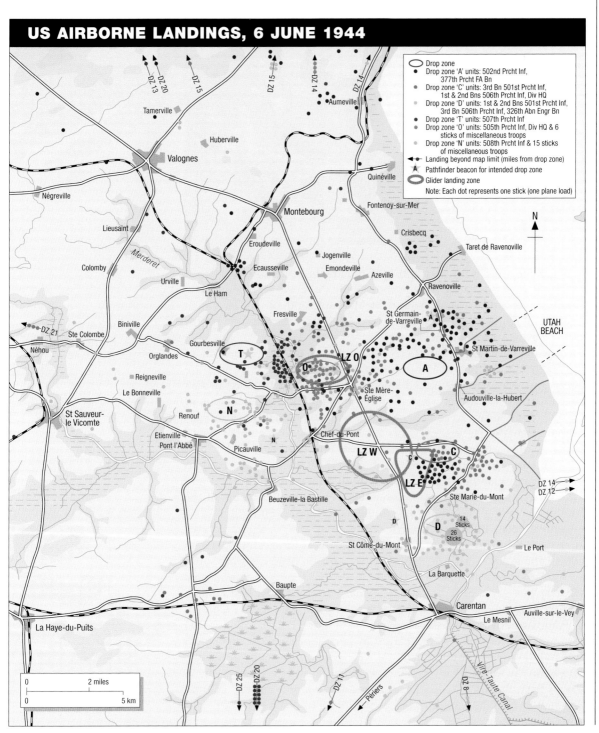

US AIRBORNE LANDINGS, 6 JUNE 1944

Drop zone
Drop zone 'A' units: 502nd Prcht Inf, 377th Prcht FA Bn
Drop zone 'C' units: 3rd Bn 501st Prcht Inf, 1st & 2nd Bns 506th Prcht Inf, Div HQ
Drop zone 'D' units: 1st & 2nd Bns 501st Prcht Inf, 3rd Bn 506th Prcht Inf, 326th Abn Engr Bn
Drop zone 'T' units: 507th Prcht Inf
Drop zone 'O' units: 505th Prcht Inf, Div HQ & 6 sticks of miscellaneous troops
Drop zone 'N' units: 508th Prcht Inf & 15 sticks of miscellaneous troops
Landing beyond map limit (miles from drop zone)
Pathfinder beacon for intended drop zone
Glider landing zone
Note: Each dot represents one stick (one plane load)

James Flanagan of C/502nd PIR displays a German flag captured during the fighting on D-Day. This scene was photographed at "Stopka strongpoint", the Marmion farm south of Ravenoville where "Mad Major" John Stopka was trying to gather troops from the 502nd and 506th PIR who had landed nearby. (NARA)

Of all the units in this sector, the 377th Parachute Field Artillery, with 12 75mm pack howitzers, was the most badly dispersed with some even landing near the marshes around St Marcouf, and others far north around Valognes. This meant there was no artillery fire support in this sector except for a single howitzer.

The southern sector was the responsibility of the two battalions of the 506th PIR, landing in Drop Zone C. The cloudbank disrupted the C-47s, and some aircraft passed over a concentration of German flak near Etienville; six aircraft were shot down and 30 damaged. In spite of the fire, some drops were concentrated, with one serial of 14 aircraft dropping almost on top of Drop Zone C and another serial of 13 bunching their sticks a mile and a half east and southeast of the drop zone. But the other serials were much further from their intended targets due to confusion over the beacons. About 140 men of the HQ and 1/506th PIR assembled in the regimental area in the first hours of the landing, including the regimental commander, Colonel Sink.

The 2/506th PIR landed north of the drop zone in the same area as the 501st PIR, but Lieutenant Colonel Robert Strayer managed to collect about 200 men by 03.30hrs. Strayer's group began moving south to seize the areas behind the Houdienville (Exit 2) and Pouppeville (Exit 1) causeways. Sink had no idea where Strayer's men had landed, and so instructed the assembled paratroopers of Lieutenant Colonel William Turner's 1/506th PIR to take control of the Pouppeville (Exit 1) causeway. Strayer's men were delayed by persistent German small arms fire and did not arrive at the Houdienville (Exit 2) causeway until early afternoon, by which time the access road had already been overrun by troops from the 4th Infantry Division moving inland. Turner's column also had tough going and it took several hours to reach the Poupeville (Exit 1) causeway.

Paratroopers of the 101st Airborne cluster around a Renault UE armored tractor that had been impressed into service to help carry supplies from the drop zone to the "Stopka strongpoint" near Ravenoville on D-Day. The troops with the circle insignia on their helmets to the left are from the divisional artillery while the paratrooper in the center with the white spade insignia is from the 506th PIR. (NARA)

Next to land were the 3/501st PIR and the divisional HQ, which was to control the planned glider-landing area near Hiesville. The 3/501st PIR lost three aircraft to flak on the approach. A force of about 300 paratroopers from the HQ and Lieutenant Colonel Julian Ewell's 3/501st PIR congregated near Hiesville. General Taylor, not knowing what was happening with Strayer's and Turner's two columns, decided to ensure that the southernmost Poupeville causeway was under US control, and so dispatched Colonel Ewell with 40 of his men around 06.00hrs. This was the first of the three paratrooper columns to actually reach the causeway around 08.00. The 2./GR.919 manned the WN6 strongpoint covering the western end of the causeway and WN2a on the beach itself. The defenses were poorly organized, but it took nearly four hours for the outnumbered paratroopers to overcome the German defenders in house-to-house fighting. The Germans surrendered around noon after suffering 25 casualties; 38 surrendered and the remainder who tried to escape across the causeway toward strongpoint WN2a on the beach were captured by advancing infantry of the 4th Division. About half of Ewell's men were casualties, but they made contact with the 2/8th Infantry at Exit 1.

Fighting flared up near the divisional CP in Drop Zone C due to the presence nearby of troops from Artillery Regiment.191 centered around Ste Marie-du-Mont. The paratroopers gradually eliminated the batteries, and the town was finally cleared of German troops by mid-afternoon when they were reinforced by GIs from the 8th Infantry advancing from the beaches.

The final groups to land were the 1/501st PIR, elements of the 2/501st PIR, the 3/506th PIR as well as engineer and medical personnel. These forces were earmarked for Drop Zone D, the southernmost of the drop zones. The approach to the drop zone was hot, with a considerable amount of light flak, searchlights, and magnesium flares. Six C-47s were shot down and 26 damaged. These drops were among the most successful in putting the paratroopers near their intended objective, but this was not entirely fortuitous, as the Germans had assumed that this area could be used for airborne landings. As this was the last of the divisional landings, the German troops in the sector were alerted and had troops near the landing zone. The 1/501st PIR commander was killed and his executive

A patrol from the 101st Airborne tows supplies from the drop zone on D-Day. The paratrooper to the right has used a captured German belt to carry a pair of German "potato masher" hand-grenades while one of his comrades carries what appears to be a German officer's service cap. (NARA)

officer captured. The regimental commander, Colonel Johnson, landed near the center of the zone and was able to rally about 150 paratroopers. He immediately set off for the primary objective, La Barquette locks controlling the flooding of the areas along the Douve River. The force brushed aside the German sentries and occupied the locks, but was soon under fire from German artillery. With the situation at the locks in hand, around 09.00hrs Johnson and about 50 paratroopers returned to the landing zone to seek reinforcements. About half of 2/501st PIR was engaged in a sharp firefight around the village of Les Droueries, and had been unable to disengage and move south to the objective. Instead of encountering the single platoon expected in this sector, they were confronted by an entire battalion, III/GR.1058. They spent most of the day fighting around the town of St Côme-du-Mont. Johnson was able to collect a few additional paratroopers and set off to seize or destroy the bridges over the Douve River below its junction with the Merderet River.

The third unit landing in Drop Zone D, the 3/506th PIR, had the roughest time. German troops were waiting in the landing area and had soaked a wooden building with fuel. They set the building on fire, illuminating the descending paratroopers. The battalion commander and his executive officer were among those killed in the first moments. Captain Charles Shettle, the battalion S-3, landed away from the main drop zone and set off to the le Port bridge with about 15 men. This small group gradually increased in size as it attracted scattered paratroops, and emplaced itself at two of the bridges by 04.30hrs. They were forced back by German counterattacks around 06.30hrs as they were nearly out of ammunition. However, they took up positions near the bridges, and were able to keep the Germans at bay. Ironically, the next day Shettle was able to call in a P-47 strike in hopes of attacking the German positions, but due to confusion, the P-47s skip bombed the bridges instead.

A pair of 82nd Airborne paratroopers from the 505th PIR eye a rabbit, though it is unclear whether they view it as a potential pet or potential lunch. This photo was taken near Ste Mère-Église on D-Day and provides some details of the paratroopers specialized garb including the jump gloves and scarves made from camouflage fabric. (NARA)

A patrol of paratroopers from the 508th PIR, 82nd Airborne move through the churchyard of St Marcouf on D-Day. (NARA)

BOSTON MISSION

The 82nd Airborne Division revised its plans on 28 May due to the discovery that the 91st Luftlande Division had moved into its planned landing area. The 82nd Airborne's new assignment was to land two regiments on the western side of the Merderet River, and one regiment on the eastern side around Ste Mère-Église to secure the bridges over the Merderet. The landings of the 82nd Airborne were even more badly scattered than those of the 101st Airborne and as a result, only one of its regiments was able to carry out its assignment on D-Day. The 82nd Airborne began landing about an hour after the 101st Airborne, around 02.30hrs.

The 505th PIR was assigned to land on Drop Zone O to the northwest of Ste Mère-Église. Unlike many other transport serials, those flying to Drop Zone O spotted the cloudbank early and managed to fly over it in coordinated fashion. The only cloud problems were over the drop zone itself, forcing some C-47 pilots to initiate the drop higher than usual at 1,000 feet. The pathfinders had done such a thorough job marking it that many aircraft circled back over the area to drop the paratroopers more accurately. This was the most precise series of jumps of any that night. Lieutenant Colonel Edward Krause's 3/505th PIR was assigned to take the town of Ste Mère-Église and managed to assemble about 180 paratroopers. The town had been garrisoned by the supply element of the divisional anti-aircraft unit Flak Regiment Hermann, but most of the 200 men of the unit left the town before the arrival of the paratroopers. Krause ordered his men into the town with explicit instructions to limit their actions to knives, bayonets and grenades to make it easier to distinguish German defenders. Krause's group quickly seized the town, killing about 10 German troops and capturing 30 others.

Lieutenant Colonel Benjamin Vandervoort's 2/505th PIR collected about half its troops and set out to establish a defense line north of the drop zone as planned. However, at 09.30hrs, the German GR.1058 staged a counterattack against Ste Mère-Église from the south. The regimental commander, Colonel William Ekman, ordered Vandervoort to return back southward to assist in the defense. Before doing so, he broke off a platoon to remain at Neuville and carry out the battalion's original mission. It proved to be a crucial decision. Shortly after establishing a defensive perimeter north of the town, Lieutenant Turner Turnbull's platoon was hit by a German infantry company but managed to hold his position during an eight-hour struggle. Only 16 of the 44 paratroopers in Turnbull's platoon survived the fighting, but the platoon's defense shielded the battalion while it faced an even greater threat to the south.

The 2/505th PIR arrived in Ste Mère-Église around 10.00hrs and took over part of the perimeter defense. The first German attack consisted of two companies from the Georgian Battalion 795 and troops of the 91st Luftlande Division with a few of the division's StuG IIIs. It was repulsed by the 3/505th PIR. Colonel Krause ordered a counterattack and about 80 men from Company I advanced southward along the road, hitting one of the retreating German convoys with a grenade attack. This was the one and only German attack of the day against the town.

The 1/505th PIR landed with the headquarters including General Ridgway. Around 04.00hrs, Company A under Lieutenant John Wisner set off for the La Fière bridge with about 155 paratroopers. This group increased in size as it approached the bridge, picking up stragglers from the 507th and 508th PIR. The advance on the bridge was slowed by frequent encounters with German troops. An initial attempt to rush the bridge failed due to entrenched German machine-gun teams, the first of several attempts that day in a confusing series of engagements.

The two other regiments of the 82nd Airborne Division landing in Drop Zones T and N on the west side of the Merderet River were hopelessly scattered. Pathfinders had been unable to mark the drop zones, in some

Another view of a group of paratroopers from the 508th PIR near the church in St Marcouf on D-Day. The sergeant in the foreground is armed with the folding-stock version of the M1 carbine, developed for the airborne forces. (NARA)

This 88mm Flak 36 anti-aircraft gun was one of a battery of four captured by the 82nd Airborne in Normandy. It appears to have been spiked with its breech removed. (MHI)

cases due to the proximity of German troops. The transport aircraft were disrupted by the coastal cloudbank, and after arriving over the drop area, the pilots had searched in vain for the signals, or in some cases homed in on the wrong beacon. Much of the 507th PIR was dropped into the marshes east of Drop Zone T while the 508th was dropped south of Drop Zone N. These swamps were deep and many of the heavily laden paratroopers drowned before they could free themselves of their equipment. In addition, a great deal of important equipment and supplies landed in the water, and valuable time had to be spent trying to retrieve this equipment. About half of the 508th PIR landed within two miles of the drop zone, but the remainder landed on the other side of the Merderet River or were scattered to even more distant locations. The 507th PIR dropped in a tighter pattern than the 508th, but many aircraft overshot the drop zone, dumping the paratroopers into the swampy fringes of the Merderet River. The most noticeable terrain feature in the area of the 507th PIR drop was the railroad line from Carentan on an embankment over the marshes. Many paratroopers gathered along the embankment.

La Fière Bridge

One of the missions of the 507th PIR was to seize the western approaches to the La Fière bridge, which connected the drop zones west of the Merderet River with Ste Mère-Église and the paratroopers on the east side. The bridge was a small stone structure over the Merderet River, but the farmland on the west side of the river had been flooded by the Germans to prevent its use as an airborne landing zone. The connection between the bridge and the hamlet of Cauquigny over the flooded area was a long, tree-lined causeway.

After the first attempt by Lt Wisner of A/505th PIR to rush the bridge, the eastern approaches became a collection point for paratroopers trying to make their way to the west side of the Merderet River, having been wrongly dropped on the eastern side. By mid-morning about 600 para-

This modest little stone bridge over the Merderet River at La Fière was the scene of some of the fiercest fighting on D-Day by the 82nd Airborne Division. This photo was taken by Gen Gavin after the fighting. (MHI)

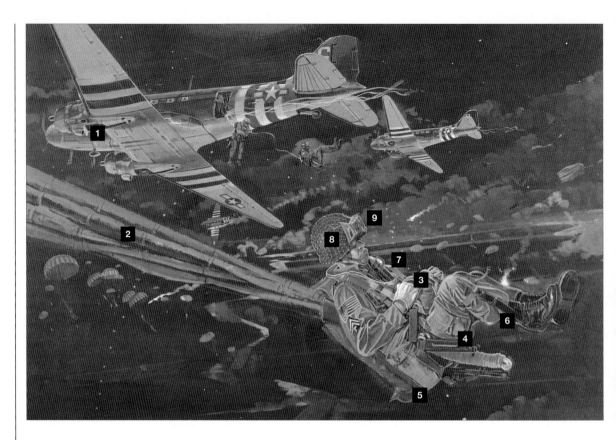

BOSTON MISSION – 82ND AIRBORNE DIVISION OVER DROP ZONE T, 02.40HRS, D-DAY (pages 124–125)

Based at Fulbock in England, the 442nd Troop Carrier Group was attached to the 52nd Wing for the D-Day airlift. The group's four squadrons made up Serial 26 of Mission Boston and arrived over Drop Zone T between 02.39 and 02.42hrs on D-Day. The serial carried 45 sticks of paratroopers: 36 from the rifle companies of the 1st Battalion, 507th Parachute Infantry Regiment, and 9 sticks of the headquarters company. The group lost one aircraft on the approach to the drop zone, and suffered damage to 31 of its aircraft due to flak over the drop zone. This shows aircraft from the 305th Troop Carrier Squadron (TCS), which carried the codes 4J on the nose (1) (the other squadrons were J7: 303rd TCS; V4: 304th TCS; 7H: 306th TCS). The C-47 was a military derivative of the Douglas DC-3 civil airliner. The main structural difference between the two types was the use of a large cargo door on the left rear side of the C-47 fuselage. The C-47 had simple, folding bench seats in the main cabin instead of conventional passenger seats. On paratrooper missions such as this, the typical load was one "stick" of paratroopers, which usually totalled 18 to 20 paratroopers. Alternatively, fewer paratroopers and more carge could be air-dropped. The paratrooper in the foreground, a Tech 5 from the 507th Parachute Infantry Regt. (PIR), is seen moments after jumpng from the aircraft. After leaving the C-47, the aircraft's slipstream tended to blow the paratrooper backward and curl him up. As the static line opened up the T-5 parachute pack,

the olive drab canopy began to deploy (2). The large surface of area of the deploying canopy tended to swing the paratrooper around again, and within seconds, the shroud lines cleared the pack and the canopy blossomed, giving the paratrooper a hard jolt. Quick deployment of the parachute was essential since the drops were conducted from only 700 feet. US paratroopers also carried a reserve chute on their chest (3). This paratrooper is armed with a .45 cal. Thompson sub-machine gun (4), which has been tucked under the waist web of the T-5 parachute harness to keep it in place. The paratroops carried a good deal of equipment into combat. Just visible under the harness is his yellow "Mae West" life vest. His musette bag hangs under the reserve chute, an ammunition bag from his right hip (5), and an assault gas mask in waterproof bag from his left hip (not visible). He has a fighting knife (6) strapped to his right leg above his jump boots. Although not visible here he also carries a .45 cal automatic in a holster on his hip with a folding knife in its scabbard in front of this. On his chest is a TL122C flashlight (7). Paratroopers on D-Day wore the M1942 paratroop battledress with its distinctive pockets. The paratrooper's M1C helmet (8) resembles the normal GI helmet, but has a modified liner and chinstrap to absorb the shock of the opening parachute. The first aid packet (9) taped to the front of the helmet for ready access contained a field dressing, tourniquet and morphine. Many paratroopers wore gloves to protect their hands during the jump.
(Howard Gerrard)

troopers had coalesced and a force under Captain F. "Ben" Schwarzwalder from the 2/507th PIR began a house-to-house skirmish to clear the manor farm on the eastern side of the bridge. When General Gavin arrived later, he split the growing force, sending a team of 75 paratroopers south to find another crossing point, while leading a second group of 75 to the bridge at Chef-du-Pont. General Ridgway arrived afterwards, and ordered Colonel Lindquist of the 508th PIR to organize the various groups near La Fière and capture the bridge.

Unknown to the force on the east side of the La Fière bridge, about 50 paratroopers of the 2/507th PIR had attempted to cross the bridge earlier in the morning from the western side. After being forced back by machine-gun fire, they established a defensive position in the Cauquigny church on the other end of the causeway. The attack against the bridge from the east side began around noon and about 80 paratroopers under Schwarzwalder pushed over the causeway and linked up with the platoon on the western side. Schwarzwalder's men were not followed by any other troops, and he decided that they should join up with the rest of their battalion under Lieutenant Colonel Charles Timmes in an orchard in Amfreville to the northwest of Cauquigny. Schwarzwalder left behind about a dozen paratroopers, believing they would be adequate to hold the bridge until other paratroopers from the east side passed over. However, before the force on the eastern side moved more paratroopers across, GR.1057 of the 91st Luftlande Division attacked with the support of a few Hotchkiss H-39 light tanks of Panzer Abteilung 100, quickly regaining control of the western side of the causeway in Cauquigny. As a result, the bridgehead over the Merderet was lost for the next two days and would be the scene of intense fighting.

The group under General Gavin that split off to seize the Chef-du-Pont bridge had no success. The bridge was stubbornly defended by a small number of German troops dug in along the causeway. Gavin's force was ordered back to La Fière to reinforce the main effort, and he left behind an understrength platoon commanded by Captain Roy Creek to cover the bridge. This unit was nearly overwhelmed by a later German counterattack, but they were rescued in the nick of time by the unanticipated arrival of a glider carrying a 57mm anti-tank gun, followed by reinforcements from La Fière. The reinforcements allowed Creek's force to clear the Germans off the bridge and cross the river to the west side.

A glider train passes over the French coast on the afternoon of D-Day, part of the re-supply missions. One of the German strongpoints is evident below in the center of the photo. (NARA)

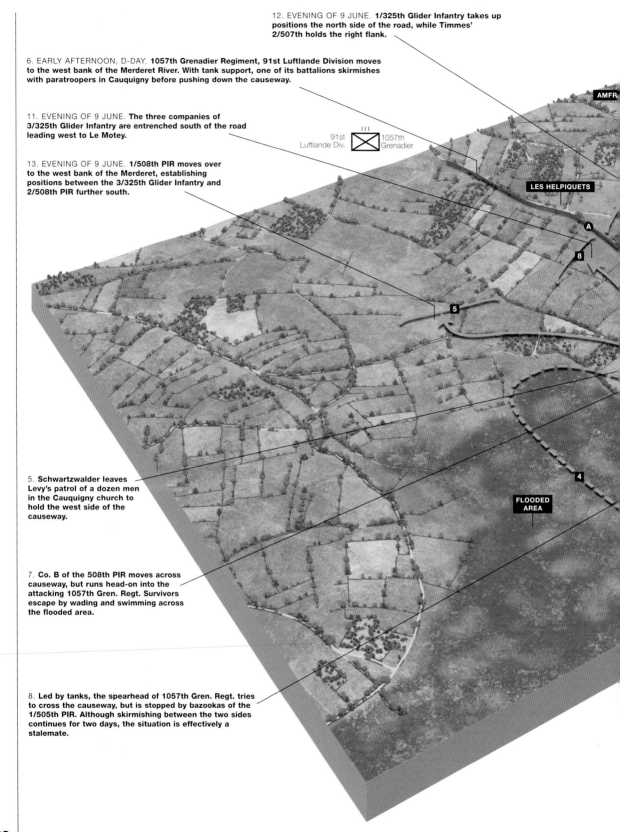

12. EVENING OF 9 JUNE. **1/325th Glider Infantry takes up positions the north side of the road, while Timmes' 2/507th holds the right flank.**

6. EARLY AFTERNOON, D-DAY. **1057th Grenadier Regiment, 91st Luftlande Division moves to the west bank of the Merderet River. With tank support, one of its battalions skirmishes with paratroopers in Cauquigny before pushing down the causeway.**

11. EVENING OF 9 JUNE. **The three companies of 3/325th Glider Infantry are entrenched south of the road leading west to Le Motey.**

91st
Luftlande Div.   1057th
Grenadier

13. EVENING OF 9 JUNE. **1/508th PIR moves over to the west bank of the Merderet, establishing positions between the 3/325th Glider Infantry and 2/508th PIR further south.**

AMFR

LES HELPIQUETS

A

8

5

5. **Schwartzwalder leaves Levy's patrol of a dozen men in the Cauquigny church to hold the west side of the causeway.**

4

FLOODED
AREA

7. **Co. B of the 508th PIR moves across causeway, but runs head-on into the attacking 1057th Gren. Regt. Survivors escape by wading and swimming across the flooded area.**

8. **Led by tanks, the spearhead of 1057th Gren. Regt. tries to cross the causeway, but is stopped by bazookas of the 1/505th PIR. Although skirmishing between the two sides continues for two days, the situation is effectively a stalemate.**

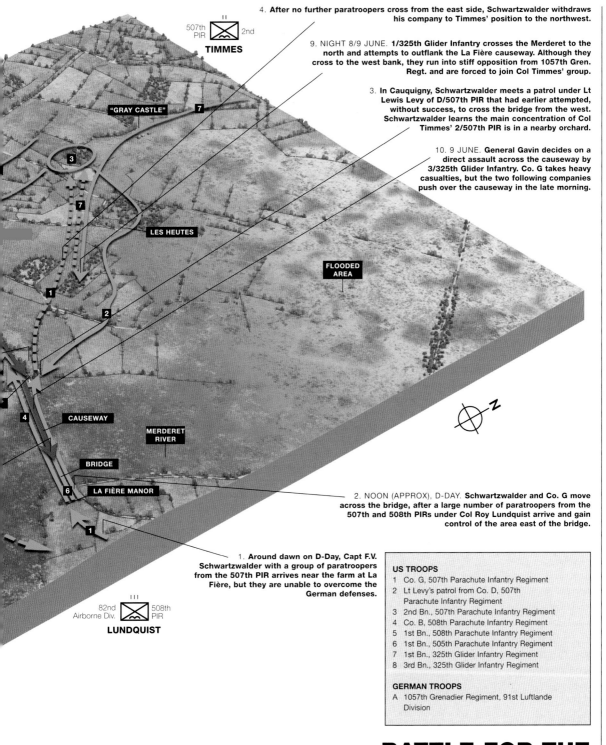

507th PIR 2nd
TIMMES

4. After no further paratroopers cross from the east side, Schwartzwalder withdraws his company to Timmes' position to the northwest.

9. NIGHT 8/9 JUNE. **1/325th Glider Infantry crosses the Merderet to the north and attempts to outflank the La Fière causeway. Although they cross to the west bank, they run into stiff opposition from 1057th Gren. Regt. and are forced to join Col Timmes' group.**

3. In Cauquigny, Schwartzwalder meets a patrol under Lt Lewis Levy of D/507th PIR that had earlier attempted, without success, to cross the bridge from the west. Schwartzwalder learns the main concentration of Col Timmes' 2/507th PIR is in a nearby orchard.

10. 9 JUNE. **General Gavin decides on a direct assault across the causeway by 3/325th Glider Infantry. Co. G takes heavy casualties, but the two following companies push over the causeway in the late morning.**

"GRAY CASTLE" 7

3

7

LES HEUTES

FLOODED AREA

1

2

4 **CAUSEWAY**

MERDERET RIVER

BRIDGE

6 **LA FIÈRE MANOR**

1

2. NOON (APPROX), D-DAY. **Schwartzwalder and Co. G move across the bridge, after a large number of paratroopers from the 507th and 508th PIRs under Col Roy Lundquist arrive and gain control of the area east of the bridge.**

1. Around dawn on D-Day, Capt F.V. Schwartzwalder with a group of paratroopers from the 507th PIR arrives near the farm at La Fière, but they are unable to overcome the German defenses.

82nd Airborne Div. 508th PIR
LUNDQUIST

US TROOPS

1 Co. G, 507th Parachute Infantry Regiment
2 Lt Levy's patrol from Co. D, 507th Parachute Infantry Regiment
3 2nd Bn., 507th Parachute Infantry Regiment
4 Co. B, 508th Parachute Infantry Regiment
5 1st Bn., 508th Parachute Infantry Regiment
6 1st Bn., 505th Parachute Infantry Regiment
7 1st Bn., 325th Glider Infantry Regiment
8 3rd Bn., 325th Glider Infantry Regiment

GERMAN TROOPS

A 1057th Grenadier Regiment, 91st Luftlande Division

BATTLE FOR THE LA FIÈRE BRIDGE, MERDERET RIVER

6–9 June 1944, viewed from the southeast, showing the bitter 4-day struggle for the La Fière Bridge. This small bridge and its associated causeway over the Merderet River proved crucial in the early operations beyond Utah Beach as they were the main link between the separated elements of the 82nd Airborne Division.

One of the few other coherent operations of the early morning on the west bank of the Merderet involved a force assembled by Lieutenant Colonel Thomas Shanley of the 2/508th PIR near Picauville. His unit's assignment was to destroy the Douve bridge at Pont l'Abbé, but his force quickly came in to contact with a German infantry battalion from GR.1057 involved in sealing off the west bank of the Merderet River. Shanley withdrew his force to the battalion assembly area on Hill 30 and they fought a day-long engagement, shielding the operations of the forces near La Fière.

By the afternoon of D-Day, there were three separated groups of paratroopers in the area around La Fière bridge: about 300 paratroopers with Shanley, 120 with Timmes and Schwarzwalder, and 400 with Col George Millett of the 507th PIR on the east side of La Fière. All three groups were short on ammunition, and under intense pressure from GR.1057. As will be detailed later, the fighting for La Fière continued for three days.

Glider Reinforcements

The next airborne missions in the early hours of D-Day were the glider reinforcement flights: Mission Detroit for the 82nd Airborne Division and Mission Chicago for the 101st Airborne Division. Mission Detroit left England at 01.20hrs with 52 Waco C-4A gliders carrying 155 troops, 16 57mm anti-tank guns, and 25 jeeps. One of these gliders, carrying the division's SCR-499 long-range radio, was lost shortly after take-off. A second aircraft and glider were lost before reaching Landing Zone E. The overloaded glider carrying the 101st Airborne deputy commander,

Table 2: D-Day Glider Operations, IX Troop Carrier Command

Mission	Chicago	Detroit	Keokuk	Elmira	Galveston	Hackensack	Total
Mission date	D-Day 04.00	D-Day 04.07	D-Day 21.00	D-Day 21.00	D+1 07.00	D+1 09.00	
Landing zone	LZ E	LZ O	LZ E	LZ W	LZ W	LZ W	
Tow aircraft sorties	52	52	32	177	102	101	516
Aborted sorties	1	0	0	2	2	0	5
Aircraft lost or missing	1	1	0	5	0	0	7
Aircraft damaged	7	38	1	92	26	1	165
Horsa sorties	0	0	32	140	20	30	222
Horsa sorties aborted	0	0	0	2	2	0	4
Waco sorties	52	53	0	36	84	70	295
Waco sorties aborted	1	1	0	0	2	0	4
Aircrew killed or missing	4	4	0	1	0	0	9
Aircrew wounded	1	3	0	8	0	0	12
Glider pilots dispatched	104	106	64	352	208	200	1,034
Glider pilots lost	14	13	0	26	0	3	56
Troops carried	155	220	157	1,190	968	1,331	4,021
Troops landed	153	209	157	1,160	927	1,331	3,937
Waco casualties*	27	30	0	15	35	16	123
Horsa casualties*	0	0	44	142	80	74	340
Artillery carried	16	16	6	37	20	0	95
Vehicles carried	25	27	40	123	41	34	290
Cargo carried (tons)	14	10	19	131	26	38	238

*troops injured or killed during landing

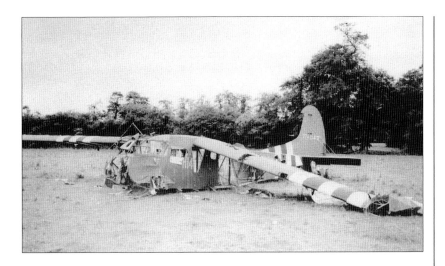

Landing in twilight in small, congested farm fields, many gliders like this Waco CG-4A made very rough landings. Although there had been hopes to retrieve and reuse the gliders after Normandy, most were damaged beyond repair. (MHI)

Brigadier General Donald Pratt, crashed on landing, killing the general. The nighttime landings at 03.45hrs were almost as badly scattered as the paratroopers with only 6 gliders on target, 15 within three-quarters of a mile, 10 further west and 18 further east. Nevertheless, casualties were modest with five dead, 17 seriously injured and seven missing.

The 46 Waco CG-4A gliders of Mission Detroit landed at 04.10hrs near the 82nd Airborne's Landing Zone O, carrying 220 troops as well as 22 jeeps and 16 anti-tank guns. About 20 of the gliders landed on or near the landing zone, while seven were released early (five disappearing) and seven more landed on the west bank of the Merderet River. The rough landings in this sector led to the loss of 11 jeeps and most of the gliders, but troop losses were less than expected, 3 dead and 23 seriously injured.

THE GERMAN REACTION

German forces on the Cotentin peninsula were not on alert on the night of 5/6 June 1944 due to the weather conditions mentioned earlier. The first hint of activity came into German intelligence around 23.00–24.00 on 5 June when signals units picked up a coded message to French resistance. Around 23.30hrs, an aircraft warning station at Cherbourg alerted the local command that ship activity and the concentration of transport aircraft at British airfields suggested an invasion was underway. This set in train a number of alerts. The first news of paratroop jumps began arriving at headquarters around 01.30hrs from the area around the Vire River. These alerts increased in number through the early morning hours. One of the sticks of pathfinders landed on top of the regimental headquarters of GR.919, located in a quarry on the road between Quineville and Montebourg. Oberstleutnant Gunther Keil commanded the battalions along the coastline, and found a map on one of the paratroopers that indicated that the main drop would be around Ste Mère-Église. At first, the regimental headquarters believed that the paratroopers were part of a raid, and not a major drop. The Georgian Battalion.795 located east of Ste Mère-Église reported around 03.00hrs that the battalion was surrounded, but Keil was a bit skeptical as the messengers had arrived at the command post without difficulty and an

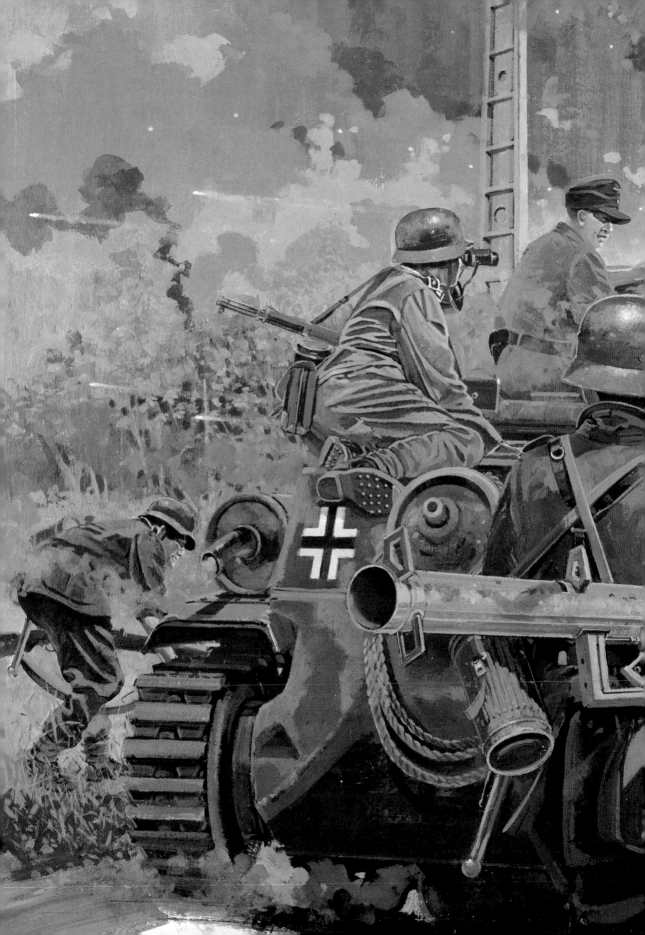

GERMAN COUNTERATTACK ON THE MERDERET RIVER,
14.00HRS D-DAY (pages 132–133)

Around 13.00hrs Grenadier Regiment.1057 of the
91st Luftlande Division began a counterattack towards the
La Fière causeway through Cauquigny. A company of
Hotchkiss H-39 tanks of PzAbt.100 spearheaded the attack,
but two were disabled in the first attack, which was beaten
off. The surviving pair of Hotchkiss tanks again took up the
lead, accompanied by infantry. Company A, 1/505th PIR had
set up a defensive position on the east side of the La Fière
bridge and earlier in the morning the paratroopers had placed
a string of anti-tank mines in plain sight on top of the road as
a deterrent to the Panzers. The Hotchkiss tanks sped ahead of
the accompanying infantry, and approached to within 40 feet
of the mines. The paratroopers had two bazooka teams in
ambush position and they immediately hit the first tank (1).
The second tank (2) had no room to maneuver on either side
of the causeway, and backed away. An infantry attack by
GR.1057 followed, which was stopped by small arms fire and
the support of some 60mm mortars. Attacks continued
through the day, with the paratrooper positions pounded by
German artillery. During a truce late in the day to recover the
wounded, a paratrooper surveyed the German positions on
the causeway and estimated they had suffered about
200 casualties in their brave but futile counterattacks. The
paratroopers had also taken heavy losses, and few of the men
holding the east side of the bridge survived D-Day. Around
02.00hrs on 7 June, the second Hotchkiss returned and
attempted to push the derelict tank off the road, but was
attacked in the dark by Sgt William Owens with Gammon

grenades, and retreated again. This was the last attempt by
Grenadier Regiment.1057 to cross the Merderet, but they
established blocking positions on the causeway that
prevented the paratroopers from crossing as well. The
Hotchkiss H-39 tank, dubbed "PzKpfw 38H 735(f)" in
Wehrmacht service, was a French cavalry tank captured in
the wake of the 1940 campaign. They were widely used by
the Wehrmacht in secondary roles, especially anti-partisan
fighting and saw combat in Finland, Yugoslavia, Russia, and
France. The Wehrmacht made several changes to the tanks,
most evidently cutting off the top of the turret cupola and
replacing it with a split hatch (3) for the tank commander.
After being rebuilt in 1941, they were repainted in standard
German dark gray, but many were camouflaged later with
the newer dark yellow color (4). Despite its name, the 91st
Luftlande Division was a regular army (Heer) division. As a
result, its uniforms were typical of those worn by the German
army in the summer of 1944. The Unteroffizier (NCO) (5),
riding on the back of the rear tank, is the squad leader (gruppen-
führer) and is armed with the ubiquitous 98k rifle, although
nominally the squad leader should be armed with a machine
pistol. His binoculars and map case set him apart from the
rest of the rifle squad. The soldier alongside him on the tank
is equipped with an MP40 machine pistol (6). Following the
tank is a richtschütze (7) armed with a Panzerschreck
anti-tank rocket launcher (8). A loader, not visible here, would
normally accompany him carrying two more rockets. The rest
of the squad includes the machine-gun team (9), consisting of
a gunner and assistant gunner and armed with a MG-42 light
machine-gun, and two more riflemen (10). (Howard Gerrard)

Troops disembark from the large side access door of a Horsa glider. These large British gliders were preferred for carrying heavier supply loads. (NARA)

officer of the Georgian battalion arrived safely by car. He gave more credence to a report from a company of the divisional engineers who reported that thousands of paratroopers were landing.

At 84th Corps headquarters, Gen Marcks became concerned that the paratroopers might create a gap between the 709th Division at Utah Beach and the 352nd Division at Omaha. The only major corps reserve was Kampfgruppe Meyer of the 352nd Infantry Division near St Lô. At 03.10, Gen Marcks ordered Meyer to advance towards the junction of the two divisions between Utah and Omaha beaches. The decision to send the reserves after the paratroopers proved to be premature and a serious mistake. Later in the morning, the force would be badly needed in the opposite direction. As a result, Kampfgruppe Meyer spent most of the morning marching westward, only to have their orders changed a few hours later and shifted in the opposite direction, all the while under air attack.

US paratroopers landed mainly in the deployment area of the 91st Luftlande Division. The reaction of the division was confused, in part due to the absence of senior divisional commanders at the Rennes wargame. General Falley was alerted to the paratrooper landings early in

The plywood construction of the Horsa made it vulnerable to break-up during hard landings as is all too evident in this case. The combination of poor light and confined landing fields led to many crashes on D-Day. (NARA)

the morning and set out by car to return to his unit. Around dawn, his car was intercepted before reaching his command post by a paratrooper patrol and he was killed after a short skirmish near Picauville. Unaware of Falley's fate and unable to contact him, the division's operations officer, General Bernhard Klosterkemper, took temporary command. On learning that the Americans had seized Ste Mère-Église, he ordered GR.1057 to begin to move east over the Merderet via the La Fière bridge, where the regiment would become entangled with the 82nd Airborne Division over control of the Merderet River crossings.

In the meantime, Oberst Keil had asked permission from 84th Corps headquarters to use Major Moch's battalion from GR.1058 of the 91st Luftlande Division located at St Côme-du-Mont to assist him in his own efforts to regain control of Ste Mère-Église from the north. Permission was granted by corps HQ at 03.30hrs and Keil hoped that Moch's battalion would arrive at Ste Mère-Église by 08.00. Instead of moving on the town, Moch's battalion was still in its garrison north of Ste Mère-Église at 08.00hrs and Keil again ordered him to attack the town, without result. Finally, around 11.00hrs, Moch sent a message indicating that the battery at Azeville had been captured and asking Keil if he should retake it. At the end of his patience, Keil told him to follow the previous orders but Moch's battalion did not reach the outskirts of the town until 13.00hrs. By the afternoon, a perimeter defense had already been established and Moch's battalion reinforced the units assaulting Lt Turnbull's platoon outside Neuville, but were unable to overcome the outnumbered but tenacious paratroopers.

The German troops south of Ste Mère-Église, including the remnants of the Georgian Battalion.795, were pressed into a pocket by the paratrooper attacks from the north, and the advance of 4th Division troops from the beaches later in the day. This pocket continued to block the road south of Ste Mère-Église through D-Day.

While Moch's battalion was sluggishly approaching Ste Mère-Église, the corps headquarters ordered a second battalion from GR.1058 to follow it southward to the town. However, it became bottled up around Montebourg. The corps headquarters also activated the Sturm-Battalion

AOK 7 and sent it along the road from St Floxel to Beuzeville-au-Plain, eventually attacking the US positions on the eastern side of Ste Mère-Église in the afternoon. Elements of the Panzerjäger Company.709 accompanied it, but were lost in the fighting with the paratroopers around Beuzeville-au-Plain.

Fallschirmjäger Regiment.6 (FJR 6) near Periers was alerted around midnight, and began encountering paratroopers who had landed far south of the intended landing areas. Von der Heydte tried reaching higher command but telephone lines in the area had been cut, probably by the French resistance. The 3./FJR 6 engaged in skirmishes with US paratroopers in the pre-dawn hours, being pushed to the southeast. Von der Heydte finally managed to reach Gen Marcks around 06.00hrs by using phones at the St Lô post office, and he was ordered to clear the Carentan area of paratroopers and begin moving his regiment northward toward Ste Mère-Église with the objective of eliminating the paratrooper concentrations there. In the days prior to the invasion, Rommel had ordered units in areas vulnerable to paratroop landing to disperse their garrison, and as a result, FJR 6 had a difficult time assembling its troops. Von der Heydte passed through Carentan ahead of his troops, finding the town devoid of German or American troops, and he reached a German battalion dug in near St Côme-du-Mont. He climbed the village church's steeple, giving him a vista of the battlefield all the way to Utah Beach. The vast armada of US ships was clearly visible, and he later recalled that the scene was oddly tranquil, like a summer's day on the shore of the Wannsee near Berlin with little evidence of fighting. This was the first time that a senior German officer learned that the paratrooper attack had been reinforced by a major amphibious landing. As 3./FJR 6 was still engaged with US forces, the other two battalions reached this assembly area in the early afternoon. The 2./FJR 6 was directed to advance on Ste Mère-Église along the main road while the 1./FJR 6 would advance further east to shield the column from US troops landing from the sea. The two advancing battalions moved out around 19.00hrs and had no serious contact with US forces until after nightfall, when both battalions were heavily disrupted by further airborne landings virtually on top of them.

The fate of the I./GR.919 stationed along Utah Beach was not recorded in detail due to its quick rout. Communications between the battalion and the division headquarters were lost before noon on D-Day as US troops captured most of its strongpoints. Of the 13 strongpoints, WN1 to WN14 along the coast, all of the southern strongpoints closest to the US landings were taken by US forces on D-Day. Those further north on the coast including WN10, WN10a, WN11 and StP12 held out for another day or two, finally surrendering after running out of food and ammunition.

THE AMPHIBIOUS LANDINGS

Task Force U under Rear Admiral Don Moon reached the transport area off Utah Beach around 02.30hrs and the command ship, USS *Bayfield*, dropped anchor. There was no significant German naval activity in the area even though Admiral Krancke had issued orders to repel the invasion force after shore radar had located the oncoming invasion fleet at 03.09hrs. Two torpedo boat flotillas operating out of Cherbourg encountered heavy seas, and returned to port before dawn without engaging the Allied landing force. The first actions of the day began around 05.05hrs when German coastal batteries began to open fire on Allied shipping as it crossed the horizon. The Morsalines battery of 6./HKAA.1261 with six French 155mm guns had been located in concrete emplacements near St Vaast, but due to air attacks, was moved to open ground near Videcosville. It began engaging a minesweeper, prompting HMS *Black Prince* to respond. The Marcouf battery of 3/HKAA.1261 and the neighboring 4/HKAA.1261 engaged the destroyers USS *Corry* and *Fitch*. While maneuvering to avoid the fire, the *Corry* struck a mine amidships, cutting it in two. The destroyers *Fitch* and *Hobson* pulled alongside while keeping the coastal batteries under fire. The Marcouf battery was subjected to the most intense fire, first by the cruiser *Quincy* and then by the battleship USS *Nevada*. *Nevada* scored a direct hit on one of the four bunkers with a 5in. round, but it was a dud, passing through the bunker and out the other side. The battery lost the first of three guns in the early morning exchange, the second at 15.57 and the last at 18.30hrs.

The preliminary naval bombardment of the beach began at H-40 (05.50hrs). As H-hour approached, the fire was redirected toward flank targets, especially remaining German naval batteries in the area. Utah Beach was scheduled for a preliminary air bombardment by IX Bomber Command. Although cloud cover threatened to

The 14in. guns of the battleship USS *Nevada* begin pounding German fortifications along Utah in preparation for the landings. One of the principal missions of the naval gunfire support was to eliminate the numerous German coastal batteries north of Utah Beach. (NARA)

In contrast to Omaha Beach where the heavy bomber attacks were completely ineffective, the attacks on Utah by B-26 Marauder medium bombers substantially disrupted the W5 strongpoint. These are B-26 bombers of the 553rd BS, 386th "Crusaders" Bomb Group and they display the white and black invasion stripes on their wings and fuselages. (NARA)

disrupt the bombardment, the attacking B-26 Marauder pilots decided to drop below the prescribed altitude to 3,500–7,000 feet. A total of 269 bombers took part, dropping 525 tons of 250lb bombs between 06.05 and 06.24hrs. This was in complete contrast to Omaha Beach where the bombers remained above the cloud cover, and ineffectively dropped their bombs far behind the beach using blind-bombing tactics. Besides the bombardment of the beach itself, a further 33 aircraft dropped 47 tons of bombs on the coastal artillery batteries near Maisy and Gefosse.

The preliminary bombardment proved to be extremely effective in suppressing the German defenses at the WN5 strongpoint. Most of the open gun pits had been knocked out by the attacks, and even some of the enclosed bunkers had collapsed or were seriously damaged. One of the few defense positions intact was the well-protected Bauform 667 casemate on the southern fringe of WN5. Although casualties from the bombardment had been low, many of the German defenders were stunned by the bomb blasts and naval gunfire.

The first landing actually occurred two hours before the main landings. Activity had been spotted on the St Marcouf islands off Utah Beach in May, so a cavalry detachment of 132 men from the 4th and 24th Cavalry Squadrons were sent ashore at 04.30hrs. In fact, there were no German troops on the islands, but minefields and later German artillery fire killed two and wounded 17.

As on Omaha Beach, the preliminary force ashore was scheduled to be amphibious Duplex Drive M4A1 medium tanks. The 32 tanks from the 70th Tank Battalion were carried toward their launch point on board eight LCTs. The run toward the beach was slowed by the headwind and steep chop. At 05.21hrs, one of the two control craft guiding in the force

An aerial view of Utah Beach taken on D-Day. The area behind the beach was flooded, and beyond that, the *bocage* typical of Normandy can be seen. (NARA)

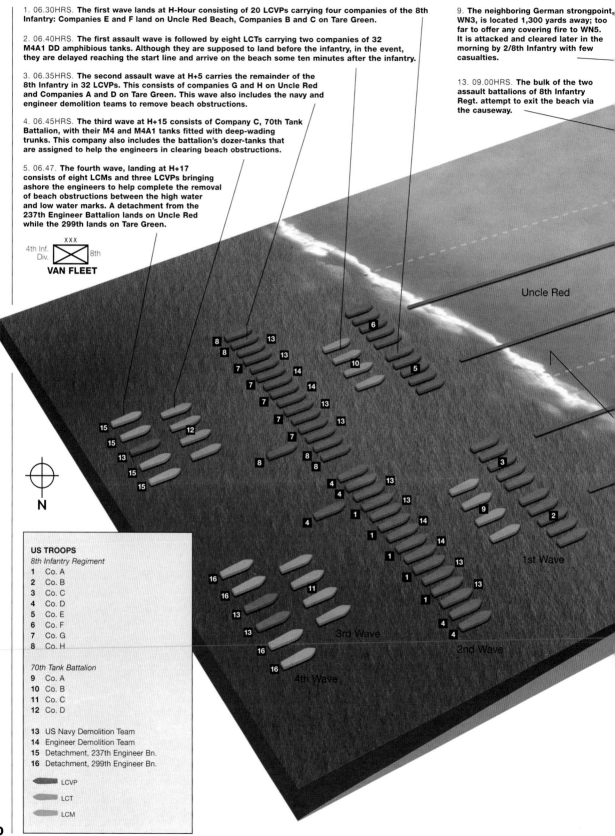

1. 06.30HRS. **The first wave lands at H-Hour consisting of 20 LCVPs carrying four companies of the 8th Infantry: Companies E and F land on Uncle Red Beach, Companies B and C on Tare Green.**

2. 06.40HRS. **The first assault wave is followed by eight LCTs carrying two companies of 32 M4A1 DD amphibious tanks. Although they are supposed to land before the infantry, in the event, they are delayed reaching the start line and arrive on the beach some ten minutes after the infantry.**

3. 06.35HRS. **The second assault wave at H+5 carries the remainder of the 8th Infantry in 32 LCVPs. This consists of companies G and H on Uncle Red and Companies A and D on Tare Green. This wave also includes the navy and engineer demolition teams to remove beach obstructions.**

4. 06.45HRS. **The third wave at H+15 consists of Company C, 70th Tank Battalion, with their M4 and M4A1 tanks fitted with deep-wading trunks. This company also includes the battalion's dozer-tanks that are assigned to help the engineers in clearing beach obstructions.**

5. 06.47. **The fourth wave, landing at H+17 consists of eight LCMs and three LCVPs bringing ashore the engineers to help complete the removal of beach obstructions between the high water and low water marks. A detachment from the 237th Engineer Battalion lands on Uncle Red while the 299th lands on Tare Green.**

9. **The neighboring German strongpoint, WN3, is located 1,300 yards away; too far to offer any covering fire to WN5. It is attacked and cleared later in the morning by 2/8th Infantry with few casualties.**

13. 09.00HRS. **The bulk of the two assault battalions of 8th Infantry Regt. attempt to exit the beach via the causeway.**

4th Inf. Div. ⊠ 8th
XXX
VAN FLEET

N

Uncle Red

6

1st Wave

2nd Wave

3rd Wave

4th Wave

US TROOPS

8th Infantry Regiment
1 Co. A
2 Co. B
3 Co. C
4 Co. D
5 Co. E
6 Co. F
7 Co. G
8 Co. H

70th Tank Battalion
9 Co. A
10 Co. B
11 Co. C
12 Co. D

13 US Navy Demolition Team
14 Engineer Demolition Team
15 Detachment, 237th Engineer Bn.
16 Detachment, 299th Engineer Bn.

⬬ LCVP
⬬ LCT
⬬ LCM

140

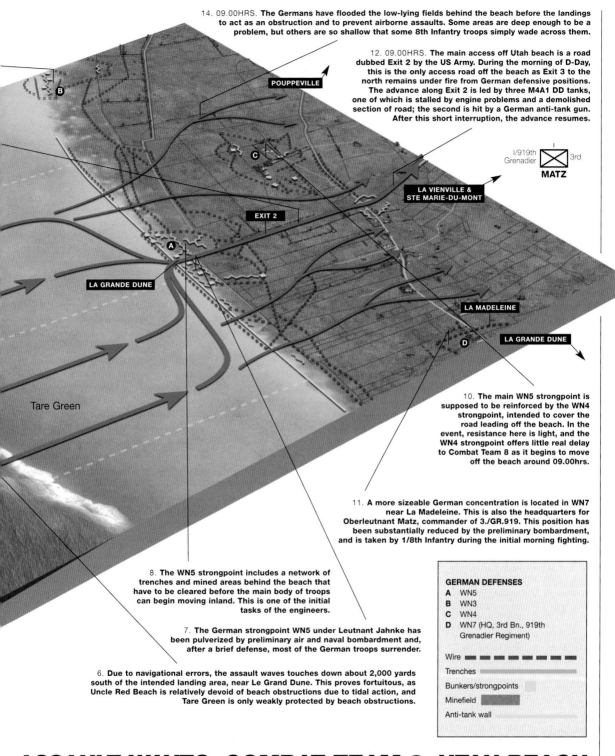

14. 09.00HRS. The Germans have flooded the low-lying fields behind the beach before the landings to act as an obstruction and to prevent airborne assaults. Some areas are deep enough to be a problem, but others are so shallow that some 8th Infantry troops simply wade across them.

12. 09.00HRS. The main access off Utah beach is a road dubbed Exit 2 by the US Army. During the morning of D-Day, this is the only access road off the beach as Exit 3 to the north remains under fire from German defensive positions. The advance along Exit 2 is led by three M4A1 DD tanks, one of which is stalled by engine problems and a demolished section of road; the second is hit by a German anti-tank gun. After this short interruption, the advance resumes.

POUPPEVILLE

I/919th Grenadier ⊠ 3rd
MATZ

LA VIENVILLE & STE MARIE-DU-MONT

EXIT 2

LA GRANDE DUNE

LA MADELEINE

LA GRANDE DUNE

Tare Green

10. The main WN5 strongpoint is supposed to be reinforced by the WN4 strongpoint, intended to cover the road leading off the beach. In the event, resistance here is light, and the WN4 strongpoint offers little real delay to Combat Team 8 as it begins to move off the beach around 09.00hrs.

11. A more sizeable German concentration is located in WN7 near La Madeleine. This is also the headquarters for Oberleutnant Matz, commander of 3./GR.919. This position has been substantially reduced by the preliminary bombardment, and is taken by 1/8th Infantry during the initial morning fighting.

8. The WN5 strongpoint includes a network of trenches and mined areas behind the beach that have to be cleared before the main body of troops can begin moving inland. This is one of the initial tasks of the engineers.

7. The German strongpoint WN5 under Leutnant Jahnke has been pulverized by preliminary air and naval bombardment and, after a brief defense, most of the German troops surrender.

6. Due to navigational errors, the assault waves touches down about 2,000 yards south of the intended landing area, near Le Grand Dune. This proves fortuitous, as Uncle Red Beach is relatively devoid of beach obstructions due to tidal action, and Tare Green is only weakly protected by beach obstructions.

GERMAN DEFENSES

A   WN5
B   WN3
C   WN4
D   WN7 (HQ, 3rd Bn., 919th Grenadier Regiment)

Wire
Trenches
Bunkers/strongpoints
Minefield
Anti-tank wall

ASSAULT WAVES, COMBAT TEAM 8, UTAH BEACH

06.30–09.00hrs, 6 June 1944, viewed from the north. As a result of the offshore current and poor visibility, Combat Team 8's first wave lands 2,000yds south of the intended landing zone. The defenses are less formidable and the assault actually easier. The German strongpoints are rapidly overcome and the troops push inland to link up with troops from the 82nd and 101st Airborne.

struck a mine and sank, followed 15 minutes later by an LCT. The naval control officer realized that the force was behind schedule, and to speed the landing, the LCTs launched the tanks from closer to shore than planned, from about 1,500 yards (1,300m) instead of 5,000 yards (4,550m). Even so, the 28 DD tanks arrived ten minutes after the first wave of troops.

The assault force for Utah Beach was Combat Team 8, formed from the 8th Infantry of the 4th Infantry Division, along with supporting engineers and other specialist troops. The initial two waves consisted of two assault battalions, more heavily equipped than normal infantry, landing in LCVPs. The first wave included 20 LCVPs with 30 troops each. The offshore current pushed the craft somewhat to the south, and the landmarks on shore were difficult to see due to the smoke caused by the heavy bombardment. As a result, the first wave of the assault force landed about 2,000 yards (1,800m) south of the intended objective around Exit 3 and Les Dunes de Varreville, landing instead near Exit 2 and the Grande Dune. The navigational error had little effect on the operation, and if anything permitted an easier landing as it transpired that there were fewer beach obstructions in this sector and the German strongpoints were less substantial. Instead of facing two major German strongpoints on the intended beach, the landing faced only a single strongpoint that had been pulverized by the aerial bombing. Several company-sized task forces set about reducing the German strongpoints along the beach, which was accomplished without difficulty aided by the newly arrived DD tanks. The tanks quickly knocked out the surviving bunkers, and began breaching the seawall using gunfire. The commander of the German defenses, Leutnant Jahnke, ordered the Goliath remote control vehicles to be launched against the tanks and landing craft, but the bombardment had severed the wire guidance cables to their hidden nests.

German resistance on Utah Beach was quickly overwhelmed except for sporadic artillery shelling from distant coastal batteries. This view from a Coast Guard LCVP shows troops wading ashore with an LCI beached to the left. The barrage balloons were intended to prevent low-altitude strafing by German aircraft.

Company C of the 70th Tank Battalion goes ashore at Utah Beach in the third wave. The first two companies of the 70th Tank Battalion used DD tanks, while this company used deep-wading trunks. (NARA)

Tank casualties on Utah Beach were due almost entirely to mines. This M4 medium tank named "Cannonball" of Co. C, 70th Tank Battalion became trapped in a hidden shell crater while driving to the beach from its LCT. The two deep-wading trunks are very evident in this view. (NARA)

The first assault wave was followed by 32 more LCVPs containing the remainder of the two assault battalions along with engineer and naval demolition parties. The demolition teams set about destroying beach obstructions to permit the landing of additional craft once the tide had turned. The engineers began to tackle the problem of minefields along the beach, and also used explosive charges to blow gaps in the seawall to allow the troops speedier passage off the beach. The third wave at H+15 consisted of 8 more LCTs containing Company C from the 70th Tank Battalion using M4 tanks fitted with wading trunks as well as four dozer-tanks to assist in the beach-clearing operation. The fourth wave consisted mainly of detachments from the 237th and 299th Engineers to assist in clearing the beaches. Two additional battalions, 3/8th Infantry and 3/22nd Infantry also followed. By this stage, German fire was limited to sporadic artillery. Most of the German defenders surrendered quickly, but Jahnke was not pulled from his command bunker until around noon during the clean-up operations.

The first senior officer on the beach was General Theodore Roosevelt Jr., the 4th Division's assistant commander. On realizing they had landed on the wrong beach, he personally scouted the exits to determine which causeway to use to exit the beach. Roosevelt met with the two infantry battalion commanders and instructed them to eliminate remaining German defenses and move out over the Exit 2 causeway. By 09.00hrs, the defenses behind the beach had been reduced and the 8th Infantry was moving inland, led by tanks from the 70th Tank Battalion. On the way down the causeway, the Germans had set off a demolition charge under a small culvert, creating a gap in the road. The lead tank had mechanical problems, stalling the second tank, which was struck by an anti-tank gun. The third tank quickly eliminated the gun and engineers from the Beach Obstacle Task Force brought up a length of treadway bridge to cover the gap. Due to congestion on the causeway, some units moved across the flooded tidal pools behind the beach.

The 1/8th Infantry moved north from the causeway and reached Turqueville by evening without encountering any serious resistance. The

COMBAT TEAM 8 ON UTAH BEACH, 07.30HRS D-DAY
(pages 144–145)

The M4A1 Sherman tanks of Company C, 70th Tank Battalion arrived on Utah Beach in the third wave aboard LCTs at H+15. Unlike the battalion's two other companies of tanks fitted with DD Duplex Drive equipment, which in theory at least allowed them to "swim" ashore, Company C relied on deep-wading trunks to get to the beach. After reaching the shoreline, the crew detached the clumsy upper trunks, but the lower adaptor trunks are still evident on this tank. The mission of the tanks on the beach was to help the infantry in overcoming any beach defenses, and to assist in exiting the beach by blasting the seawall with their guns. Here "Colombia Lou" (1), one of the company's M4 medium tanks, engages a German Bauform 667 bunker (2) with GIs from the 8th Infantry (3) taking cover behind the advancing tank. These ferro-concrete bunkers were so thick that naval gunfire or bombs could not easily knock them out. The only effective method to silence them was to engage them at relatively close quarters, firing directly into the bunker's embrasure. Assault troops of the 8th Infantry wore distinctive battledress on D-Day. Due to the suspicion that the Germans might use chemical weapons to defeat the landings, the troop's uniforms were impregnated with a solution that prevented the chemical agent from soaking into the clothing. On Omaha beach, the usual battledress was impregnated with this chemical preparation. On Utah Beach, the assault troops wore a set of chemically impregnated HBT (herringbone tweed) battledress (4) over their normal uniforms. They could then discard the HBTs after the landings. The black waterproof bag (5) they are carrying contains an assault gas mask. Another item specially developed for the D-Day landings was the assault vest (6), which was intended to take the place of normal webbing, ammunition pouches, and musette bags all in a single garment. In the event, the assault vest proved to be cumbersome and unworkable and the concept was discarded. All the members of the fire team seen here are armed with the M1 Garand rifle (7) except for one team member who is armed with a BAR (Browning Automatic Rifle) (8). The GI on the right has a rifle grenade adapter fitted to his rifle (9), and is preparing to fire a rifle grenade at the German defenses. Due to the recoil from launching these grenades, the prescribed method of firing them was to place the butt of the rifle on the ground.
(Howard Gerrard)

3/8th Infantry headed directly west from the causeway, and ran into elements of the 14th Company of GR.919, the regimental anti-tank unit, with a platoon of 75mm anti-tank guns deployed in field positions along with infantry from the I./GR.919. A short firefight ensued in which about 50 Germans were killed and about 100 surrendered. The battalion reached the area north of Les Forges and sent out a platoon to link up with the 82nd Airborne Division near Chef-du-Pont. The 2/8th Infantry headed south toward Pouppeville along the seawall rather than crossing the causeway. There was almost continuous skirmishing with isolated German riflemen along the coast, but the battalion overwhelmed the weakly defended WN2a strongpoint and made their way to Exit 1 and the road junction near Pouppeville. They linked up with Colonel Ewell of the 3/501st PIR who had already cleared the town of troops from GR.1058. Besides the actions by the 8th Infantry, A/49th Engineer Combat Battalion was assigned to seize a lock near Grand Vey that controlled the flooding of the tidal pools. In the process, they took about 125 German prisoners.

The remainder of the 4th Infantry Division landed on D-Day, along with the first elements of the 90th Division. Both the 12th and 22nd Infantry were directed toward the northern side of the beachhead area. Starting from a position further south than the planned landing area, they did not reach their objectives on D-Day. They formed a defensive perimeter emanating westward from St Germain-de-Varreville towards Ste Mère-Église.

Reinforcement of the airborne divisions continued through the day. Howell Force, a reserve of troops from 82nd Airborne Division under Colonel E. Raff, landed by sea and followed 3/8th Infantry, planning to join up with their parent unit. On reaching the area near Les Forges where the 3/8th Infantry had set up its nighttime bivouac, Raff was told that the infantry planned to advance no further that night as they were already in possession of their objective and had run into German defenses north of their position. Raff wanted to link up with airborne forces in Ste Mère-Église, and was also concerned about the safety of Landing Zone W, the destination of Mission Elmira, another glider supply effort. Attempts to budge the German defenses had not succeeded by the time that the gliders appeared over the landing zone around 21.00hrs, and the fields were in no-man's land. The first wave consisted of 54 Horsa and 22 Waco CG-4A gliders with 437 troops, 64 vehicles, 13 57mm anti-tank guns and 24 tons of supplies. In the declining light, the gliders landed under fire from scattered German positions. The main hazard was the difficulty of landing the gliders in confined farm fields at dusk, and many gliders crashed on landing. The casualties were surprisingly light considering the circumstances. The second wave of the Elmira mission consisting of 86 Horsa and 14 Waco CG-4A gliders landed about an hour and a half later in Landing Zone O north of Ste Mère-Église. The third and smallest glider landing of the evening, Operation Keokuk, crunched into Landing Zone E, west of Hiesville.

D-Day at Midnight

By midnight on D-Day, Utah Beach was securely in American hands and the 4th Infantry Division had reached its initial objectives, at a very modest cost, only 197 casualties. The startling contrast in the casualties compared to the more than 2,000 suffered on neighboring Omaha Beach were due to the weak defenses on Utah Beach and the total disruption of German defenses by the airborne landings. Omaha Beach was defended by 11 strongpoints instead of the one at Utah, and the defending forces there had 26 anti-tank guns and field guns aimed at the beach compared to only 5 at Utah Beach. There was a similar discrepancy in machine-guns and mortars. In addition, the Utah Beach bunkers were heavily damaged by the preliminary bombardment, while the Omaha bunkers were never bombed. Utah Beach was defended by only about a company of infantry, while Omaha Beach had portions of two infantry regiments. Tanks also

The W5 strongpoint at Utah Beach had a French 47mm Model 1937 anti-tank gun among its defenses that was knocked out by the preliminary bombardment. The Wehrmacht made extensive use of captured equipment in its Normandy defenses as well as older German equipment deemed obsolete for the Russian front. (NARA)

A view of Utah Beach after the initial landings. The most common anti-tank defensive work at Utah Beach was the Bauform 60 50mm anti-tank gun pit seen to the right. There were about 1,800 of these guns used for coastal defense in 1944. (NARA)

This 50mm anti-tank gun in the Bauform 667 casemate was knocked out by a direct hit on its shield by tank gun fire. These ferro-concrete bunkers were nearly impervious to bombing and naval gunfire, and had to be eliminated by close combat assault. (USAOM)

landed in force on Utah, with nearly three intact companies on the beach in the opening hour of the fighting.

The air landings by the 82nd and 101st Airborne Divisions had not gone according to plan, due to dispersion of the drops. Only about ten per cent of the paratroopers landed on their drop zones, a further 25 per cent within a mile, and another 20 per cent within two miles. The remainder were more scattered: about 25 per cent were within five miles, 15 per cent were between five and 25 miles from their drop zones, and about five per cent were missing. By dawn, the 82nd Airborne Division had only about 1,500 paratroopers near their divisional objectives and the 101st Airborne had only about 1,100. By midnight, the situation was not much better, only about 2,000 under divisional control with the 82nd and 2,500 with the 101st Airborne Division of the 13,350 dropped. While the serious dispersion accounts for the problems in the morning, the continued difficulties collecting troops during the course of the day was due to the unexpected isolation of small groups of paratroopers by the maze of hedgerows and flooded farmlands and the lack of sufficient radios to link the dispersed groups. Casualties sustained by the airborne units on D-Day have never been accurately calculated as so many troops were missing for days afterwards. Nevertheless, it is evident that casualties in these units were considerably higher than those suffered by the 4th Infantry Division during the beach landings. Indeed, total casualties in the Utah sector were comparable to the 2,000 casualties on Omaha Beach, but a significant portion of these casualties were paratroopers captured by the Germans and non-combat injuries sustained during the night drops.

As a result of the difficulties in assembling the paratroopers, the objectives of the airborne divisions were not met on D-Day. The airborne divisions did secure some of the access routes off the beach, but the

As the 8th Infantry began exiting Utah Beach over the Exit 2 causeway, one of the DD tanks from Co. A, 70th Tank Battalion was hit by a hidden anti-tank gun. The damaged tank was pushed off the causeway to clear it for following troops. As can be seen, the canvas flotation screens on this DD tank had been folded down. (MHI)

only causeway that really mattered was seized by the 8th Infantry. Bridges over the Merderet were not secured, and large portions of the 82nd Airborne remained cut off on the west side of the river. Equally worrisome, the airborne divisions did not manage to create an effective defensive screen on the southern edge of the VII Corps lodgment, leaving the bridgehead vulnerable to attack by German reserves. This had no consequence due to the weak German response.

By the perverse logic of war, the airborne assault actually did accomplish its mission even if specific objectives were not achieved. The paratroopers were so widely scattered that they disrupted and tied down most German forces on the eastern side of the Cotentin peninsula. If the US airborne commanders were unhappy over their failures, the German senior commanders were baffled. Some German officers believed that the airborne assault represented a clever new tactical approach they dubbed "saturation attack", intended to disrupt defensive efforts by the German army rather than to control specific terrain features. Although the Germans may have been impressed by the airborne landings, senior Allied leaders were not. The problems with the Normandy landings convinced them that nighttime landings were inherently too risky given the limitations of contemporary navigation technology, and subsequent Allied airborne operations were conducted in daylight.

German defensive operations on D-Day had been passive and unsuccessful. The vaunted Atlantic Wall in this sector had been breached within an hour with few casualties. The combat performance of German infantry units, not surprisingly, was quite mixed. Some units, such as GR.1057 along the Merderet, attacked and defended with tenacity and skill. Many of the static defense units surrendered to the paratroopers even though they outnumbered the attackers, especially those with conscripted Poles and "volunteer" Soviet prisoners. In general, the Utah Beach sector received relatively little attention from German corps and army head-quarters due to the perception that other sectors were far more dangerous, especially the British beaches. Indeed, it was not apparent to senior German commanders until late in the day that a major amphibious landing was under way at Utah Beach.

Troops from the 8th Infantry wade through some of the inundated farm fields behind Utah Beach. The cylindrical devices the two lead GIs are carrying are their inflated floatation belts. These troops are also carrying the distinctive assault gas-mask bags so typical of the Normandy landings. (NARA)

CONSOLIDATING THE BEACHHEAD

General Collins, commander of VII Corps, realized that his first mission would be to consolidate the beachhead area due to the lingering dispersion of the paratroop forces. He was still not in touch with General Ridgway from the 82nd Airborne Div., and the first communications were not received until late on D+1. The primary mission of the day was to eliminate the German pocket south of Ste Mère-Église, and to relieve the pressure on the northern sector of the town's defenses. The pocket contained the remnants of the Georgian Battalion.795 and GR.919. By dawn, the 8th Infantry was poised along its southern and eastern flank, and

Fighting went on for several days to clear the German strongpoints along the coast north of Utah Beach. This is a sniper patrol from 3/22nd Infantry checking out a farm in the Dunes des Varreville area on 10 June 1944. (NARA)

The Georgian Battalion.795 Ost was stationed immediately behind Utah Beach and involved in the D-Day fighting. This Georgian captain was captured after their positions were overrun. Curiously enough, he had featured in a series of German propaganda photos taken before D-Day of Hitler's new allies. (NARA)

attacks began that morning. Although the Georgians resisted the initial attacks, a Russian-speaking GI was able to convince them to surrender. About 250 troops gave up to the 1/8th Infantry. The two other battalions of the 8th Infantry had a much harder fight against German units holding a ridge that covered the access road to Ste Mère-Église, but this was overcome, and the two battalions fought their way into town. In the meantime, Collins had already ordered a column of tanks of C/746th Tank Battalion to Ste Mère-Église along the eastern road, and these arrived in time to beat back an early afternoon attack by GR.1058, supported by StuG III assault guns. The 82nd Airborne was reinforced during the day by additional air-landings of the 325th Glider Infantry at 07.00 and 09.00hrs in the Les Forges area. Fighting continued around the La Fière bridge, with the paratroopers repulsing German attacks. But at the end of D+1, a substantial portion of the 82nd Airborne Div. remained cut off on the western side of the Merderet. Nevertheless, the fighting on D+1 solidified the 82nd Airborne positions on the eastern bank, with the division now in firm control of Ste Mère-Église and connected to the seaborne invasion force.

The other two regiments of the 4th Division pushed northward out of the beachhead along the coast. The most difficult fighting took place around the fortified German coastal gun positions at Azeville and Crisbecq. Although the two regiments were able to push about two miles northward during the day, they were unable to overcome the two fortified areas and suffered heavy casualties. The 3/22nd Infantry advanced along the coast and reduced the surviving German beach strongpoints. Naval fire-control parties helped direct the gunfire of warships against the bunkers. By the evening of D+1, the battalion had fought its way through all of the German defenses up to WN11 when it was ordered inland to serve as a reserve for the other two battalions of the 22nd Infantry that had been battered that day in the fighting with the coastal artillery fortifications. While moving across the inundated tidal flats westward, a German prisoner reported that most of his comrades in the WN13 strongpoint wanted to surrender after a day of pounding from naval gunfire. As a result, the 3/22nd Infantry swung behind WN11 and occupied WN13 further to the north, leaving behind a company to prevent the garrison of WN11 from escaping. This strongpoint surrendered the following day.

The 101st Airborne Div. was involved for most of D+1 in securing the southern flank of the beachhead, especially around St Côme-du-Mont and the Douve River north

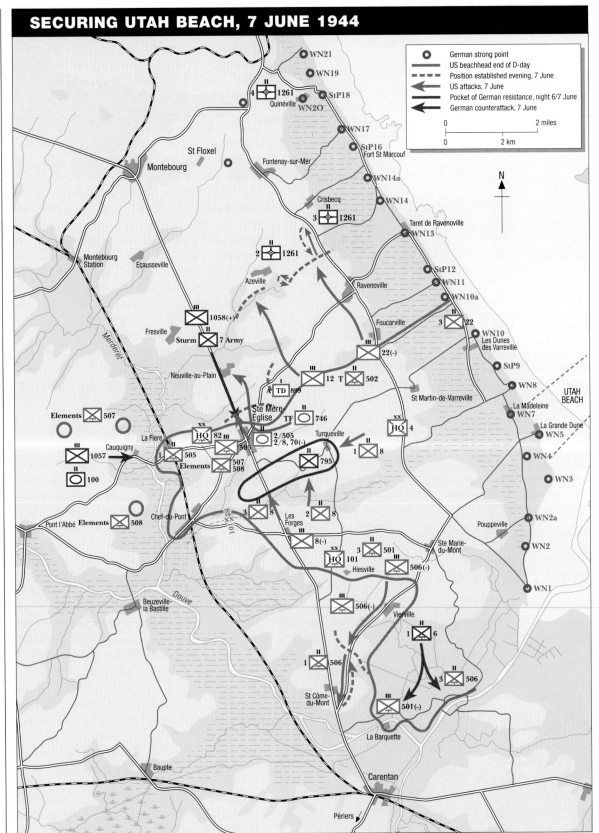

SECURING UTAH BEACH, 7 JUNE 1944

Legend:
- German strong point
- US beachhead end of D-day
- Position established evening, 7 June
- US attacks, 7 June
- Pocket of German resistance, night 6/7 June
- German counterattack, 7 June

0 — 2 miles
0 — 2 km

N

WN21
WN19
StP18
4 — 1261
Quinéville
WN2O
WN17
St Floxel
StP16
Fort St Marcouf
Montebourg
Fontenay-sur-Mer
WN14a
Crisbecq
WN14
3 — 1261
Taret de Ravenoville
WN13
2 — 1261
StP12
WN11
Azeville
Ravenoville
WN10a
Montebourg Station
Ecausseville
Foucarville
3 — 22
WN10
Les Dunes des Varreville
1058(+)
Sturm — 7 Army
22(-)
Fresville
StP9
Neuville-au-Plain
12 T — 502
WN8
A — TD — 899
St Martin-de-Varreville
Ste Mère-Église
TF — 746
UTAH BEACH
La Madeleine
WN7
Elements — 507
La Grande Dune
WN5
Turqueville
HQ — 4
WN4
La Fiere
HQ — 82
505
2/505
2/8, 70(-)
Cauquigny
1 — 505
795
1057
Elements
507
508
1 — 8
WN3
100
Chef-du-Pont
3 — 8
Les Forges
2 — 8
WN2a
Pont l'Abbé
Elements — 508
Pouppeville
8(-)
HQ — 101
3 — 501
Ste Marie-du-Mont
WN2
Hiesville
506(-)
Beuzeville-la Bastille
Douve
506(-)
Vierville
WN1
1 — 6
1 — 506
3 — 506
St Côme-du-Mont
501(-)
La Barquette
Baupte
Carentan
Périers

152

of Carentan. Two battalions of German paratroopers from FJR 6 had been advancing through this area on D-Day, with 1./FJR 6 reaching the area of Ste Marie-du-Mont and 2./FJR 6 reaching within a mile of Ste Mère-Église from the east. Von der Heydte, after seeing the scale of the American operation, realized that his attack on Ste Mère-Église with a mere two battalions was a fool's errand, and during the night of 6/7 June, ordered both battalions to withdraw. The 2./FJR 6 received the order and withdrew but the other battalion did not respond. It belatedly withdrew southward during D+1 toward the rear of the defensive positions of the 101st Airborne Division along the Douve River. It nearly bumped into a column from 1/506th PIR heading out of Vierville, but the American column hesitated to fire as the identity of the force was very unclear. By late afternoon, about 300 German paratroopers from the 1./FJR 6 began approaching the rear of Captain Shettle's force of about 100 paratroopers from 3/506th PIR. The American paratroopers responded with a series of aggressive patrols that convinced the Germans they were facing a much superior force. About 40 Germans were killed in the skirmishes, but platoon-sized units began surrendering, eventually totaling 255 men by evening, outnumbering their captors by a large margin. The remainder of the 1./FJR 6, numbering about 500 German paratroopers, began approaching the defensive perimeter held by 250 paratroopers under Colonel Johnson who were positioned near the La Barquette locks and the Le Port bridge. Not realizing that US forces held the area, the German paratroopers marched carelessly into an ambush and were halted by a blast of small arms fire at 350 yards. Skirmishing followed, and Johnson finally sent an ultimatum, ordering the Germans to surrender or be annihilated by his "superior forces". Small groups of German paratroopers began

Troops from Utah Beach pass through Ste Mère-Église on 10 June while infantrymen cast a wary glance for snipers. From their uniforms, these are troops of the 4th or 90th Division rather than paratroopers. There were still isolated German soldiers near the beach for several days after the landings. (NARA)

surrendering and by nightfall about 150 Germans had been killed or wounded, and another 350 surrendered at a cost of ten US paratroopers killed and 30 wounded. Only 25 German paratroopers survived the debacle and made it over the river to Carentan.

While this fighting was going on, other elements of the 101st Airborne were making their way toward St Côme-du-Mont in a series of small skirmishes with the Sturm-Abt. AOK 7 and elements of 3./FJR 6. By the end of the day, the force around St Côme-du-Mont included five airborne battalions, two artillery battalions and a company of light tanks. These would form the core of an assault force to strike south to the key town of Carentan to help link up Utah and Omaha beaches.

Although the VII Corps had made solid progress on D+1, it was still behind schedule. Under the original plan, Collins had hoped that the 4th Division could rapidly exit the beachhead and begin advancing north toward Cherbourg. However, the fighting was progressing much more slowly than hoped due to the inability of the 82nd Airborne Division to control the Merderet River crossings, the unexpected difficulties of infantry combat in the coastal hedgerows, and the three-day delay in consolidating the badly scattered paratroopers. During a visit to Normandy on D+1, Eisenhower expressed his concern to Bradley that the Germans might exploit the gap between the V Corps on Omaha Beach and the VII Corps on Utah. As a result, Bradley instructed Collins to focus his immediate attention on closing this gap by seizing Carentan.

Rommel had originally believed that the main Allied effort was on the Calvados coast, especially in the British sector around Caen.

Infantry from the 4th Division move a column of German prisoners back to the beach as an M4 medium tank passes by near Ste Mère-Église on 10 June 1944. By this stage, there were two tank battalions ashore: the 70th, which had landed on D-Day morning, and the 746th Tank Battalion, which landed later. (NARA)

**Paratroopers from the
101st Airborne Division pass
through Ste Marie-du-Mont on
12 June 1944. Aside from
the divisional patches, the
paratroopers can be distinguished from the regular infantry
units by their distinctive
battledress including the cargo
pockets on their trousers. (NARA)**

On 8 June he received a set of orders for the US VII Corps that had been
found by a German unit near Utah Beach. This made it clear that the Allies
intended to push northward out of Utah Beach toward Valognes and
eventually take Cherbourg. As a result, he diverted a first-rate unit, the
77th Infantry Division, which had been intended to prevent the link-up
of Omaha and Utah beaches, and ordered it instead into the Cotentin
peninsula to reinforce the Cherbourg front. The task of preventing the
link-up of the two American beaches in the Carentan sector was assigned
to the new and inexperienced 17th SS-Panzergrenadier Division "Gotz von
Berlichingen".

THE BATTLE FOR CARENTAN

The force attacking Carentan was placed under command of Brigadier
General Anthony McAuliffe, better known for his later role in the defense
of Bastogne. The plan was to seize St Côme-du-Mont, which controlled
the highway to Carentan. The defense of Carentan fell mainly to the two
surviving battalions of FJR 6 under Oberstlt von der Heydte. He gathered
a number of withdrawing German infantry companies to the defense,
and on 9 June the corps attached a further two Ost battalions, which he
deployed on the eastern side of the town due to their dubious potential.

After a preliminary artillery preparation on the morning of 8 June,
one glider infantry and three paratroop battalions began the assault.
The survivors of Sturm-Abt. AOK 7 began to retreat out the west side of
St Côme-du-Mont, but then veered southward toward the main road,

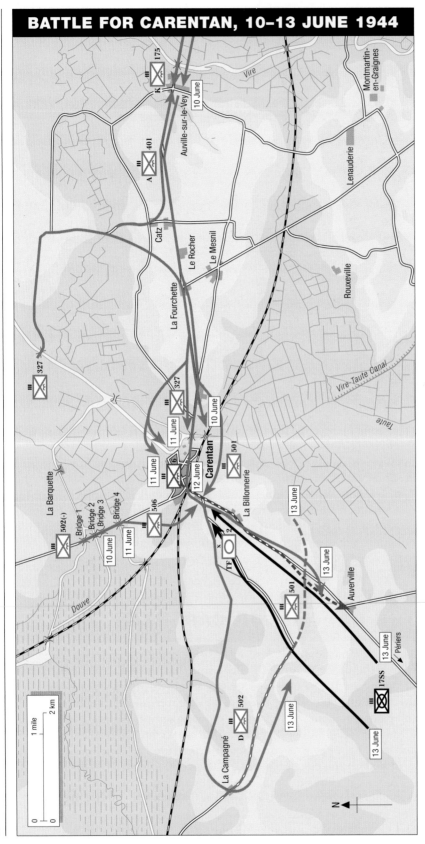

BATTLE FOR CARENTAN, 10–13 JUNE 1944

K 175

401 A

175

10 June

Auville-sur-le-Vey

Vire

Montmartin-en-Graignes

Lenauderie

Catz

Le Rocher

Le Mesnil

La Fourchette

Rouxeville

327

327

11 June

10 June

11 June

Carentan

501

10 June

12 June

6

11 June

La Barquette

502(–)

Bridge 1

Bridge 2

Bridge 3

Bridge 4

506

10 June

11 June

La Billonnerie

13 June

13 June

Auverville

TF

2

x

501

13 June

Périers

13 June

Douve

Vire-Taute Canal

Taute

17SS

13 June

La Campagné

D 502

13 June

1 mile

2 km

0

0

N

After von der Heydte's battered FJR 6 retreated out of Carentan, the 17.SS-Pz.Gren. Division tried to retake the town on 13 June 1944. In the foreground is a 57mm anti-tank gun of the 82nd Airborne while behind it to the right is one of the StuG IV assault guns of 1./SS-Pz.Abt. 17 that was knocked out during the fighting about 3.5km (2.2 miles) outside Carentan on the Periers road near the crossroads with the D223 leading to Baupte and La-Haye-du-Puits. The paratroopers used the light-weight airborne Mk. 3 version of the British 6-pdr instead of the standard US Army 57mm anti-tank gun. (NARA)

colliding with the 3/501st PIR. A series of skirmishes ensued that were finally settled when two more paratroop battalions pushed past the town. By the end of the day, McAuliffe's forces had gained control of the northern side of the causeway leading to Carentan over the Douve and Madeleine rivers. The nature of the fighting that ensued was determined by the terrain. The area on either side of the causeway consisted of marshes and flooded farmland that was mostly impassable to infantry. As a result, the fighting had to be conducted down the narrow causeway itself and across each of its four bridges. The retreating German force had blown the first bridge over the Douve River, and so the advance along the bridge did not begin until the night of 9/10 June while the engineers attempted to span the gap. A boat patrol that night reached as far as the fourth and final bridge over the Madeleine River, but came under intense fire from Carentan. An artillery barrage preceded the attack by the 3/502nd PIR in the early evening of 10 June. The battalion was stretched out in a thin column from the second to fourth bridge, when German machine-gunners began to open fire. Advance across the Madeleine River bridge was inhibited by a Belgian gate obstacle that the paratroopers had managed to move, creating a single 18in. gap. As a result, only one soldier at a time could pass over the bridge. The fighting continued after dark, and was marked by a strafing run by two Luftwaffe aircraft, a rare appearance in the Normandy skies.

By dawn, about 250 paratroopers had reached the final Madeleine bridge, which was overlooked by a stone farmhouse. At 06.15hrs, Col Cole and the battalion executive officer, Major John Stopka, led a bayonet charge by 70 paratroopers into the farm. Although the farm was taken, by this stage the 3/502nd PIR had taken such heavy casualties that the 1/502nd PIR was brought forward to carry on the attack. In fact, the position was so tenuous that the 1/502nd could do no more than reinforce Cole's men to hold the farm against repeated German counterattacks. An afternoon attack almost succeeded in overwhelming the US paratroopers, but an artillery barrage placed almost on top of the American positions broke the German attack. Around 20.00hrs, the 2/502nd PIR was brought forward to relieve the other two battered battalions. By now, von der Heydte's German paratroopers were beginning to show the strain of combat as well, experiencing serious shortages of machine-gun ammunition and receiving few reinforcements. All rifle ammunition was collected and turned over to the machine-gun crews, and the paratroopers were forced to rely on pistols, grenades or whatever else was at hand. A request to airlift small arms ammunition to the beleaguered garrison was granted on 11 June, but the drop zone was in a field nearly nine miles (14km) behind the front, taking time to collect and distribute.

During the two days of intense fighting by the 502nd PIR along the causeway, the 327th Glider Infantry had crossed the Douve further east in the early morning hours of 10 June. It was then reinforced by 1/401st Glider Infantry, which began moving south to seize the roads leading

The initial defenders of Carentan were Fallschirmjäger Regiment 6, which had already lost one of its battalions in the first days of fighting against the US paratroopers. This photo shows a team of German paratroopers on an exercise on 1 June 1944 shortly before the invasion, wearing their distinctive helmets. (MHI)

A GI inspects one of the StuG IV assault guns of SS-Pz.Abt. 17 knocked out along the Carentan–Periers road. This was a less common version of the standard German assault gun, based on the PzKpfw IV chassis. The ubiquitous StuG III was based on the PzKpfw III chassis. (NARA)

out of Carentan toward the east. One of its companies moved east toward Isigny, meeting up with scouts from the 29th Division, marking the first contact between Utah and Omaha beaches. By the end of 10 June, the 327th Glider Infantry set up a defensive perimeter covering the east side of Carentan, where it was joined by elements from the 401st Glider Infantry. In contrast to the frustrating assault over the causeway, this advance proceeded so well that McAuliffe ordered the 501st PIR to reinforce the glider infantry on 11 June in preparation for a final assault on 12 June. The situation of the German garrison had become so perilous that on the afternoon of 11 July, von der Heydte decided to withdraw his force rather than face certain annihilation. During a lull in the fighting in the late afternoon, the garrison began to slip out to the southwest.

The attack on the city in the early morning hours of 12 July consisted of a drive by the glider infantry from the northeast directly into Carentan and a pincer movement by the 501st and 506th PIR to cut the roads to the southwest to prevent the garrison from escaping. The city was captured quickly, but aside from a small rearguard, the garrison had already withdrawn. After Carentan was taken, the VII Corps set about reinforcing the connections with V Corps to the east.

As Von der Heydte's paratroopers made their way southwest from Carentan on 11 July, they bumped into the lead elements of the 17th SS-Panzergrenadier Division. Von der Heydte later claimed that he had not been informed of the reinforcement, but senior German commanders blamed him for the unauthorized and premature abandonment of the city after he had been informed several times about the plans. Generalleutnant Max Pemsel, the Seventh Army chief of staff, later wrote that von der Heydte had suffered a temporary mental and physical breakdown due to the savage and uninterrupted fighting of the previous several days. The only reason he was not relieved for such a "misguided" decision was the outstanding performance of his outnumbered regiment up to that point.

17.SS-Pz.Gren.Div. had been formed in November 1943, and was not complete when sent into action in June 1944. Although near strength in personnel, it had only about 60 percent of its officers and NCOs, and was very short of motor transport. The divisional commander, SS-Gruppenführer Werner Ostendorf, decided to retake Carentan by attacking down two roads on the western side of city. The attack would not be preceded by reconnaissance or artillery fire in order to gain tactical surprise, and would be spearheaded by SS-Panzer Abteilung 17 equipped with 48 StuG IV assault guns. Ostendorf felt that the sudden appearance of large numbers of armored vehicles would carry the day since, to date, the fighting in this sector had been conducted by light infantry on both sides with few anti-tank weapons. The Panzers would serve as the spearhead for the main attack by SS-Panzergrenadier Regiment 37.

McAuliffe had planned to deploy the 506th PIR into the same area on the morning of 13 June to deepen the defenses, but they had not begun to advance when the German attack began around 07.00hrs. The German columns started from the divisional assembly areas, and due to the congestion on the country roads, the advance was slow in progressing. No contact was made with the paratroopers until around 09.00hrs when the lead StuG IV assault guns had approached to within 875 yards (800m) of the southwestern side of Carentan. In the confined terrain southeast of the city, the 506th PIR was able to slow the attack by using the hedgerows to good effect. They were reinforced by the 2/502nd PIR on the right flank.

There had been growing indications from Enigma decryption that Rommel planned to deploy the 17th SS-Panzergrenadier Div. against Carentan, prompting Bradley to deploy a task force from the newly arrived 2nd Armored Division including a company of medium tanks, a company of light tanks, and an armored infantry battalion into the area. When the paratroopers reported the Panzer attack around 09.00hrs, the task force

The 90th Division began to move forward to replace the 82nd Airborne Division once the bridges over the Merderet had been cleared. This is a .30 cal machine gun team moving forward, the gunner in front with the .30 cal Browning light machine-gun, and his assistant behind carrying the tripod and ammunition. (NARA)

The 82nd Airborne was once again committed to action in mid-June to help speed the attack across the Contentin peninsula. This is Lt Kelso Horne, commander of 1st Platoon, Co. I, 508th PIR, near St Sauveur-le-Vicomte. (NARA)

began moving and reached the town around 10.30. The German attack petered out by noon. The inexperienced Panzergrenadiers had a hard time adjusting to the *bocage* fighting, and a combination of officer and NCO shortages as well as combat losses left many units leaderless. Some units began to retreat on their own, forcing von der Heydte and his adjutant to round up many of them, sometimes at gunpoint. The left flank of the German attack was supposed to be defended by the surviving Hotchkiss H-39 tanks of Panzer-Abteilung 100, but the battered force evaporated. The US armored counterattack began around 14.00hrs down the Carentan–Baupte road. This threatened to cut off the German attack force, especially when it was followed by a second tank–paratrooper thrust down the Carentan–Periers road. Von der Heydte, finding the SS-Panzergrenadier Regiment 37 commander dazed, took command and ordered the Panzergrenadiers as well as his force to withdraw to a line he had reconnoitered earlier. Losses in the 17th SS-Panzergrenadier Div were 79 killed, 316 wounded and 61 missing. In addition, only about half of the division's 48 StuG IV assault guns were still operational with seven lost, and 13 damaged.

Infuriated by the debacle, Ostendorf attempted to make von der Heydte the scapegoat for his division's failure, and had him arrested and sent before an SS military judge that night. General Meindl, in temporary command of this sector after General Marcks had been killed in an air attack the day before, ordered von der Heydte released. The Seventh Army staff concluded that the counterattack at Carentan had failed due to the 17th SS-Panzergrenadier Div.'s inexperience. The rebuff of the German counterattack allowed Collin's VII Corps to consolidate the link-up with Gerow's V Corps on 14 June.

A GI from the 9th Division, armed with a .45 cal Thompson sub-machine gun, moves along a shallow road embankment near St Sauveur-le-Vicomte during the effort to cut off the Cotentin peninsula. (NARA)

One of the more common German tank destroyers in the Normandy fighting was the Marder III Ausf. M, which consisted of the highly effective 75mm PaK 40 anti-tank gun mounted on the rear of the Czech PzKpfw 38 (t) tank chassis. This one from Panzerjäger Abt. 243 was captured by the 82nd Airborne Division during the fighting on the Cotentin peninsula. A knocked-out M4 medium tank can be seen ahead of it. (MHI)

CUTTING OFF THE COTENTIN

Although it had been Collins' intention to shift the emphasis of VII Corps to a rapid assault on Cherbourg, by D+3 the focus was changed again. The slow pace of the advance in the *bocage* convinced both Bradley and Collins that a quick capture of Cherbourg was unlikely. Under such circumstances, it became imperative to cut off the Cotentin peninsula from any further German reinforcements. The first issue was completing the link-up of the elements of the 82nd Airborne Division on either side of the Merderet River.

With the positions on the east bank of the Merderet at La Fière bridge secure, on D+1 Gavin sent the 3/508th PIR to Chef-du-Pont to link up with Col Shanley's isolated force on the west bank. The fire directed against the causeway during the daylight hours made it impossible to

LEFT A fine character study of a typical young German *landser* of the 353rd Infantry Division during the Normandy fighting, wearing a shelter segment that doubled as a poncho. In front of him is his entrenching shovel and mess kit. This photo was taken on 25 June 1944 near La Haye-du-Puits during efforts by the Wehrmacht to prevent the American beachhead from pushing south out of the Cotentin peninsula. (MHI)

RIGHT GIs of the 9th Division use a roadside drainage ditch for cover during a skirmish near St Sauveur-le-Vicomte on 21 June 1944. In the background to the right is their 1¹/₂-ton weapons carrier while to the left is an abandoned German truck. (NARA)

carry out this mission, though Shanley was able to send a patrol across the causeway at night.

On D+2, the focus again returned to La Fière bridge. On the night of 8 June, two paratroopers from Col Timmes' group found a partially submerged road across the inundated fields north of the bridge, and crossed to the east bank. A plan was developed for Colonel Millett's group to join Col Timmes' group, and then link up with a battalion from the east bank moving across the newly discovered crossing. Col Millett's column began moving before daylight on 9 June, but were discovered and raked by German machine-gun fire. Colonel Millett was captured and the column retreated. The 1/325th Glider Infantry was able to make it across the inundated river and join Timmes' group, but attempts to push southward to the La Fière bridge were repulsed by German troops in a stone building dubbed the "Gray Castle".

Under growing pressure from senior commanders, Gavin was forced to execute a direct assault across the La Fière causeway from the east bank. He moved a few M5A1 tanks and a company of the 507th PIR to the forward edge of the bridge to provide covering fire. The force chosen for the assault was the 3/325th Glider Infantry. After a preliminary artillery bombardment and under a partial cover of smoke, Company G led the attack off at 10.45hrs on 9 June. The glidermen were told to make the 500-yard crossing in one sprint, but only a handful of men were able to do so in the face of intense German machine-gun fire. Those who hesitated were caught in the open on the exposed stretches of the causeway, and casualties soon mounted. One of the M5A1 light tanks attempted to push across the causeway, but hit a mine. This tank, along with a German Hotchkiss H-39 knocked out in earlier fighting, further congested the narrow passage. Company E tried the crossing next, but along the northern bank

The approaches to Cherbourg were studded with bunkers and other fortifications. This team of GIs from the 79th Division pose near a pillbox they had knocked out with a bazooka during the fighting outside the port. (NARA)

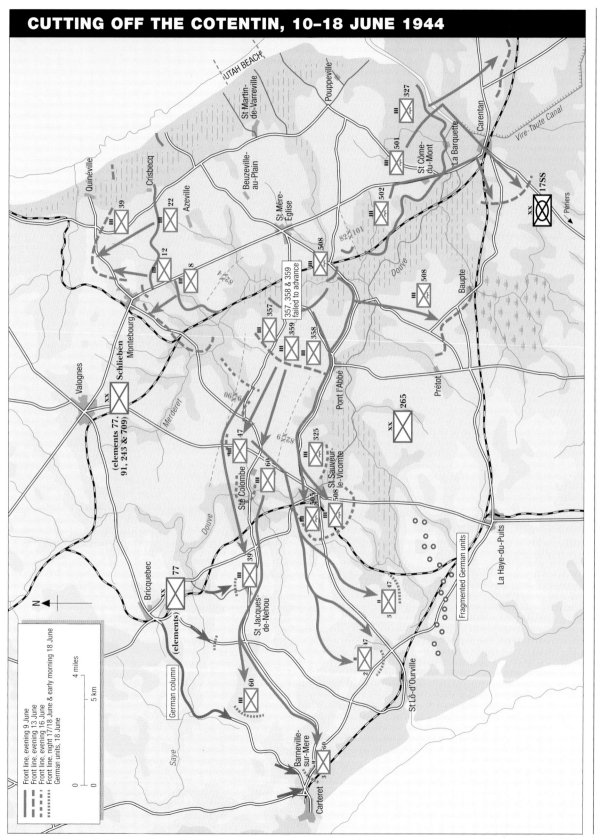

CUTTING OFF THE COTENTIN, 10–18 JUNE 1944

UTAH BEACH

St Martin-de-Varreville

Pouppeville

327

501

St Côme-du-Mont

La Barquette

Carentan

Vire-Taute Canal

175ss

Périers

Quinéville

Crisbecq

Beuzeville-au-Plain

Azeville

St Mère-Eglise

39

22

502

12

8

508

Douve

508

Baupte

357

357, 358 & 359 failed to advance

359

358

Montebourg

Schlieben

Valognes

xx

(elements 77, 91, 243 & 709)

Merderet

265

Pont l'Abbé

Prétot

47

60

325

St Sauveur-le-Vicomte

508

Ste Colombe

Douve

505

508

39

Bricquebec

77

xx

(elements)

St Jacques-de-Néhou

47

3

Fragmented German units

La Haye-du-Puits

St Lô-d'Ourville

German column

47

2

60

Saye

Barneville-sur-Mere

60

Carteret

3

N

4 miles

5 km

0

0

Front line, evening 9 June
Front line, evening 13 June
Front line, evening 16 June
Front line, night 17/18 June & early morning 18 June
German units, 18 June

165

of the causeway instead of on top of it. They made their way toward the church in Cauquigny, and the German positions were suppressed by small arms fire from Timmes' group. After this company made its way over the bridge and began clearing buildings on the north side of the exit, it was followed by Company F, which pushed beyond the bridgehead toward Le Motey. Due to the usual radio problems, Gavin was unsure of the progress of the 3/325th Glider Infantry and ordered his reserve company from the 507th PIR across the causeway. Further advances westward towards Le Motey were brought to a halt when US artillery continued its fire missions into the area, unaware that US troops had pushed that far. In spite of the many problems, the attacks on 9 June finally cleared the La Fière bridge and causeway.

With passage of the Merderet River open, Collins moved the 90th Division forward to take over the task of moving westward. On 10 June two regiments of the 90th Division began a westward advance over the La Fière and Chef-du-Pont bridges aiming to establish a bridgehead over the Douve River. The 357th Infantry moved over the La Fière bridge but ran into the defenses of GR.1057 past Le Motey. Inexperienced in *bocage* fighting, its lead battalion retreated into the positions of the 325th Glider Infantry. A second attack at dusk by another battalion was equally unsuccessful. The 358th Infantry was assigned to reach Pont l'Abbé, and its lead battalion dug into defense positions short of the objective after coming under heavy fire. GR.1057 launched a counterattack in mid-afternoon, without success.

A squad of GIs advance through a farm field on the outskirts of Cherbourg. They are probably from the 4th Division as the NCO to the left armed with the M1 carbine is still wearing one of the assault vests issued to combat teams involved in the initial D-Day landings. (NARA)

The attacks continued the following day with 357th Infantry still unable to overcome the German defensive positions around Les Landes, and the 358th Infantry on the fringe of Pont l'Abbé. The following day, the 359th Infantry rejoined the division from other assignments and reinforced the attack. The 12 June attack was further reinforced by the 746th Tank Battalion and additional artillery fire support. In spite of the reinforcements, the advance on 12 and 13 June was measured in hundreds of yards. In frustration at the slow pace of the advance in four days of fighting, General Collins visited the division on 13 June. After visiting the divisional command post, Collins was aggravated when he could find no regimental or battalion headquarters, nor much evidence of fighting.

Exasperated by the 90th Division's poor performance, Collins telephoned Bradley about his plans to relieve the division's commander and two regimental commanders. He felt that the main problem was the division's poor training and lackluster leadership. They decided to pull the division out of the line in favor of an experienced unit and Bradley agreed to the use of the 9th Division, regarded as being one of the two best

divisions in theater along with the 1st Division at Omaha Beach. This delayed the advance, so the attack resumed toward the Douve on 15 June with the 82nd Airborne Division on the left and the 9th Division on the right. The 82nd Airborne Division reached St Sauveur on the Douve on 16 June while the 9th Division's 60th Infantry reached the Douve near Ste Colombe. With German resistance crumbling, Collins urged Eddy to push to the sea as rapidly as possible. During the night of 16/17 June, a company from 3/60th Infantry riding on tanks and other armored vehicles reached the hill overlooking the coastal town of Barneville-sur-Mer before dawn. Early in the morning, the company advanced into the town, unoccupied except for a few startled German MPs. The rapid advance by the 9th Division had severed the Cotentin peninsula and cut off Cherbourg.

The sudden isolation of Cherbourg caused a major row among senior German leaders. Rommel had moved the 77th Infantry Division into the Cotentin peninsula on 9 June, but was unwilling to lose the best division in 84th Corps. On 15 June he ordered the amalgamation of the remnants of the 709th Infantry Div. and 243rd Infantry Div. into Kampfgruppe Schlieben with a mission to defend the port of Cherbourg. The 77th Infantry Division, along with the few surviving elements of the 91st Luftlande Division, were formed into Kampfgruppe Hellmich and instructed to withdraw southward if the Americans cut off the peninsula with an aim to prevent any further American penetration south. The capture of St Sauveur prompted Rundstedt and Rommel to begin the withdrawal of Kampfgruppe Schlieben into the Cherbourg area. Rommel

A pair of M4 medium tanks advance along the battered Rue du Val-de-Saire in the Tourlaville district of Cherbourg on 26 June 1944. The 746th Tank Battalion supported the 9th Division during the fighting in Cherbourg. (NARA)

and Rundstedt met with Hitler on 16 June at the W2 Battle HQ in Margival, France. Hitler insisted that the largest possible forces be committed to the defense of "Fortress Cherbourg" but he finally agreed to allow Kampfgruppe Hellmich to withdraw southward starting on 17 June. The order proved difficult to implement after both General Hellmich and the commander of the 77th Infantry Division, General Rudolf Stegmann, were killed during air attacks on 17 June. The first unit to begin the withdrawal was GR.1049, which ran into 1/39th Infantry on the morning of 18 June near St Jacques-de-Nehou and was stopped. The neighboring GR.1050 had more success, gaining control of a bridge over the Ollande River near St Lô-d'Ourville from the hapless 357th Infantry of the 90th Division, capturing about 100 GIs and breaking out with about 1,300 men before the gap was finally sealed. In the event, this was the only major group to escape the encirclement, and the 77th Infantry Division lost most of its artillery in the breakout attempt.

NORTH TO CHERBOURG

On 18 June 1944, Field Marshal Bernard Montgomery laid out the immediate tasks for the Allied forces in Normandy. The First US Army was to take Cherbourg while the British Second Army was to take Caen. The breakthrough to the west coast led Bradley to reorganize the forces on the Cotentin peninsula. The new VIII Corps under Major General Troy Middleton was given the 82nd Airborne and 90th Division with an assignment to defend toward the south and prevent any German forces from reinforcing the Cotentin peninsula. Collins' VII Corps now consisted of three infantry divisions, the 4th, 9th and 79th Divisions, which had the mission of advancing on Cherbourg. Eddy's 9th Division began an abrupt change in direction from west to north, moving against the western side of Cherbourg. Barton's 4th Division continued its push up along the eastern coast to Cherbourg, while the newly deployed 79th Division would push up the center. The initial aim was to seize the Quineville ridge, which dominated the terrain southward.

The 4th Division had been fighting northward since D-Day, its advance hampered by the presence of many fortified coastal artillery batteries along the eastern coast. On the left flank, 82nd Airborne's 505th PIR and 4th Division's 8th Infantry Regiment finally reached positions from the Montebourg railroad station to the western outskirts of Montebourg by 11 June. Barton decided against taking the city for fear of tying down too many troops in street fighting. Instead, on 13 June, the 8th Infantry set up defensive positions around the city to contain any German forces within it.

The 22nd Infantry had a much more difficult time, confronting both the Crisbecq and Azeville coastal batteries, which had been reinforced by infantry from the 709th Infantry Division and Sturm.Abt. AOK 7. After repeated attacks, the Azeville position was finally overwhelmed on the afternoon of 9 June by an attack on the command blockhouse with satchel charges and flame-throwers. Frustrated by the failure of previous attacks on Crisbecq, Gen Barton formed Task Force Barber from the 22nd Infantry, reinforced with M10 3in. tank destroyers of the 899th Tank Destroyer Battalion, and tanks of the 746th Tank Battalion. He instructed Barber to skirt around Crisbecq and seize the high ground around **169**

Quineville after taking Ozeville. The attack was frustrated by the thick *bocage*, heavy German artillery fire, and determined counterattacks. The Crisbecq fortifications finally fell on 11 June when 57mm anti-tank guns of K/22nd Infantry fired through the embrasures of the two remaining strongpoints. To gain momentum, Collins took the newly arrived 39th Infantry from the 9th Division and sent it to deal with the many strongpoints along the coast. This freed up Task Force Barber to concentrate on positions further inland, and both air support and naval gunfire support resumed after several days of bad weather. Quineville was finally taken on 14 June, along with the ridgeline to the west, which had been the anchor of German defenses in this sector. Besides clearing the gateway to Cherbourg on the east coast, the operations in the week after D-Day finally ended the threat of German artillery fire into Utah Beach, which had been hampering unloading operations there.

The drive on Cherbourg began on the evening of 19 June with the 4th Division kicking it off at 03.00hrs followed by the 9th and 79th Divisions at 05.00. The 4th Cavalry Group was assigned to protect the right flank of the 4th Division and move up along the eastern coast. German defenses by this stage of the campaign were the disorganized remnants of four divisions. The 9th Division was facing portions of GR.920 and GR.921 from the 243rd Infantry Division along with the surviving elements of the 77th Infantry Division that had failed to escape southward during the breakout attempt two days before. The 79th Division in the center faced parts of the 77th Infantry Division as well as remnants of the 91st Luftlande Division. The 4th Division was facing most of the 709th Infantry Division, the survivors of Sturm.Abt. AOK 7, and large parts of the 243rd Infantry Division.

The initial attacks made steady progress as the German units tended to withdraw after first contact. After the peninsula had been isolated on

17 July, the Cherbourg garrison had been cut off from most outside communication. On 19 July General von Schlieben decided to disengage his forces from the front, and pull them back into a fortified zone on the outskirts of Cherbourg in hopes of conducting a protracted defense. As a result, the American advance only encountered rearguard units or outposts that had lost contact with headquarters. On 20 June Eddy began steps to cut off the Cap de la Hague peninsula from the rest of the Cherbourg defense. German resistance stiffened considerably, and Eddy realized that the 9th Division had finally run into the main line of defense for Fortress Cherbourg.

Von Schlieben reorganized his disparate forces into four battle-groups (*kampfgruppe*) that formed a semicircular defensive line outside the city. The German defenses were based on a series of hills and ridges located four to six miles from the port. Many of the defenses included bunkers, while others included concrete structures of the abandoned V-1 buzz bomb bases. The attack on Cherbourg was preceded by an intense air preparation conducted by the IX Tactical Air Command. The ground attack on the afternoon of 22 June was preceded at 12.40hrs by 25 minutes of rocket attacks and strafing by ten squadrons of Typhoons and Mustangs of the 2nd Tactical Air Force (RAF), 55 minutes of bombing and strafing by 562 P-47s and P-51s, followed at H-Hour (14.00) by bombing runs of 11 groups of B-26 Marauders of the Ninth Air Force. The air attacks proved

A group of GIs and French civilians celebrate the capture of Cherbourg, driving around the city in a captured Renault UE tractor. (NARA)

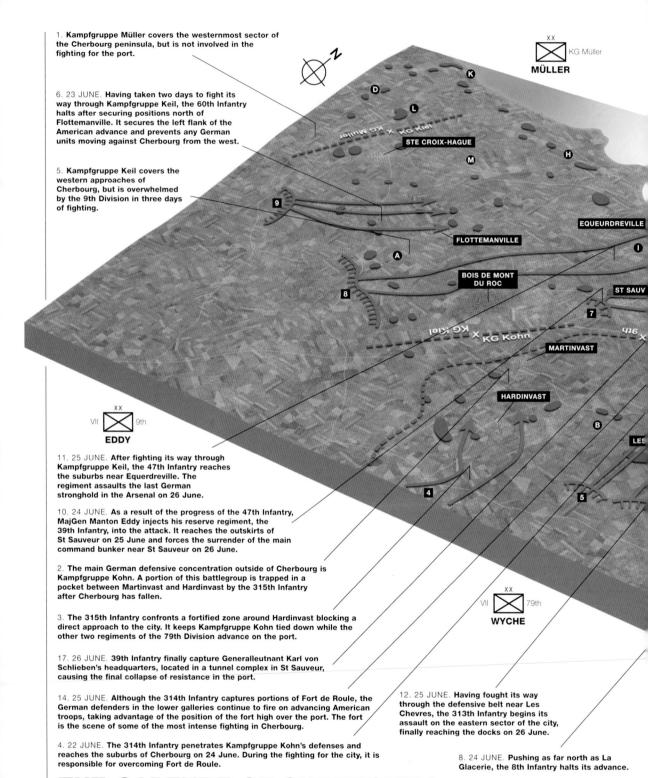

1. **Kampfgruppe Müller** covers the westernmost sector of the Cherbourg peninsula, but is not involved in the fighting for the port.

6. **23 JUNE. Having** taken two days to fight its way through Kampfgruppe Keil, the 60th Infantry halts after securing positions north of Flottemanville. It secures the left flank of the American advance and prevents any German units moving against Cherbourg from the west.

5. **Kampfgruppe Keil** covers the western approaches of Cherbourg, but is overwhelmed by the 9th Division in three days of fighting.

11. **25 JUNE. After** fighting its way through Kampfgruppe Keil, the 47th Infantry reaches the suburbs near Equerdreville. The regiment assaults the last German stronghold in the Arsenal on 26 June.

10. **24 JUNE. As** a result of the progress of the 47th Infantry, MajGen Manton Eddy injects his reserve regiment, the 39th Infantry, into the attack. It reaches the outskirts of St Sauveur on 25 June and forces the surrender of the main command bunker near St Sauveur on 26 June.

2. The main German defensive concentration outside of Cherbourg is Kampfgruppe Kohn. A portion of this battlegroup is trapped in a pocket between Martinvast and Hardinvast by the 315th Infantry after Cherbourg has fallen.

3. The 315th Infantry confronts a fortified zone around Hardinvast blocking a direct approach to the city. It keeps Kampfgruppe Kohn tied down while the other two regiments of the 79th Division advance on the port.

17. **26 JUNE.** 39th Infantry finally capture Generalleutnant Karl von Schlieben's headquarters, located in a tunnel complex in St Sauveur, causing the final collapse of resistance in the port.

14. **25 JUNE. Although** the 314th Infantry captures portions of Fort de Roule, the German defenders in the lower galleries continue to fire on advancing American troops, taking advantage of the position of the fort high over the port. The fort is the scene of some of the most intense fighting in Cherbourg.

4. **22 JUNE.** The 314th Infantry penetrates Kampfgruppe Kohn's defenses and reaches the suburbs of Cherbourg on 24 June. During the fighting for the city, it is responsible for overcoming Fort de Roule.

12. **25 JUNE. Having** fought its way through the defensive belt near Les Chevres, the 313th Infantry begins its assault on the eastern sector of the city, finally reaching the docks on 26 June.

8. **24 JUNE. Pushing** as far north as La Glacerie, the 8th Infantry halts its advance.

MÜLLER · KG Müller

EDDY VII · 9th

WYCHE VII · 79th

STE CROIX-HAGUE
EQUEURDREVILLE
FLOTTEMANVILLE
BOIS DE MONT DU ROC
ST SAUV
MARTINVAST
HARDINVAST
LES

KG Müller
KG Keil
KG Kohn
9th

THE CAPTURE OF CHERBOURG

22–30 June 1944, viewed from the southeast, showing the assault on this vital strategic port by US 4th, 9th, and 79th Infantry Divisions. The city was captured amid bitter fighting, but comprehensive destruction of facilities by the German defenders rendered the port of Cherbourg useless to the Allies for many weeks.

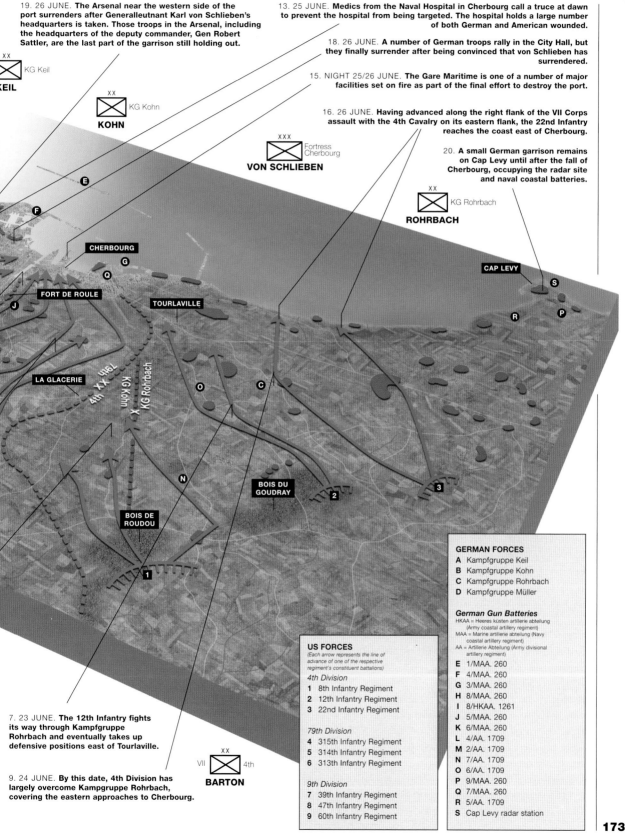

19. 26 JUNE. The Arsenal near the western side of the port surrenders after Generalleutnant Karl von Schlieben's headquarters is taken. Those troops in the Arsenal, including the headquarters of the deputy commander, Gen Robert Sattler, are the last part of the garrison still holding out.

13. 25 JUNE. Medics from the Naval Hospital in Cherbourg call a truce at dawn to prevent the hospital from being targeted. The hospital holds a large number of both German and American wounded.

18. 26 JUNE. A number of German troops rally in the City Hall, but they finally surrender after being convinced that von Schlieben has surrendered.

15. NIGHT 25/26 JUNE. The Gare Maritime is one of a number of major facilities set on fire as part of the final effort to destroy the port.

16. 26 JUNE. Having advanced along the right flank of the VII Corps assault with the 4th Cavalry on its eastern flank, the 22nd Infantry reaches the coast east of Cherbourg.

20. A small German garrison remains on Cap Levy until after the fall of Cherbourg, occupying the radar site and naval coastal batteries.

XX
KG Keil
KEIL

XX
KG Kohn
KOHN

XXX
Fortress Cherbourg
VON SCHLIEBEN

XX
KG Rohrbach
ROHRBACH

CAP LEVY

E
F

CHERBOURG
G
Q

FORT DE ROULE
J

TOURLAVILLE

S

R
P

LA GLACERIE

4th XX 79th
KG Kohn
KG Rohrbach

O
C

N

BOIS DU GOUDRAY
2

3

BOIS DE ROUDOU

1

7. 23 JUNE. The 12th Infantry fights its way through Kampfgruppe Rohrbach and eventually takes up defensive positions east of Tourlaville.

9. 24 JUNE. By this date, 4th Division has largely overcome Kampfgruppe Rohrbach, covering the eastern approaches to Cherbourg.

VII XX 4th
BARTON

US FORCES
(Each arrow represents the line of advance of one of the respective regiment's constituent battalions)

4th Division
1 8th Infantry Regiment
2 12th Infantry Regiment
3 22nd Infantry Regiment

79th Division
4 315th Infantry Regiment
5 314th Infantry Regiment
6 313th Infantry Regiment

9th Division
7 39th Infantry Regiment
8 47th Infantry Regiment
9 60th Infantry Regiment

GERMAN FORCES
A Kampfgruppe Keil
B Kampfgruppe Kohn
C Kampfgruppe Rohrbach
D Kampfgruppe Müller

German Gun Batteries
HKAA = Heeres küsten artillerie abteilung (Army coastal artillery regiment)
MAA = Marine artillerie abteilung (Navy coastal artillery regiment)
AA = Artillerie Abteilung (Army divisional artillery regiment)
E 1/MAA. 260
F 4/MAA. 260
G 3/MAA. 260
H 8/MAA. 260
I 8/HKAA. 1261
J 5/MAA. 260
K 6/MAA. 260
L 4/AA. 1709
M 2/AA. 1709
N 7/AA. 1709
O 6/AA. 1709
P 9/MAA. 260
Q 7/MAA. 260
R 5/AA. 1709
S Cap Levy radar station

173

less effective than anticipated, and many infantry units radioed that they were being inadvertently attacked. The best results had been obtained on the western side where the 9th Division artillery had suppressed German flak positions in anticipation of the air missions. None of the main defenses were cracked on 22 June, and it took two days of hard fighting before the first portions of the defensive belt were finally overcome. The first penetrations past the outer defenses took place in the 9th Division's sector near the Flottemanville–Hague strongpoints late in the evening of 23 June.

Although von Schlieben was in command of the four divisions holding the city, the actual command of the port was under Generalmajor Robert Sattler until 23 June when Hitler appointed von Schlieben as the commander of Fortress Cherbourg. Requests for further ammunition and reinforcements went unanswered, but senior German commanders felt that the garrison could hold out for months due to the geography and the extensive fortifications around the port.

The final assaults into the town were made by infantry–tank teams, with each of the divisions receiving a separate tank battalion for support. These were essential to deal with the many bunkers and defenses encountered. Although German resistance on 24 June continued to be intense, there was a growing tendency for the defenses to crumble once vigorously assaulted. By the end of the day, breaches had been made in the final layer of outer defenses, allowing the first access to the city itself. At dawn on 25 June, a German medical officer accompanied by a captured American pilot came out under a flag of truce to ask that the naval hospital be spared from shelling and for a supply of plasma. They were allowed to return to the city with the plasma, and with a demand for the immediate surrender of the city. By the time the demand had reached von Schlieben, the 314th Infantry was already assaulting Fort de Roule overlooking the city. The intensity of the fighting for the fort is evident from the fact that two Medals of Honor for bravery were awarded for the action. By midnight, the 314th Infantry had broken into the fort and occupied the upper levels, but with German troops still occupying the lower galleries. The 47th Infantry made the first penetration into the suburbs of Cherbourg on 25 June after overcoming the defenses at Equeurdreville. By nightfall the city was illuminated by the fires of the burning port facilities that the Germans had set as the final stage of the destruction of the port.

The final assault into the city by the 9th and 79th Division occurred on 26 June. US patrols in the city continued to be harassed by artillery fire from the lower levels of Fort de Roule, which were still in German hands. These lower levels were not immediately accessible to the troops from 2/314th Infantry on top of the fort, and they began to try to lower charges down ventilation shafts. A demolition team snaked its way along the cliff face on the western side of the fort and blasted one of the tunnel openings with pole charges and bazookas. Troops below the fort began firing into the embrasures with 57mm anti-tank guns. Resistance finally collapsed in the early evening and several hundred prisoners were taken.

Fighting in the city remained intense through the day, and the presence of many large concrete structures and coastal gun positions greatly complicated the American attacks. The 39th Infantry learned from prisoners that Gen Schlieben was in a bunker in St Sauveur, and by mid-afternoon Companies E and F had fought their way to the tunnel entrance of the command bunker. A prisoner was sent in to demand surrender, which was refused. M10 tank destroyers were brought forward, and a few 3in. high explosive rounds were enough to cause the Germans to reconsider. About 800 officers and troops began to pour out including General von Schlieben, Admiral Walter Hennecke, and their staffs. The surrender was made to Gen Eddy, but von Schlieben refused to order the surrender of the rest of his garrison. Nevertheless, the forces still holding the City Hall surrendered after learning of von Schlieben's surrender. The last major defensive position in the city was the Arsenal, which was protected by a moat and strongly defended by anti-aircraft and anti-tank guns on parapets. The 47th Infantry was assigned to take it on the morning of 26 June, and began by picking off two of the 20mm Flak parapets with tank fire. Before the main assault at 08.30hrs, a psychological warfare unit brought up a loudspeaker, urging the garrison to surrender. General Sattler, the deputy commander of Cherbourg, agreed to surrender the 400 men under his command, and the rest of the arsenal surrendered by 10.00hrs. This ended the organized resistance in the port, though mopping-up operations continued for two days. About 10,000 prisoners were captured on 25–26 June. Two more days were spent eliminating outlying forts in the harbor, mainly by air attack and tank gun fire. There were also isolated garrisons on Cap Levy that were taken by the 22nd Infantry, and about 3,000 Germans had retreated to Cap de la Hague. The 9th Division assaulted these positions and overran the final defenses on 30 June. A total of 6,000 prisoners were captured in the final operations in late June. On 1 July, the 9th Division reported to Collins that all organized resistance on the Cotentin peninsula had ended.

The total casualties of the VII Corps from D-Day to the fall of Cherbourg at the end of June was about 22,000. The large number of missing was due to scattered airborne landings that accounted for 4,500 of the missing, some of whom were captured. German casualties are not known with any precision although prisoners totaled 39,000. The allies had hoped to capture Cherbourg by D+15, so its capture on D+21 was not far behind schedule, especially compared to the plans for Caen in the neighboring British sector. The capture of Cherbourg did not provide any immediate benefit to the Allied supply situation, as the Germans had thoroughly demolished the port facilities prior to the surrender. Their one failure in this regard was the large fuel storage facility in the port, which remained intact and quite valuable to the Allies. It took almost two months to clean up the port, but it was back in operation by September 1944.

Table 3: US VII Corps Casualties D-Day to 1 July 1944

Unit	killed	wounded	missing	captured	Total
4th Div.	844	3,814	788	6	5,452
9th Div.	301	2,061	76		2,438
79th Div.	240	1,896	240		2,376
90th Div.	386	1,979	34		2,399
82nd Abn. Div.	457	1,440	2,571	12+	4,480
101st Abn. Div	546	2,217	1,907	?	4,670
Corps troops	37	157	49	61	304
Total	**2,811**	**13,564**	**5,665**	**79**	**22,119**

The fall of the port shocked Hitler and the senior German leadership who believed that such a heavily fortified facility could hold out for months. They seriously overestimated the paper strength of their own forces and seriously underestimated combat efficiency of the US Army. With the capture of the Cotentin peninsula, hope evaporated that the Allies could be dislodged from France.

THE BATTLEFIELD TODAY

In contrast to Omaha Beach, where most of the combat action occurred on the beach itself, the fighting for Utah Beach was over very quickly. The most intense D-Day fighting in this sector consisted of small skirmishes by the paratroopers scattered in the farmland behind the beach. There is a museum near the beach itself, and a significant number of German fortifications remain, including some preserved artillery emplacements. The "Musee de Debarquement d'Utah Beach" is located in Ste Marie-du-Mont adjacent to the beach and includes many exhibits of weapons and equipment associated with the landing. The area behind the beach that was flooded at the time of D-Day has long since been drained and is now farmland.

Of all the sites connected with the paratrooper actions, Ste Mère-Église is no doubt the most popular, due in no small measure to the dramatic depiction in the well-known film "The Longest Day". None other than John Wayne depicted (the much younger!) LtCol Benjamin Vandervoort. The images of Red Buttons in the film, depicting Pvt John Steele hanging by his parachute from the church steeple, is one of the most memorable in the movie. For years, the church in Ste Mère-Église has had a mannequin hanging from a parachute draped from the roof to commemorate the airborne landings. The church also contains a stained glass window commemorating the 505th PIR, which was added on the 25th anniversary. There is a large museum in the town, the "Musee des Troupe Aeroportees", devoted to the airborne landings.

This picture of Utah Beach was taken in 1947, and the area is very similar today. Compared to the photo on p.53, which shows the beach on D-Day, the flooded areas behind the beach have been drained and returned to use as farmland. (MHI)

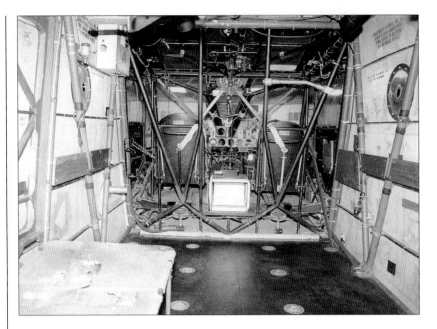

The 82nd Airborne Division Museum at Ft. Bragg has preserved one of the few surviving Waco CG-4A gliders. In spite of their canvas covering, their tubular fuselage construction proved to be relatively robust for such a light airframe. The canvas bench seat for the glider infantry can be seen in the left foreground. (Author)

The countryside around Ste Mère-Église is dotted with dozens of small markers, monuments, shrines, and plaques. Some of these are memorials to various units that took part in the fighting, while some commemorate individuals, such as a plaque at the site where General Pratt was killed. It is helpful to have a guidebook or map to seek out these memorials, as many are remote from the main roads. La Fière bridge still exists, though it is still as inconspicuous as in 1944. Nearby is the famous "Iron Mike" monument to the paratroopers. There are markers nearby showing the depth of the water of the flooded farm fields, but it takes some imagination to recall how difficult the fight along the causeway must have been.

The numerous concrete fortifications erected by the Germans along the coast in many cases still exist, as the larger bunkers are so difficult and costly to remove. Many of these are on private land, and tourists should take extreme care when visiting such sites as many contain sub-basements that present a real hazard to the unprepared. Some of the most impressive fortifications are the Crisbecq and Azeville batteries and there is a museum (La Batterie d'Azeville) open in the summer months nearby. Cherbourg has been heavily rebuilt since the war, and the Fort de Roule has been converted into the "Musee de la Liberation".

American servicemen killed in action were interred in the American Cemetery and Memorial, located in Colleville-sur-Mer near the St Laurent draw on Omaha Beach. There are two German military cemeteries near Utah Beach, the Orglandes cemetery about seven miles from Ste Mère-Église and the larger cemetery at La Cambe, which is about 17 miles southeast of Ste Mère-Église.

FURTHER READING

The D-Day landings have proven to be one of the most popular topics of World War II history, and there are hundreds of titles on this subject of varying quality. There was a flood of new books around the time of the 1994 anniversary. Paratroop operations are of particular fascination to many military history buffs, and many surveys of airborne operations cover the D-Day jumps. The list below is by no means exhaustive and consists mainly of more recent titles that the author has found to be particularly useful. Besides the commercially published books, there are a number of limited-circulation books by US Army commands that are particularly useful for those looking for more in-depth coverage, and can be found in specialist military libraries. The two most relevant to the Omaha landings are the First US Army and the V Corps report of operations. For Utah Beach and the airborne landings, in contrast to the V Corps history, the VII Corps history is weak and not worth the effort to locate. Of the semi-official divisional histories, several have been reprinted by Battery Press, including the 9th, 79th, and 101st Airborne. The multi-volume 4th Division History has not been reprinted, but is not as detailed as other divisional histories dealing with D-Day. There are also many after-action reports on the D-Day landings that are more difficult to find except at archives. The author consulted the collections at the Military History Institute at the Army War College at Carlisle Barracks, Pennsylvania, and the US National Archives and Records Administration (NARA) at College Park, Maryland. Some of the better reports include the "Operation Report Neptune: Omaha Beach" by the Provisional Engineer Special Brigade Group, and "Amphibious Operations: Invasion of Northern France: Western Task Force June 1944" by the US Fleet HQ. One of the most useful studies of the airborne landings is USAF Historical Study No. 97, prepared at the Air University in 1957, entitled "Airborne Operations in World War II: European Theater", which provides an excellent account and pointed critique of the conduct of the D-Day airborne landings. There are also numerous after-action reports by the various US Army units located in Record Group 407 at NARA, College Park.

There have been a number of films devoted to D-Day, including Darryl Zanuck's memorable epic "The Longest Day", which devotes considerable time to the airborne landings around Ste Mère-Église. A more contemporary depiction of the airborne operations is included in Steven Spielberg's multi-part TV-movie "Band of Brothers" based on the excellent Stephen Ambrose book about a company of the 101st Airborne.

Ambrose, Stephen, *D-Day, June 6, 1944* (Simon & Schuster, 1994). This account of the D-Day landings by the popular historian is based on many interviews with veterans that presents the soldiers' perspectives of the fighting.

Balkoski, Joseph, *Beyond the Beachhead: The 29th Infantry Division in Normandy* (Stackpole, 1989). This is an excellent account of the formation and training of the 29th Division and its actions in the Normandy campaign.

Bando, Mark, *101st Airborne: The Screaming Eagles at Normandy* (MBI, 2001). This is an excellent photographic portrait of the 101st Airborne in Normandy with many detailed accounts of individual actions based on interviews with veterans.

Berger, Sid, *Breaching Fortress Europe* (Society of American Military Engineers, 1994). This book looks at the role of US Army engineer troops in the D-Day landings.

Bernage, George, *Debarquement à Utah Beach* (Heimdal, 1984). This short but useful photographic portrayal of Utah Beach on D-Day has excellent details on the German beach defenses.

Bernage, George, *Premiere Victoire Americaine en Normandie* (Heimdal, 1990). Another useful Heimdal photo book by this prolific French specialist on Normandy; this time covering the battle for Cherbourg.

Bernage, George, *Omaha Beach* (Heimdal, 2002). This is an excellent photographic portrayal of Omaha Beach on D-Day, and the best single volume detailing the configuration of the German beach defenses.

Collins, J. Lawton, *Lightning Joe* (LSU Press, 1979). An excellent autobiography by the VII Corps commander with insightful comments about the conduct of the fighting.

Esvelin, Philippe, *D-Day Gliders, Les planeurs Americains du Jour J* (Heimdal, 2002). A short and excellent photographic account of the glider operations on D-Day.

Ewing, Joseph, *29 Let's Go!: A History of the 29th Division in World War II* (Infantry Journal 1948; Battery Press reprint 1979). This is one of the better semi-official divisional histories published immediately after the war with a very good account of the division at Omaha Beach.

Gawne, Jonathan, *Spearheading D-Day* (Histoire & Collections, 1998). This is a superb, and lavishly illustrated examination of the US special units deployed during the Normandy landings with excellent coverage of their specialized equipment, and uniforms.

Harrison, Gordon, *Cross-Channel Attack* (US Army CMH, 1951). This is the official US Army "Green Book" history of the Normandy landings and remains one of the best available accounts.

Isby, David, *Fighting the Invasion: The German Army at D-Day* (Greenhill, 2000). This is the best single volume on the German army on D-Day and consists of a collection of essays written by senior German leaders for the US Army's Foreign Military Studies program after the war based on their recollections of the campaign.

Isby, David, *Fighting the Invasion: The German Army from D-Day to Villers Bocage* (Greenhill, 2001). This is a follow-on to the first volume and takes the action into mid-June. It has good coverage of several of the German units prominent in the Cotentin peninsula fighting, especially FJR 6 and the 709th Infantry Division.

Kilvert-Jones, Tim, *Omaha Beach* (Leo Cooper, 1999). This is one of the popular Battleground Europe paperbacks combining a tour guide of the battlefield with an excellent short narrative of the battle.

Koskimaki, George, *D-Day with the Screaming Eagles* (1970, Casemate reprint 2002). A classic by Gen Taylor's radioman, who has collected a wealth of fellow veterans accounts.

Knickerbocker, H.R. et. al., *Danger Forward: The Story of the First Division in World War II* (1947, Battery Press reprint 2002). This is one of the better divisional histories published immediately after the war covering the division at the center of the US landings.

Lewis, Adrian, *Omaha Beach: A Flawed Victory* (University of North Carolina, 2001). This is an excellent academic study of the planning of the D-Day landings.

Masters, Charles J., *Glidermen of Neptune* (S. Illinois University Press, 1995). An account of the glider operations on D-Day by the son of one of the glider infantrymen.

Morison, Samuel E., *The Invasion of France and Germany 1944–1945* (Little, Brown, 1957). This is the volume in Morison's multi-volume history of the US Navy in World War II, and remains the best single account of US Navy actions on D-Day.

Omaha Beachhead (US Army CMH, 1945, numerous reprints) This is the earlier and shorter official history of the Omaha Beach landings, and is available in a paperback edition from the US Government Printing Office, including an excellent set of maps.

Winston Ramsey, *D-Day Then and Now, Volume 2* (After the Battle, 1995). This is a typically lavish and massive "After the Battle" treatment with an excellent selection of historical photos, complemented by photos of the same sites today.

Rapaport, Leonard, Northwood, A., *Rendezvous with Destiny* (Infantry Journal; Battery Press Reprint). A classic divisional history of the 101st Airborne and one of the best studies of a US WWII division.

Friedrich Ruge, *Rommel in Normandy* (Presidio, 1984). This is an account of Rommel's efforts in Normandy by his naval aide, and provides an inside view of the debates over German defensive strategy in 1944.

Shilleto, Carl, *Utah Beach: Ste Mère-Église* (Leo Cooper, 2001). This is one of the popular Battleground Europe paperbacks combining a tour guide of the battlefield with a short narrative of the battle.

Stillwell, Paul, *Assault on Normandy* (US Naval Institute, 1994). This is an excellent collection of essays by US Navy participants of the D-Day landings.

Utah Beach to Cherbourg (US Army Center for Military History, 1946; many reprints). This short account of Utah Beach preceded the "green book" history but still remains valuable.

Wolfe, Martin, *Green Light: A Troop Carrier Squadron's War from Normandy to the Rhine* (Univ. Of Pennsylvania Press, 1983). An account of the Normandy airdrops from the perspective of one of the C-47 pilots provides an interesting contrast to the paratrooper accounts which are often critical of the transport pilots.

INDEX

Figures in **bold** refer to illustrations.

1st Army 98, 169
1st Infantry Division **19, 25**, 37, 39, 65–6, **67, 68**, 83, 168
1st US Army (FUSA) plan 109, 110
2nd Armored Division 160
2nd Army (British) 169
2nd Fallschirmjäger Division (Wehrmacht) 105 *see also* Fallschirmjäger Regiment 6 (FJR6) (Wehrmacht)
2nd Infantry Division **91**
2nd Ranger Battalion **27**, 38, 48, 49, 52, 68–78, **69, 70–2, 77**
4th Cavalry Group 170
4th Infantry Division 99, **104**, 106–7, 115, 118, 119, 136, 142, 143, 147, **147**, 148, 149, 154, 169, 170, 179
5th Ranger Battalion 38, 52–3, **58–60**, 77, 82
V Corps 98, 154, 159, 161, 179
6th Fallschirmjäger Regiment (FJR6) (Wehrmacht) 100, 105, 137, 153, 154, 155, **158**
7th Army (Wehrmacht) 97, 161
VII Corps 98, 99, 115, 150, 154, 155, 159, 161, 163, 169, 175, 176, 179
8th Infantry Regiment 119, 142, 143, 147, **147**, 149, 150, **150**, 151
VIII Corps 169
9th Infantry Division 99, 108, **161, 163,** 167, 168, 169, 170, 171, 174, 175, 179
IX Tactical Air Command 171
IX Troop Carrier Command 114, 115, 130–1
12th Infantry Regiment 147
XII Corps 99
16th Infantry Regiment **4, 16,** 16–17, **19, 25,** 27, 36–7, **38,** 39, **41,** 49–50, **50, 51, 54–6,** 57, 61, 83
17th SS-Panzer Abteilung 160
17th SS-Panzergrenadier Division 'Gotz von Berlichingen' 155, 157, 159, 160, 161
18th Panzer Division (Wehrmacht) 97
XVIII Airborne Corps 99
22nd Infantry Regiment 143, 147, 151, 169, 170, 175
26th Infantry Regiment 39
29th Infantry Division 37, 39, 65, 82, 159
33rd Field Artillery Battalion 39
37th SS-Panzergrenadier Regiment 160, 161
39th Infantry Regiment 170, 175
47th Infantry Regiment 175
49th Engineer Combat Battalion 147
50th Troop Carrier Wing 114
52nd Troop Carrier Wing 114
66th Corps (Wehrmacht) 97
70th Tank Battalion **104**, 107, 139, 142, **142**, 143, **146,** 149, 154

77th Infantry Division (Wehrmacht) 155, 168, 170
79th Infantry Division 99, 108, **164,** 169, 170, 175, 179
81st Chemical Weapons Battalion **83**
82nd Airborne Division 98, 99, 106, 107, 110, 113, 114, **120, 121,** 122, **122, 126,** 130, 136, 147, 149, 150, 151, 154, 157, 160, 163, 168, 169
84th Infantry Corps (Wehrmacht) 97, 135, 136, 168
87th Corps (Wehrmacht) 97
90th Infantry Division 99, 107, 147, **160,** 166, 167, 169
91st Luftlande Division (Wehrmacht) 97, 104–5, 110, 111, 113, 121, 122, 127, 134, 135, 136, 168, 170
100th Panzer Abteilung Division (Wehrmacht) 105, 127, 134, 161
101st Airborne Division 99, **105,** 106, 110, **112,** 114, 115, **119, 120,** 130, 149, 151, 152, 153, 154, **155,** 179
101st Jäger Division (Wehrmacht) 97
101st Panzer Abteilung Division (Wehrmacht) 103
116th Infantry Regiment 17, 18, **22,** 27, 37, 39, 48–9, 49, 51, 52–3, 57–61, **58–60,** 60, 61, 65, 82
175th Infantry Regiment 39
206th Panzer Abteilung Division (Werhmacht) 104
237th Engineers 143
243rd Infantry Division (Wehrmacht) 97, 100, 103, 104, 111–13, 168, 170
299th Engineers 143
314th Infantry Regiment 174, 175
325th Glider Infantry **107,** 151, 164, 166
327th Glider Infantry 158, 159
337th Infantry Division (Wehrmacht) 97
352nd Artillery Regiment (Wehrmacht) 35
352nd Fusilier Battalion (Wehrmacht) 35
352nd Infantry Division (Wehrmacht) **31, 34,** 34–5, 82, 135
353rd Infantry Division (Wehrmacht) **163**
357th Infantry Regiment 166, 167, 169
358th Infantry Regiment 166, 167
359th Infantry Regiment 167
377th Parachute Field Artillery 118
401st Glider Infantry 158, 159
442nd Troop Carrier Group 126, **126**
501st Parachute Infantry Regiment 118, 119, 120, 147, 157, 159
502nd Parachute Infantry Regiment **107,** 115–16, **118,** 157, 158, 160
505th Parachute Infantry Regiment 121, 122, 123, 134, 169, 177
506th Parachute Infantry Regiment 115, 118, 119, 120, **121,** 153, 159, 160
507th Parachute Infantry Regiment 122, 123, 127, 130, 164, 166

508th Parachute Infantry Regiment **121,** 122, **122,** 123, 127, 130, 163
701st Infantry Division (Wehrmacht) 105
709th Infantry Division (Wehrmacht) 97, 102–3, 104, 135, 168, 169, 170
716th Infantry Division 28, 34, 73
740th Tank Battalion **167**
741st Tank Battalion 37, 45–8, 50, 57, 61, 65, 66, 82, **83**
743rd Tank Battalion 37, 44, 52, 57, 64, 78, 82, 85
746th Tank Battalion 151, 153, 167, **168,** 169
899th Tank Destroyer Battalion **105,** 169
919th Grenadier Regiment (Wehrmacht) 111, 112–13, 116, 131, 138, 147, 150
920th and 921st Grenadier Regiments (Wehrmacht) 170
1040th and 1050th Grenadier Regiments (Wehrmacht) 169
1057th Grenadier Regiment (Wehrmacht) 127, 130, 134, 136, 150, 166
1058th Grenadier Regiment (Wehrmacht) 113, 120, 121, 136, 147, 151, 153

air power 7–9, **21,** 87, 108, 114, 115, 120, 138–9, 171 *see also* Luftwaffe
operations 21, 41, 44, 87, 88–9
Rommel's views on 9
airborne landings 115–31, **117**
Albany, Operation 114, 115–20
Aldis lamps 114
Allied forces *see also* air power; British Army; US Army; US Army Air Force
combat effectiveness 8–9
command structure 14–15
intelligence 9
naval 138, 151
plans 19–28, **22, 26**
amphibious beach landings
Omaha Beach **4,** 45, 49, **52,** 65, **67, 68, 80**
Utah Beach 109, 138–55, **140–1, 142**
amtracs (amphibious tractors) 25
Ancon, USS 78
anti-tank vehicles and weapons **30,** 32, 34, **67, 68, 81,** 82, **100, 134, 148, 149** *see also* weapons
Anvil, Operation 5, 7
Anzio landing 94
Arkansas, USS **20**
Army Group B (Wehrmacht) 12–13, 96
artillery *see also* German coastal strongpoints and batteries
German 34–5
  50mm PaK 38 anti-tank guns **30,** 32
  88mm PaK 43/41 'Scheunentor' **31**
  105mm leFH 18/40 **31**
decoys 76

gun casemates **29, 76, 109, 110,** 112, 139, **149**
   Omaha dispositions 31–3
   WW1 field guns **87**
   US **68,** 80–1, **83**
'Atlantic Wall' 12, 13, 93–4, **94, 109,** 150 *see also* German coastal strongpoints and batteries
Audouville-la-Hubert 116
Augusta, USS **15, 40**
Azeville coastal battery 106, **109,** 138, 151, 169, 178
   museum 178

B-26 Marauder bombers 21, 138, **139**
Band of Brothers (motion picture) 179
Barbarossa, Operation 97
Barton, MajGen Raymond 'Tubby' 98, **98,** 99, 105, 169
Bauform 60, 50mm anti-tank gun **148, 149**
Bauform casemate batteries **29, 76, 109, 110,** 112, 139, **149** *see also* German coastal strongpoints and batteries
beach defenses **8, 11, 12,** 20, 28–36, **29** *see also* German coastal strongpoints and batteries
   anti-tank ditches **81**
   clearing 78–80
   gun pits **30**
   trenches **32,** 32–3
beach landings
   Omaha **4,** 45, 49, **52,** 65, **67, 68, 80**
   Utah 109, 138–55, **140–1, 142**
Belgian gates **29**
Bingham, Maj Sidney 53, 57, 61
bombardment by US Navy 20–1, 44, **63,** 63–5, 69, 87
Boston, Operation 114, 121–31
Bradley, LtGen Omar **15,** 15–16, 28, 65, 67, 98, **98,** 106, 110, 154, 160, 163, 167, 169
British Army Commandos **70–2, 77**
British 'Funnies' (tanks) 22–4
Brittany 93, 94
Bryant, Adm 63–4
bulldozers 23, 50, 61, **81**

C-47 troop transports **111, 112,** 114, 115, **116,** 118, 119, 121
C-54 troop transports 114
Cabourg 61, 84
Canham, LtCol Charles 'Stoneface' 17–18, 53, 60, 82
Carentan, battle for 154, 155–61, **156**
Carmick, USS 64
casemate batteries **29, 76, 109, 110,** 112, 139, **149** *see also* German coastal strongpoints and batteries
Cassidy, LtCol Patrick 116
casualties
   German 87, 175–6
   US **48,** 79, 80, 81, 85–7, 175–6
    first and second wave 52, 57
    Gap Assault Teams 51
cemeteries 178
Channel Islands 111

Char B1 tank 104, 105
Charlie beach **45,** 78
Cherbourg 93, 104, 105, 109, 111, 113, 155, 163, 168
   capture of 169–76, **172–3**
Churchill tanks 23, 27
Cobra, Operation 108
Cointet gates 29
Cole, LtCol Robert 116, 158
Colleville 64, 66, 85
Colleville draw, E-3 **7,** 32, **64, 66**
   attacks on 50, 61, 79–80
   landings near 49, **64,** 65
Collins, MajGen J. Lawton 'Lightning Joe' 25, 98, **98, 99,** 150, 151, 154, 161, 163, 166, 167, 169, 170, 175
Combat Team '8' 104, **140–1,** 142, **146**
Commandos, British **70–2, 77**
communications
   German 66
   US 62, **63, 77**
Corlett, MajGen Charles 25
Cota, BrigGen Norman 'Dutch' **17,** 18, 53, **58–60, 78**
Cotentin peninsula 93, 94, 97, 100, **101,** 103, 104, 105, 106, 108, 109, 110, 111
   German order of battle 106
   isolation of Wehrmacht by US 163–9, **165**
   US order of battle 108
Crisbecq 169–70
Crisbecq coastal battery 106, **109,** 138, 151, 169, 178

D-Day (6 June 1944) 40–84, 114–76
   chronologies 10, 95
   weather conditions 114, 115
DD tanks 142, 143, **149** *see also* M4A1 Duplex Drive Sherman amphibious tank
destroyers **20, 63,** 63–5
Dog Green beach 44, **45,** 48, 52, 78
Dog Red beach 44, 53, **58–60**
Dog White beach 51, 52, **85**
Dollman, Genobst Friedrich 13, 40, 97, 111
Douve River 110, 115, 120, 153, 157, 158, 168
Doyle, USS 64
dozer-tanks 23, 50, 61, **81**
draws (gullies) 31–2
   D-1 Vierville 44, **45,** 63, 78–9, 91
   D-3 Les Moulind 32, 48, 51, 52–3, **57, 61, 62,** 64, 79
   E-1 St. Laurent 49, 65, 79, **79, 84, 91**
   E-3 Colleville **7,** 32, 49, 50, 61, **64,** 65, **66,** 79–80
   F-1 50, 61
Driscoll, Maj Edmond **16**
DUKW's (trucks) **53,** 80–1

Easy Green beach **57,** 79
Easy Red beach **29, 57**
   clearing 78–9
   landings **4,** 45, 49, 65, **67, 68, 80**
   operations 57–61
Eddy, MajGen Manton 99, **99,** 171, 175

Eisenhower, Gen Dwight D. 14–15, **15,** 16, **17,** 20, **98, 107,** 110, 154
Ekmann, Col William 122
Element C 29
Emmons, USS 64
engineers (Engineer Special Brigades) 65, 78–80, **80,** 84, **85**
engineers (Gap Assault Teams) **24,** 27, 38, 49–51
Enigma code 113, 160
equipment, US Army **19, 27,** 38
Eureka radar beacon 114
Ewell, LtCol Julian 119

Falley, GenLt Wilhelm 97, 135–6
Fallschirmjäger Regiment 6 (FJR6) (Wehrmacht) 100, 105, 137, 153, 154, 155, **158**
First US Army (FUSA) plan 109, 110
Flak 36, 88mm, anti-aircraft gun **122**
Flak Regiment Hermann 121
Flanagan, James **118**
Fort du Roule **170**
Fortitude, Operation 7, 20
Fox Green beach 49, **50,** 61, **64, 66, 79**
Fox Red beach 64
Führer Directive '51' 12, 100

Gap Assault Teams **24,** 27, 38, 49–51, 51
gas masks **27**
Gavin, Gen 127, **129,** 166
Gebelin, LtCom A.L. **20**
Gebirgs-haubitz 40, 105mm mountain gun 105
Gee navigation aid 114
Georgian Battalion 795 Ost 113, 122, 150
Gerhardt, MajGen Charles 17
German Army *see* Wehrmacht
German coastal strongpoints and batteries **5,** 12, 13, **29,** 31–3, **32,** 36, 50, **50, 51,** 52, 53, 61, **61,** 62, 63, 64, 65, 66, **76,** 79, 82, 88, 91, 93–4, **94,** 106, **109, 110,** 112, 138, 139, 142, 147, 148, **149,** 150, 151, **152,** 169, 178 *see also* Bauform casemate batteries
German naval forces 12, 89, 113, 138
Gerow, MajGen Leonard 16, 17, 24, 65, **98,** 161
Geyr von Schweppenburg, Gen Leo Freiherr 13
Gibbs, LtCol **16**
glider troop carriers **111,** 127, 130–1, **131, 135, 136, 137,** 148
Gold Beach 62, 66, 88
Goliath remote control demolition vehicles **102,** 112, 142
Gorenc, Joseph **111**
Göring, Reichsmarschall Hermann 11
Granville 106
Grenadier Regiment 726 (Wehrmacht) 34, 35, 36, 66, 73–6, 82
Grenadier Regiment 914 (Wehrmacht) 35, 77–8, 82
Grenadier Regiment 915 (Wehrmacht) 35, 67, 83

Grenadier Regiment 916 (Wehrmacht) 35, 62, 66, 67, 73, 82

Grenadier Regiment 919 (Wehrmacht) 111, 112–13, 116, 131, 138, 147, 150

Grenadier Regiments 920 and 921 (Wehrmacht) 170

Grenadier Regiments 1049 and 1050 (Wehrmacht) 169

Grenadier Regiment 1057 (Wehrmacht) 127, 130, 134, 136, 150, 166

Grenadier Regiment 1058 (Wehrmacht) 113, 120, 121, 136, 147, 151, 153

Hall, Adm 20–1

harbors, artificial 91, 93, 109

'hedgehogs' 29

Heeres-küsten-artillerie-abteilung (coastal artillery regiments)
HKAA 1260 36
HKAA 1261 106, 112, 138
HKAA 1262 106

Hellmich, GenLt Heinz 97, 169

helmet markings **58–60, 69, 70–2, 80, 85**

Hemmkurven (ramp obstacles) 29

Hennecke, Adm Walter von 175

Heydte, Col Oberstlt von der 100, 101, 105, 137, 153, 155, 158, 159, 161

Hicks, LtCol Herbert **16**

Hiroshi, Oshima 9

Hitler, Adolf 12, 13, 89, 113, 169, 174, 176
as commander 8, 11, 96, 97

Hoge, BrigGen William 17

Horne, Lt Kelso **161**

Horner, LtCol Charles **16**

Horsa glider troop carrier **135,** 148

Hotchkiss H-39 tank **103,** 104, 105, 127, 134, **134,** 161, 164

Houdienville 118

Howell Force 147

Hueber, MajGen Clarence **15, 16–17**

insignia, Allied
116thInfantry **58–60**
British Commandos **70–2**
engineers **80, 85**
Rangers **58–60, 69**

intelligence 9

Iron Mike monument 178

Janke, Lt 142, 143

Johnson, Col 120

Kampfgruppe Hellmich 168, 169

Kampfgruppe Meyer 35, 41, 51, 62, 85, 88, 135

Kampfgruppe Schlieben 168

Keil, ObstLt Gunther 112

Keitel, GFM Wilhelm 11

Kirk, RAdm Alan **15**

Klosterkemper, GenMaj Bernhard 98, 136

König, GenMaj Eugen **97,** 98

Kraiss, GenLt Dietrich 14, **14,** 35, 51, 62, 66–7, 77, 82, 87–8

Krancke, Adm Theodor 12, 113, 138

Krause, LtCol Edward 121, 122

Kriegsmarine (German naval forces) 12, 89, 113, 138

Kriegsspiel, (German wargames exercise) Rennes 97, 113, 135

La Fière bridge, battle for 122, **123,** 123–30, **128–9,** 136, 151, 163, 164, 166, 177 *see also* Merderet River

Landing Craft 25, **79**
crew of **54–6**
LCA 69
LCI (Landing Craft, Infantry) **37, 53, 64–6, 92**
LCI-554 66
LCT (Landing Craft, Tank) **53, 80,** 139, 142, 143, 146
LCT-30 66
LCVP (Landing Craft, Vehicle/Personnel) **4, 38, 40, 41, 44, 54–6, 66,** 142, 143
loading of 38, 48, **54–6**
LST (Landing Ship, Tank) **92, 105**

Lanker, Lt Albert 11

Le Garde Hameau 83

Le Havre, coastal guns **5**

Le Motley 166

leFH 18/40, 105mm gun **31**

Les Moulind draw, D-3 32, **57, 61, 62**
attacks on 48, 51, 52–3, 64, 79

Lettau, Maj 113

life belts **19**

The Longest Day (motion picture) 177, 179

Luftwaffe 9, 12, 33, 35, 36, 88–9, 105, 113, 157
weather forecasting by 113

M4 tank **85, 104,** 143, **143, 154, 167, 168**

M4A1 Duplex Drive Sherman amphibious tank **4, 23,** 23–5, **54–6, 65, 66, 83, 104,** 107, 139, 142, **146** *see also* DD tanks

M4A3E2 assault tank 25, 27

M5A1 tank 164

M10 gun motor carriages/tank destroyer **105,** 169

McAuliffe, BrigGen Anthony 155, 159

McCook, USS 63, 64

MacKelvie, MajGen Jay 99

Madeleine River 157, 158

Marauder bombers **21,** 138, **139**

Marcks, Gen d.Inf Erich 13–14, 41, 97, 101, 135, 137, 161

Marder III Ausf. M tank **163**

Marine-artillerie-abteilung (MAA 260, naval coastal battery) 106

Marine-artillerie-abteilung (MAA 608, naval coastal battery) 106

Market Garden, Operation 99

Marshall, George C. 14, 16

medical treatment 61, **79–81**

Meindl, Gen 161

Merderet River 110, 121, 122, 123–30, 129, 130, 131, 134, **134,** 136, 150, 151, 154, 163, 166 *see also* La Fière bridge, battle for

Mésières 116

Meyer, ObstLt 88

Michaels, LtCol John 116

Middleton, MajGen Troy 169

Millett, Col 164

mines and mine clearance 29, 40, 78–80, **85**

Model 1937, 47mm, anti-tank gun **148**

Montgomery, FM Bernard 109, 169

Morsalines coastal battery 138

Mulberry artificial Harbors 91, 93, 109

Musee de Debarquement d'Utah Beach 177

Musee de la Liberation 178

Musee des Troupe Aeroportees 177

naval bombardment 20–1, 44, **63,** 63–5, 69, 87

Naval Shore Fire Control Parties (US) **63**

Neptune, Operation 98, 109, 114

Nivens, Coxswain D. 44, 45

Normandy 93, 94, 104, 105, 110, 114

North Africa campaign 108

Oberkommando der Wehrmacht (OKW) 11

Office of Strategic Service (OSS) 114

Ohmsen, OLt zur See 109

Omaha Beach **7, 19, 45, 88,** 93, 106, 109, 112, 139, 148, 159, 177
chronology 10
geography of 30–1
operations **4, 42–3, 46–7, 52, 53, 54–6, 58–60, 70–2, 74–5**
reasons for selection of 19

Organization Todt **11,** 12, **28**

Ostendorf, SS-Gruf Werner 160, 161

Overlord, Operation 5–7, 109
strategy 93–4

P-47 strike aircraft 120

PaK 38, 50mm anti-tank guns **30,** 32

PaK 43/41, 88mm 'Scheunentor' gun **31**

Panzer Abteilung 100th Division (Wehrmacht) 105, 127, 134, 161

Panzer Abteilung 101st Division (Wehrmacht) 103

Panzer Abteilung 206th Division (Wehrmacht) 104

Panzer deployment 13, 89

Panzerjäger 35R anti tank gun 103, **103,** 104, 105

Panzerjäger Company 709 (Wehrmacht) 137

Panzerschreck anti-tank rocket unit **100, 134**

paratroops **111, 112,** 114, **116, 119, 120, 121, 122, 126, 137,** 153 *see also* Fallschirmjäger Regiment 6 (FJR6) (Wehrmacht)

Parker, Lt Charles 53, 77

Pas de Calais 7, 9, 12, 93, 94, 96

pathfinders 114, 121, 122–3, 131

Pemsel, GenLt Max 159

Pointblank, Operation 7

Pointe-du-Hoc 33, 36, **69, 73, 76,** 90
operations at 20, 38, 41, 53, 68–78, **70–2, 77**

strategic importance 28
Pointe-et-Raz-de-la-Percée **7**, 20, 31, 33, 38, **45**, 63
Polish recruits in Wehrmacht 102, 150
Pont l'Abbé 130
Pouppeville 118, 147
Pratt, BrigGen Donald 178
Priller, ObstLt Josef 'Pips' 89
PzKpfw III tank 105

Quineville 170

Raaen, Capt John 60
radar 114
radios **63**
Raeder, Adm Erich 11
Raff, Col E. 147
ramp obstacles 29
Ranger Battalions **27**, 48, 49, 52–3, 68–78, **70–2**, 77, **77**, 82
   commanders 18
   equipment 38
   insignia **58–60, 69**
   objectives 28, 37–8
Rebecca radar 114
Red Army recruits in Wehrmacht 100, **100**, 102, 103, 150, 151
Renault R-35 infantry tank 103, **103**, 104, 105
Renault UE armored tractor **119**
Rennes
   German wargames exercise at 97, 113, 135
Ridgway, MajGen Matthew **98**, 98–9, 110, 122, 127, 150
Rieve, KAdm 113
rocket craft **21**
roller-grenades 31
Rommel, GFM Erwin 96, **96**, 102, 104, 110, 111, 113, 137, 154–5, 160, 168
   on air power 9
   and beach defenses **12**, 28–9, **29**, 87
   on D-Day 40
   responsibilities re western defenses 12–13
   and troop deployment 35
'Rommel's Asparagus' 29
Roosevelt Jr., BrigGen Theodore 99, 143
Royce, Gen Ralph 15
Rudder, LtCol James E. 18, 68, **77**
Rundstedt, GFM Gerd von 11, 12, 96, 100, 110, 168, 169

St. Côme-du-Mont 120, 136, 154, 155
St. Laurent 82
St. Laurent draw, E-1 49, 65, 79, **79, 84, 91**
St. Lô 97
St. Marcouf coastal battery 106, **109**, 138, 139, 151, 169, 178
St. Marie-du-Mont 119, **155**, 177
St. Mère-Église 116, 117, 121, 122, 123, 131, 136, 137, 147, 148, 150, 151, 153, 154, 177, 178

Samel Chase, USS 44, 45, 66
Satterlee, USS 69, 76
Sattler, GenMaj Robert 174, 175
Saving Private Ryan (motion picture) 49
Schlieben, GenLt Karl Wilhelm von 97, **97**, 101–2, 111, 171, **174**
Schwartz, Lt Stanley 60
Schwarzwalder, Capt F. 'Ben' 127
Shanley, LtCol Thomas 130, 163, 164
Sherman tank *see* M4A1 Duplex Drive Sherman amphibious tank
Shettle, Capt Charles 120, 153
Sicily campaign 108, 110
signal lamps **77**
Sink, Col 118
Somua S-35 tank 104, 105
Soviet recruits in Wehrmacht 100, **100**, 102, 103, 150, 151
Spalding, Lt John 50
Sperrle, GFM Hugo 12, 88
Stegmann, Gen Rudolf 169
Stopka, Maj John 158
Strayer, LtCol Robert 118, 119
Streczyk, Sgt Philip 50
Struble, RAdm A.D. **15**
StuG III Ausf. G. assault gun **102**, 104, 122, 151, **153, 157, 159**, 160, 161
Sturm-Abteilung AOK 7 (Wehrmacht) 105, 112, 136–7, 154, 155, 169, 170
Swordhilt, Operation 25

Talley, Col 78
tanks **4**, 22–7, **23**, 37, 61, 65, **65**, 66, **66**, 78, **81, 83**, 85, 103, **103**, 104, **104**, 105, 107, 127, 134, **134**, 139, 142, **142**, 143, **146**, 149, **149**, 151, 153, 154, 161, **163**, 164, 167, **167, 168**, 169
   landing of 23–4, 44–8, 56
   losses of 82
   operations 50, 52, 53–7, 61, 64, 82
   wading trunks **23**, 24, **54–6**
Task Force Barber 170
Task Force U **92**, 138
Taylor, LtCol George **16**, 17, 61
Taylor, MajGen Maxwell 99, 119
Texas, USS 69, 78, **167**
Thompson, USS **20**
Timmes, LtCol Charles 127, 164, 166
trenches **32**
trucks, amphibious **53**, 80–1
Tschechenigel ('Rommel's Asparagus') 29
Turner, LtCol William 118, 119

U-boats 113
uniforms and clothing
   British Commandos **70–2**
   chemical-weapon protection 56
   US Army **19, 25, 70–2**
US Army 36–9, **104**
   airborne landings 115–31, **117**
   amphibious beach landings **4**, 45, 49, **52**, 65, **67, 68, 80**, 109, 138–55, **140–1, 142**

artillery battalions 80–1
   commanders 14–18
   Naval Shore Fire Control Parties 63
   offensive plans 109–10
   order of battle 39, 108
   uniforms and equipment **19, 25**, 38, **70–2**
US Army Air Force 8–9, 21, **21**, 87
US Navy bombardment 20–1, 44, **63**, 63–5, 69, 87
Utah Beach **139, 177**
   chronology 95
   consolidation on D-Day+1 **152**
   landings on D-Day 109, 138–55, **140–1, 142**

Vandervoort, LtCol Benjamin 121
Vierville 53, 82
Vierville draw, D-1 44, **45**, 63, 78–9, 91
Vire River 105, 109, 131
Volkliste III 102

Waco CG-4A glider troop carrier 131, **131**, 148
Wall, Capt Herman 80
wargames exercise (Kriegsspiel), Rennes 97, 113, 135
Wayne, John 177
weapons **54–6** *see also* anti-tank vehicles and weapons; tanks
   bangalore torpedoes **24, 25, 58–60**
   bazookas **25, 69**
   Browning Automatic Rifles (BARS) **69**
   charges **24, 25**
   chemical, protection against **54–6**
   'Goliath' 30
   M1 carbines **25**
   Sten guns **70–2**
   water proofing of **25, 41, 54–6, 58–60**
Wehrmacht in France 34–6
   Army Group B 12–13, 96
   combat effectiveness 8–9, 100–6
   command effectiveness 96
   commanders 11–14, 96–8
   D-Day reaction 131–8
   defense plans 12–14, 96–8, **101**, 109, 110–13
   deployment in 1944 8
   intelligence 9
   Mobile Brigade 66, 82, 88
   Omaha dispositions **6**
   order of battle 36, 106
   Panzer deployment 13, 89
   plans 28–33
   Polish recruits 102, 150
   prisoners of war **79, 84**
   Red Army recruits 100, **100**, 102, 103, 150, 151
   surrender in Cherbourg 174–5
Weymouth **27, 69**
Wyche, MajGen Ira 99

Ziegelmann, Col Fritz 88